Cognitive Psychology

FOR

DUMMIES

A Wiley Brand

Cognitive Psychology

FOR

DUMMIES®

A Wiley Brand

by Dr Peter J Hills and
Dr J Michael Pake

FOR

DUMMIES®

A Wiley Brand

Cognitive Psychology For Dummies®

Published by: **John Wiley & Sons, Ltd., The Atrium, Southern Gate, Chichester,** www.wiley.com

This edition first published 2016

© 2016 by John Wiley & Sons, Ltd., Chichester, West Sussex

Registered Office

John Wiley & Sons, Ltd., The Atrium, Southern Gate, Chichester, West Sussex, PO19 8SQ, United Kingdom

For details of our global editorial offices, for customer services and for information about how to apply for permission to reuse the copyright material in this book, please see our website at www.wiley.com.

For general information on our other products and services, please contact our Customer Care Department within the U.S. at 877-762-2974, outside the U.S. at 317-572-3993, or fax 317-572-4002. For technical support, please visit www.wiley.com/techsupport.

Wiley publishes in a variety of print and electronic formats and by print-on-demand. Some material included with standard print versions of this book may not be included in e-books or in print-on-demand. If this book refers to media such as a CD or DVD that is not included in the version you purchased, you may download this material at http://booksupport.wiley.com. For more information about Wiley products, visit www.wiley.com.

A catalogue record for this book is available from the British Library.

Library of Congress Control Number: 2016930757

ISBN 978-1-119-95321-0 (pbk); ISBN 978-1-119-95390-6 (ebk); ISBN 978-1-119-95391-3 (ebk)

Manufactured in the United States of America

10 9 8 7 6 5 4 3 2 1

Contents at a Glance

Table of Contents

Part V: Thinking Your Way around Thought 253

Chapter 17: Uncovering How People Solve Problems 255

Chapter 18: Thinking Logically about Reasoning................267

Introduction

The fact that you're reading this book implies that you have an interest in cognitive psychology or you're studying it for a course. In either case, you probably think that you know what cognitive psychology is: the study of all mental abilities and processes about knowing. Clearly, the subject covers a huge range whose contents would barely fit into 50 books the size of this one – with more being written every day!

We think that everybody should be interested in cognitive psychology, because it's fascinating. We know that all aficionados say that (from bell ringers to beer-mat collectors), but cognitive psychology really is! By scientifically studying how people see, remember, know, speak and think, you can truly understand what being human means and what makes all humans special.

About This Book

Cognitive Psychology For Dummies is designed as an introduction to the subject. We cover the historical perspective on cognitive psychology, but also draw on interesting, more recent work.

We adopt an informal writing style, but one that remains technically appropriate and scientifically accurate. We write in plain English (which is tricky, because cognitive psychologists love jargon!). Where we do use technical language you can assume that it's the only way to express something, but overall we make the tone as friendly as possible. We even include some jokes (if you don't spot any, it's because we're not very funny!). At no point are we making fun of anyone (except ourselves).

We endeavour to relate everything in this book to everyday reality, using real-world examples to anchor the more technical information. Nevertheless, cognitive psychologists like to create highly controlled, laboratory-based experiments that, on the surface, bear little resemblance to the real world. Don't fear though; everything cognitive psychologists study has some benefit to humanity.

Most chapters also cover instances of 'when things go wrong'. These discussions show how a particular cognitive ability can go haywire in healthy people (such as visual illusions) or those with brain damage.

This book is for people who need and want to know about cognitive psychology. For the former, we present all the information covered in school and the first year of a university course (anywhere in the world) in a highly accessible way. We map the content onto the most common courses of cognitive psychology. If you simply want to know about cognitive psychology, we present some of the most interesting and fun psychology here too. We pack the book with examples and exercises you can try out and demonstrate on your friends and family to amaze them!

Conventions Used in This Book

We use conventions to help you find your way around this book easily:

- ✔ *Italic* text highlights new, often specialist, terms that we always define nearby. These include elements of jargon we just can't escape, though we also use italics for emphasis.
- ✔ **Boldfaced** text indicates part of a list or numbered steps.

Unlike most textbooks in psychology, we don't include references or in-text citations. We mention the name of a researcher when we feel that the person's work is important and worth remembering.

We sometimes describe a few of the most important and influential studies, but not always. Be assured, however, that all the results and effects we describe in this book are based on empirical research – we simply don't want to get bogged down in such detail too often.

We also provide a number of sidebars, containing additional information with more detailed theories, methodologies or clinical examples. You can skip over these without missing anything essential, but we think they're interesting and add a lot to the text.

Foolish Assumptions

Hundreds of books on cognitive psychology exist. Many are technical, long, dry, specialised or cover a very narrow area of cognition. We wrote *Cognitive Psychology For Dummies* assuming the following:

✔ You want to understand how people think, see and remember things.

✔ You have questions about how the human mind works.

✔ You're starting a course in cognitive psychology and haven't studied it before.

✔ You've found other textbooks too complicated, dry or technical.

✔ You're simply interested in people.

✔ You have a basic understanding of psychology, probably from an introductory course or reading *Psychology For Dummies*.

✔ You want to discover a few tips on improving your own cognition.

Icons Used in This Book

Throughout this book, we use icons in the margins to help you find certain types of information. Here's a list of what they mean.

When you see this icon, we're giving you a bit of information that may come in handy someday.

Don't forget the information by this icon! It shows what you need to pick up from the particular paragraph.

Like most sciences, cognitive psychology has a lot of terms and particular usages. We highlight them with this icon so that you can join in the conversation wherever cognitive psychologists gather.

This icon flags text that rises above what you need for a basic understanding of the topic at hand. You can skip these paragraphs if you prefer without harming your comprehension of the main point. We often use this icon when describing studies in detail or the brain regions involved in cognition.

We use this icon to point out how the information under discussion has applications or is observed in reality.

This icon indicates a task or exercise to perform on yourself or someone you know. The exercises are based on examples we provide in the text or on an Internet resource.

Beyond the Book

The area of cognitive psychology is so vast that its contents would fill far more than this book. Given that it's really interesting and exciting, we want to give you as much chance to learn about it as possible, and so we put some extras on the Internet. In addition to the printed chapters, you can find loads more (free!) *Cognitive Psychology For Dummies* information at www.dummies.com/extras/cognitivepsychology.

In an online cheat sheet found at www.dummies.com/cheatsheet/cognitivepsychology, we include a quick guide to some central cognitive psychology ideas on memory, language and problem solving, among other topics.

Where to Go from Here

We organise this book in a logical representation of how the human brain works (information comes in, is remembered, spoken and thought about), but each chapter is self-contained so that you can dip in and out at your leisure. Except for the first and last parts, each part deals with a different element of cognitive psychology, so you can pick out the sections that you're most interested in or are struggling with the most.

Use the table of contents and index to find what's most relevant to you. If you're new to the subject, you may want to start with Chapter 1 and read the book in sequence, but you don't have to read it cover to cover.

We hope that you find the book educational, informative and entertaining. We think that you'll like it and learn a lot about yourself as you go. If you do, tell your friends about it!

Part I
Getting Started with Cognitive Psychology

getting started
with

Cognitive
Psychology

In this part . . .

- Understand what cognitive psychology is and why it's so darn important.

- Realise how cognitive psychology influences every aspect of the human experience that involves thinking.

- Find useful tips on how cognitive psychology can improve your cognitive skills in school, college, university and almost all walks of life.

Chapter 1

Understanding Cognition: How You Think, See, Speak and Are!

*H*ow do you know that what you see is real? Would you notice if some-one changed her identity in front of you? How can you be sure that when you remember what you saw, you're remembering it accurately? Plus, how can you be sure that when you tell someone something that the person understands it in the same way as you do? What's more fascinating than looking for answers to such questions, which lie at the heart of what it means to be . . . well . . . you!

Cognitive psychology is the study of all mental abilities and processes about knowing. Despite the huge area of concern that this description implies, the breadth of the subject's focus still sometimes surprises people. Here, we intro-duce you to cognitive psychology, suggesting that it's fundamentally a science. We show how cognitive psychologists view the subject from an information-processing account and how we use this view to structure this book.

We also describe the plethora of research methods that psychologists employ to study cognitive psychology. The rest of this book uses the philoso-phies and methods that we describe here, and so this chapter works as an introduction to the book as well.

Introducing Cognitive Psychology

Cognitive psychologists, like psychologists in general, consider themselves to be *empirical* scientists – which means that they use carefully designed experiments to investigate thinking and knowing. Cognitive psychologists (including us!) are interested in all the seemingly basic things that people take for granted every day: perceiving, attending to, remembering, reasoning, problem solving, decision-making, reading and speaking.

To help define cognitive psychology and demonstrate its 'scientificness', we need to define what we mean by a science and then look at the history of cognitive psychology within this context.

Hypothesising about science

Although many philosophers spend hours arguing about the definition of science, one thing that's central is a systematic understanding of something in order to make a reliable prediction. The *scientific method* commonly follows this fairly strict pattern:

1. **Devise a testable hypothesis or theory that explains something.**

   An example may be: how do people store information in their memory? Sometimes this is called a *model* (you encounter many models in this book).

2. **Design an experiment or a method of observation to test the hypothesis.**

   Create a situation to see whether the hypothesis is true: that is, manipulate something and see what it affects.

3. **Compare the results obtained with what was predicted.**

4. **Correct or extend the theory.**

Philosopher Karl Popper suggested that science progresses faster when people devise tests to prove hypotheses wrong: called *falsification*. After you prove all but one hypothesis wrong about something, you have the answer (the Sherlock Holmes approach – if you exclude the impossible, whatever remains must be true!). This is also called *deductive reasoning* (see Chapter 18 for the psychology of deduction).

The scientific method has some clear and obvious limitations (or strengths, depending on the way you look at it):

✔ **You can hypothesise and test only observable things.** For this reason, many cognitive psychologists don't see Sigmund Freud, Carl Rogers and others as scientists.

✔ **You must conduct experiments to test a theory.** You can't do research just to find out something new.

Cognitive psychology employs the scientific method vigorously. Everything we describe in this book comes from experiments that have been conducted following this method. Although this does sometimes limit the questions you can ask, it establishes standards that all research must follow.

Describing the rise of cognitive psychology

Before cognitive psychology, people used a variety of approaches (or *paradigms*) to study psychology, including behaviourism, psychophysics and psychodynamics. The year 1956, however, saw the start of a cognitive renaissance, which challenged, in particular, behaviourism. For more background on how cognitive psychology emerged from other scientific disciplines, chiefly behaviourism, check out the nearby sidebar '1956: The year cognitive psychology was born'.

We don't intend to minimise the importance of behaviourism: it ensured that the scientific method was applied to psychology and that experiments were conducted in a controlled way. Cognitive psychology took this strength and carried it into more ingenious scientific studies of cognition.

1956: The year cognitive psychology was born

The behaviourist approach dominated psychology until 1956, when enough people found that it was insufficient to understand human behaviour. Specifically, behaviourism couldn't explain cognition. Part of the issue was that virtually all behaviourist research was conducted on animals (usually rats and pigeons), and perhaps humans are different to animals. Interest in new areas also proved difficult for the behaviourist model to deal with. Imagery, short-term memory, attention and the organisation of knowledge can't be easily interpreted within the behaviourist model, because behaviourists are only interested in observable behaviour.

The attack on behaviourism became venomous, with American linguist Noam Chomsky leading the charge. He claimed that the behaviourist analysis for language learning was wrong (for reasons we discuss in the chapters in Part IV). His attack coincided with a series of other key papers that showed behaviourism was waning and cognitive science was the way forward: George Miller's paper on the magic number seven (see Chapter 8), Allen Newell and Herb Simon's problem-solving model (Chapter 17), and the birth of artificial intelligence. All this happened in 1956. This *cognitive renaissance* culminated in the first textbook on cognitive psychology in 1967 by Ulric Neisser, a German-American cognitive psychologist. He described this book as an attack on behaviourism.

Looking at the structure of cognition (and of this book)

Fittingly, we're writing this book to bring cognitive psychology to a wider audience around the 50th anniversary of the first published cognitive psychology textbook (in 1967).

Applications

In Part I, we review the applications of cognitive psychology and why studying it is important. Cognitive psychology has produced some incredibly exciting and interesting findings that have changed how people view psychology and themselves (as you can discover in Chapter 2). But also, people have learnt a great deal about how best to teach, learn and improve themselves from cognitive psychology, something we address in Chapter 3. The applications of cognitive psychology are so wide that studies are used in such disparate fields as computing, social work, education, media technology, human resources and much more besides.

Information-processing framework

In this book, we follow the *information-processing* model of human cognition. In many ways, this approach to cognition is based on the computer. The idea is that human cognition is based on a series of processing stages. In 1958, Donald Broadbent, a British psychologist, argued that the majority of cognition follows the processing stages we depict in Figure 1-1. The boxes represent stages of cognition and the arrows represent processes within it.

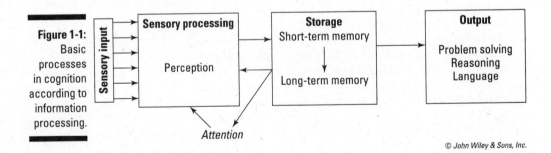

Figure 1-1: Basic processes in cognition according to information processing.

© John Wiley & Sons, Inc.

All cognition fits within this framework. Cognitive psychologists research each box (stage) and each arrow (process) in Figure 1-1 in many different domains. In other words, this framework provides a good structure for how to think about and learn about cognitive psychology (and oddly matches the framework of this book).

Your leg bone's connected to your knee bone

Cognitive psychology's favoured information-processing framework corresponds well with how the brain seems to process information. People have sensory organs that detect the world. These connect to parts of the brain devoted to perception (in the case of vision, the *occipital lobe* in the back of the head). The information then passes forward from the perception centres to the attention centres (the *parietal*

cortex, just in front of the occipital lobe) and then to the memory centres (the *temporal lobe*, in the middle of the head). Higher-level reasoning and thinking are primarily processed in the *frontal lobes* at the front of the head. Although a gross oversimplification, this description is a nice fit with the information-processing account of cognition.

Information processing may not be as simple as Figure 1-1, progressing in perfect sequence from the sensory input to long-term storage. Existing knowledge and experience may cause some processing to be in reverse. These two patterns of processing are often referred to as follows:

- ✔ **Bottom-up processing:** Physical environment and sensation drive brain processing.
- ✔ **Top-down processing:** Existing knowledge and abilities drive responses.

All forms of cognitive psychology are based on the interaction between bottom-up and top-down processing. No processing is strictly driven by the stimulus or by knowledge.

Cognitive psychologists like the information-processing framework, because people's interactions with the world are guided by internal mental representations (such as language) that can be revealed by measuring the processing time. Neuroscientists have also found parts of the brain responsible for different cognitive behaviours.

Input

In Part II of this book, we look at the first stage of cognition: input of information. In the computer analogy, this would be a camera recording information or the keyboard receiving key presses.

Cognitive psychologists call the input of information *perception*: how the brain interprets the information from the senses. Perception is different from *sensation*, which is exactly what physical information your senses record. Your brain then immediately changes and interprets this information so that it's easy to process. This process highlights a linear progression from sensation (Chapter 4) to perception (Chapters 5 and 6).

Attention follows information input (see Chapter 7). *Attention* is the first distinct process of the information-processing account, and it's what links perception with higher-level cognition. Without it, people would simply react to the world in an involuntary manner.

Storage

After you attend to information, it enters your brain's storage system (see the chapters in Part III). The brain has a number of mechanisms for storing and using information, collectively called *memory*. We cover short-term memory in Chapter 8 and long-term memory in Chapter 9. You also have stored knowledge and skills (Chapter 10). Although all this knowledge is highly useful, we can't forget(!) to consider forgetting (Chapter 11), as well as how memory works in everyday life and some of the applications of memory research (Chapter 12).

In the computer analogy of cognition, short-term memory is the RAM: it has limited capacity and simply keeps the information you're currently using available to you. Just as you can't have too many applications or windows open on a computer simultaneously without slowing it down, the same applies to human short-term memory. Long-term memory and knowledge is the hard-disk space – a vast store of information.

Language and thought

Sensation and perception are quite low-level cognitive functions: they're fairly simple processes that many animals can do. Memory is a slightly higher-level cognitive function, but the highest-level functions are the ones that animals can't do, according to some psychologists – language and thought (see Parts IV and V):

- ✔ **Language:** The first output stage of information processing. Some psychologists describe it as a human form of communication and it's typically the vocal form of exchanging ideas with other people. We describe language and its relation to other forms of communication in Chapter 13. We cover its structure and the steps needed to produce it in Chapters 14 and 15. We discuss how language relates to other parts of cognition and perception in Chapter 16.

- ✔ **Thought:** The second output stage of information processing. Problem solving, reasoning and decision-making (Chapters 17, 18 and 19, respectively) are complex, highly evolved abilities that are an accumulation of extensive experience, knowledge and skill. Plus, don't forget how cognition is affected by emotions (Chapter 20).

Researching Cognitive Psychology

People have devised a number of methods for researching cognitive psychology. Plus, technological advances allow psychologists to explore how the brain functions. In this section, we describe how experiments, computational models, work with patients and brain scanning helped psychologists to understand how the cognitive system works.

Testing in the laboratory

The tightly controlled laboratory experiment is one of the most commonly used techniques for researching cognitive psychology. Psychologists take normal people (like those exist!) – usually university students (narrowing the definition of normal to those generally well-educated and intelligent) – place these *participants* in small cubicles and show them things on a computer. Each person is tested in exactly the same way and the experimenters have complete control over what the person sees (as long as the computers follow the given instructions!).

Participants are usually unaware of exactly what they're going to do. They're given instructions to follow a set of tasks on the computer, often in the form of a game. (Indeed, a few years ago Nintendo released a brain game that included several cognitive psychological tasks, such as the Stroop effect task we describe in Chapter 7.) Participants make responses on the keyboard, mouse or other specially designed equipment.

The experimenters take the participants' responses, usually in terms of measures of response speed and their accuracy, and use statistics to work out whether the hypothesis and cognitive psychological model is correct or not. These statistics allow researchers to see whether the sample tested reflects the whole population of people that could've been tested. Then the psychologists tell the world!

Crucially, experimenters must test lots of people to get reliable results. If you only test a few people, you may get very odd results, because the world contains lots of odd individuals and they usually turn up for experiments! After testing enough people, you can see the average of lots of people, which tells you whether to trust your hypothesis or not.

Being ethical in research

Cognitive psychologists have to conduct all their research following the appropriate ethical standards, as guided by the Helsinki Principle (an internationally recognised standard for ethics). The key issue is getting *informed consent* during experiments: participants must know what's going to happen to them and permit it to happen. Experimenters don't need to tell participants everything (for example, if you want to test implicit learning or memory [Chapter 9] you wouldn't tell participants about a later memory test), but they need to know enough about what they're going to do.

Informed consent is more difficult to obtain from children and people with a brain injury.

In all cases, the person responsible for the participant must give consent. Psychologists then ensure that the participant wants to take part. If a person can't say, the psychologists look for cues to indicate whether the person wants to take part (say, a baby looking away from a computer).

Other ethical concerns exist (such as maintaining participants' health and wellbeing), but they come up less frequently in cognitive psychology. Download the British Psychological Society's guidance (www.bps.org.uk/system/files/documents/code_of_ethics_and_conduct.pdf).

Modelling with computers

One approach to testing cognitive psychology doesn't use people at all! Researchers can employ computers to mimic human cognition in what's called *computational modelling*. A good computational model is specific enough to predict human behaviour. These kinds of theories are more precise than the often vague verbal theories that earlier cognitive psychologists used.

Computational models are based around different types of structure (or *architecture*). *Connectionist models* are by far the most common of cognitive models. They work by having layers of nodes connected to each other by links that either promote or stop activity. Nodes in the same layer are usually *inhibitory* to each other (they prevent other nodes in the same layer from activating). We draw out a simple connectionist model in Figure 1-2, representing concepts and knowledge as a pattern of activation within the model. We go into much more detail in Chapter 10.

Production models are based around formal logic (Chapter 18). They rely on a series of 'if . . . then' statements. The idea is that stored knowledge exists in terms of 'if this happens, then this will'. Another technique – *artificial intelligence* – involves constructing a computer to produce intelligent outcomes, though it doesn't have to reflect human processing.

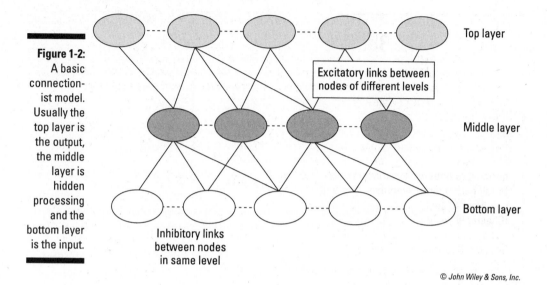

Figure 1-2:
A basic connection-ist model. Usually the top layer is the output, the middle layer is hidden processing and the bottom layer is the input.

Top layer

Excitatory links between nodes of different levels

Middle layer

Bottom layer

Inhibitory links between nodes in same level

Computational modelling can be hugely successful at explaining human behaviour, but the models created often run the risk of being incredibly complex and difficult to understand. Also, they can be modified too easily to account for a very limited set of data, making them not very useful.

Working with brain-damaged people

Cognitive neuropsychology is the study of brain-damaged patients in an attempt to understand normal cognition. Often the ingenious studies that cognitive psychologists devise are run on people with various types of brain damage to see whether they perform differently. The aim is to identify what processes take place where in the brain, and what groups of tasks are related in terms of cognitive functioning.

The neuropsychological approach has been around since the end of the nineteenth century. It has several key assumptions, as Max Coltheart, a noted Australian neuropsychologist, indicated:

- ✔ **Modularity:** The cognitive system contains separate parts that operate largely on their own.

- ✔ **Domain specificity:** Modules only work for one type of stimulus.

- ✔ **Anatomical modularity:** Each cognitive module is located in a specific part of the brain.

- ✔ **Uniformity of functional architecture across people:** Every brain in the world is the same.

- ✔ **Subtractivity:** Damage to the brain only removes abilities, but doesn't add to or change the brain in any other way. This assumption is largely wrong, especially in children, whereas the other points are at least defendable.

Neuropsychologists are always looking for dissociations or even double dissociations as the best form of evidence:

- ✔ **Dissociation:** Where they find a group of patients who perform poorly on one task but normally on others.

- ✔ **Double dissociation:** Where they have two groups of patients who show complementary patterns of impairment (so that one group is impaired on task A but not B, and the other group is impaired on B but not A). This approach shows that the two tasks are functionally different (and based on different brain structures).

Often, neuropsychologists use case studies. They look at individuals with a certain type of brain damage to understand what different parts of the brain do to a wide range of tasks. Certain people have been extensively researched and so have contributed to the knowledge of the brain more than many researchers! Chapter 21 has ten case studies for you to read.

Analysing the brain

Cognitive neuroscience is where researchers use expensive equipment to measure the brain when it's doing something. The brain consists of 100 billion neurons and each neuron is connected to up to 10,000 other neurons (that's a complex lump of goo inside your head). Yet researchers using neuroimaging have done a wonderful job of shedding light on it.

The German neurologist, Korbinian Brodmann, was the first to map the brain directly. He named 52 different brain areas and his descriptions are still used today. The assumption is that each area does a slightly different thing (based on the modularity assumption of the cognitive neuropsychologists we describe in the preceding section).

Neuroscientists use a number of ways to study cognitive psychology:

- ✔ **Single cell recording:** An electrode records the activity of single cells, which usually requires drilling into the skull and brain (so not something to undergo while eating lunch).

- ✔ **Electroencephalography (EEG):** Electrodes placed on the surface of the scalp measure the electrical activity of the brain. Electrical spikes occur due to the presentation of certain stimuli, called *event-related potentials* (ERPs). This technique records brain activity quickly but isn't good at finding the source of the activity.

- ✔ **Positron emission tomography (PET):** Radioactive substances are absorbed into the blood and a scanner picks them up when the blood enters the brain.

- ✔ **Functional magnetic resonance imaging (fMRI):** A large (and noisy) scanner detects the level of oxygen in the blood as it enters the brain. The more blood in certain areas, the more it's assumed to be active. This technique isn't good at measuring the speed of brain processing, but it can localise the source quite accurately.

- ✔ **Magneto-encephalography (MEG):** Similar to EEG, this method measures magnetic fields produced by the brain's electrical activity.

- ✔ **Transcranial magnetic stimulation (TMS):** A large magnetic pulse is sent into part of the brain, which stops that part working for a brief period.

- ✔ **Transcranial direct current stimulation (TDCS):** This method involves sending a small electrical current through parts of the brain to see how enhanced or reduced activity to a particular region affects performance on certain cognitive tasks.

These techniques can be useful in establishing which part of the brain is responsible for processing certain things, although none of them are completely accurate. To use neuroimaging techniques appropriately, you need to run a good, well-controlled cognitive test that really measures only one ability (to pinpoint which part of the brain is responsible for that ability – see the next section).

 These methods also suffer from the fact that completing research while having your brain measured is an odd experience. In the case of fMRI, it involves lying down inside a big magnet – hardly the typical position when completing any form of cognition. Therefore, these techniques may change participants' behaviour.

Acknowledging the Limitations of Cognitive Psychology

Cognitive psychologists' clever experiments (refer to the preceding section) have produced exciting findings that can help society greatly. We even use evidence from cognitive psychological research in Chapter 3 to help you in your studies!

But although cognitive psychology is generally awesome, we have to acknowledge two (minor) weaknesses to this approach:

✔ **Task impurity:** Many tasks that cognitive psychologists devise may not measure only the one intended aspect. For example, a researcher may be interested in response inhibition and use the Go/No-Go test (see Chapter 8), but this task also involves response conflict (a related, but subtly different cognitive process). The researcher's results may therefore reflect two different types of cognition, which is called task impurity.

Furthermore, results from one task are sometimes not repeated in a similar task. This *paradigm specificity* reflects the problem that some cognitive psychological effects are limited to the very precise experimental procedures used to find them.

✔ **Lack of ecological validity:** In the attempt to be highly scientific, psychologists take people out of the real world and create artificial environments where they control every aspect of their behaviour. This is unrealistic, and so results may not occur in the real world.

Cognitive psychologists are interested in the internal mental processes that occur during cognition, but these processes aren't directly observable. As a result, the evidence they collect is only indirect. Indeed, many cognitive psychologists' theories are limited in scope and only focus on a small aspect of the human experience. Therefore, many areas of cognitive psychology don't relate to other areas of cognitive psychology.

Chapter 2

gnitive Psychology
lying the Everyday

. . . .

psychology

wrong

e journey

. . . .

psychology they tend to focus on the more
findings, such as explaining unusual behaviour.
:d with every aspect of people's mental life, not
ents of most cognitive psychology books feature
– such as seeing, remembering, using language
eople do all the time without a second thought.

aviour is useful, because when you're studying
st when it's relevant to you. Therefore, a good
nitive psychology's topics is to think about how
life and how you can use the knowledge to
igs. Fortunately, cognitive psychologists have
of fascinating findings that alter how people
)ter, you read about just some of the many ways
ty plays an important role in the real world – as

Recognising the Relevance of Cognitive Psychology

This section describes four main areas that cognitive psychology investigates:

- ✔ **Perception:** How you see and comprehend the surrounding world.
- ✔ **Memory:** How you process and recall events and experiences.
- ✔ **Language:** How you understand what others tell you and how you communicate with them.
- ✔ **Thinking:** How you reason and solve problems.

Paying attention in the real world

Studies of how people perceive and make sense of the world emphasise two key ideas about human perception – one good and one bad.

The good

Human perception is amazing – the ability to make sense of a visual scene seems so effortless that you can underestimate the difficulty of the task. But attempts to program computers to make sense of visual scenes as humans do have increased the appreciation of how difficult the perception process is.

Studying how the human brain solves the problem of perception allows psychologists to find out how to copy the clever mechanisms in the brain and so produce more effective learning.

 Companies such as Google are employing techniques such as *deep learning*. This approach aims to find *higher-order features* (those key visual aspects that define the image – in a face, the pattern of two eyes above a nose above a mouth) in visual images so that they can, for example, identify images that illustrate a particular concept (such as a cute kitten). Deep learning came out of insights gained from studying human cognition and how the human brain develops perceptual understanding in response to experience.

The bad

People's amazing ability to make sense of the world around them, however, has its limits. These limitations to human perception can cause problems.

When a new road tunnel opened in the Netherlands connecting Schiphol airport to Amsterdam, the result was a higher than normal rate of traffic accidents. Cognitive psychologists identified the issue (and called it the Schiphol Tunnel problem). The tunnel had a tapered design – both ends were rectangular shapes but the entrance from the airport was bigger and the tunnel sloped in towards a smaller exit. The motorists' visual systems interpreted what they were seeing as the exit being farther away (rather than being smaller), because normally tunnels are the same size at both ends. As a result, they reached the end of the tunnel faster than they were expecting, which made them think they were going too fast and they braked suddenly. This sudden braking increased the number of accidents.

Similarly, a number of major accidents have been linked to overly complicated control systems. For instance, confusing controls were a main contributing factor to the Three Mile Island nuclear plant disaster in 1979.

By understanding the limits on how much information a person can process at one time, as well as how to attract attention and present information in an easy-to-assimilate way, cognitive psychology has had a major impact on how interfaces are designed (similar to ergonomics). This understanding applies not only to critical systems, such as nuclear power plant control systems, but also to everyday systems such as mobile phones or ovens. The cognitive psychologist Don Norman wrote a classic book called *The Design of Everyday Things* in which he devotes considerable time pointing out bad design in everyday objects from doors to ovens!

Cognitive psychology shows that you need to understand your limits and to recognise when your perceptual and attentional abilities are overstretched.

Understanding memory in the real world

Cognitive psychology provides lots of relevant insights into your everyday memory, such as information relating to academic learning. In Chapter 3, we review what cognitive psychology offers in improving your study skills, but the impact of this subject goes far wider than your revision.

Wondering whether you really 'saw' what you 'saw'

Some of the most famous cognitive psychology studies are those conducted by Elizabeth Loftus and her colleagues, which look at how memory can be flawed and misled, particularly in eyewitness testimony. As we describe in Chapter 12, the ways in which questions are phrased to witnesses can affect their memory of traffic accidents.

In a similar vein, cognitive psychologists helped to develop an interview technique for police called the *cognitive interview*. This approach emphasises several important findings from the experimental research:

- ✔ **Avoid leading questions:** Such questions after the event can alter memory for the event.

- ✔ **Reinstate context:** Memory works through association and context. People tend to remember things better if they're in the same state of mind as when the event happened. So getting witnesses to recall how they were feeling, what they were doing and so on, even if it's not obviously relevant, helps them to recall important facts.

- ✔ **Adopt different perspectives and orders:** Asking witnesses to recall events in reverse order or from a perspective other than their own can prompt additional recall.

Dealing with traumatic memories

After experiencing traumatic events such as terrorist attacks, people sometimes develop post-traumatic stress disorder (PTSD). A major symptom of PTSD is intrusive memories that can cause great distress and disruption to a person's everyday life.

Understanding how memories are stored and changed allows cognitive psychologists to contribute to developing new therapeutic techniques that attempt to reduce the incidence and effect of traumatic memories.

The approach uses knowledge of how the human brain lays down a long-term memory, called *consolidation* (flip to Chapter 9 for more). Psychologists know that sleep helps consolidation (which is why you should sleep after studying and before an exam – see Chapter 3 for more exam tips), but, conversely, being deprived of sleep can interfere with the consolidation process. Sometimes, as in a traumatic event, people may benefit from not forming such lasting memories.

For example, recent research in the UK found that preventing a person from sleeping in the aftermath of a traumatic event may reduce the subsequent harmful psychological effects. For ethical reasons, this study looked at a simulated rather than a real traumatic event and so it remains to be seen whether this finding would translate to the real world, where events may be much more intense and emotionally disturbing.

An intriguing recent finding is that each time humans recall an event, it's restored, or *reconsolidated*, and can be altered. Therefore, the potential exists that a person can recall a traumatic event and then alter it in some way so that the reconsolidated version of the memory is less troubling. Just as an eyewitness's 'memory' for an event can be altered by subsequent questioning, by exploiting knowledge of the cognitive processes underlying memory clinical approaches may be able to alter a traumatic memory after the event.

Reading about language in the real world

Cognitive psychologists have had a great impact on the educational system through their advice on how best to teach reading. Researchers, such as the late Keith Rayner, used cunningly designed experiments and sophisticated eye-tracking technology to study the cognitive processes that the brain carries out when people read. This evidence was then used to inform governments' educational policies through the advice of expert panels.

Whole-word versus phonics

Two main but contrasting approaches are used to teach reading:

- **Whole-word approach:** Emphasises meaning by teaching words as whole units to be learned in meaningful contexts.
- **Phonics approach:** Focuses on the relationship between letters and sounds.

The evidence from cognitive psychology suggests that the whole-word approach is useful for gaining children's attention and interest, but the phonics approach is most successful in teaching reading effectively.

Understanding how people read led to the increased use of phonics-based approaches in schools. These emphasise that teachers (of English at least) should focus on the *alphabetic principle* – the idea that written letters are associated with spoken *phonemes* (the sounds comprising a language) – and on teaching the child the necessary *letter-to-sound mappings* (or *grapheme* – the letter that represents a sound – to phoneme correspondences) for the language: children learn the way spelling corresponds to sounds.

Understanding the cognitive psychology of language is fascinating in its own right. People use language constantly and yet many are unaware of how it works. Knowing a bit more about the mechanics of language can make them much more aware of the difficulties faced when learning to read and how to help others to understand the patterns of language.

Talk to me, Siri!

The development of mobile phone apps that allow users to ask questions in normal speech and have them answered is a remarkable achievement; it has taken many decades of research in computer science, linguistics and cognitive psychology. From the basic understanding of speech to the ability to make pragmatic inferences (for example, if someone asks 'Do you know the time?', replying 'yes' isn't appropriate!), these systems use knowledge gained from cognitive psychology experiments to emulate this amazing human ability.

Debating language processing

In 2012, an interesting debate took place about two approaches to language processing between Noam Chomsky, a founder of the so-called cognitive revolution in the 1950s, and Peter Norvig, Google's head of research. The debate centred on the modern approach that emphasises learning from experience and amassing vast amounts of statistics about relationships in the world versus the older approach that emphasised innate knowledge and logical systems.

Put simply, Norvig contends that people can learn languages simply by identifying the statistical relationships between words: some words occur more frequently near other words and this information is required to learn a language. Chomsky believes, however, that people have a degree of innate knowledge about the structure of language and that detecting statistical patterns doesn't pick this up. Fascinatingly, in one lifetime this argument has changed from being a philosophical debate to one about everyday computer science.

Thinking in the real world

Clearly, how people think, reason and solve problems is a central concern of cognitive psychology (we devote the whole of Part V to it).

Work by two famous duos set the tone in this area, and both pairs made contributions to psychology and economics. Allan Newell and Herb Simon established much of the fundamental research into how people solve problems and make decisions. They pioneered the computational modelling of human problem-solving as well as various techniques for understanding how people solve problems. They indicated that when solving problems, people develop a problem space in which they map out their current state, the goal and all steps in between based on logic. Later, Daniel Kahneman and Amos Tversky carried out a range of experiments that demonstrated the use of *heuristics* (mental short-cuts such as stereotypes) in human decision-making and the resulting biases these cause in people's reasoning.

Early research in cognitive psychology emphasised thinking *problems*, but recent years have seen a more positive focus: how can people apply knowledge of cognitive psychology to improve decision-making? Research by Gerd Gigerenzer and colleagues shows that if people reason using methods more suited to the human brain, they can improve their decision-making. For example, in just a few hours cognitive psychologists can train doctors to make more effective interpretations of patients' test results by teaching them a method that suits the brain's 'natural' way of working.

Research in this area of cognitive psychology suggests that you can improve your thinking by making simple changes to the way you approach problems – read more about applying this knowledge to your study skills in Chapter 3.

Studying Cognitive Systems to See What Goes Right . . . and Wrong

A common theme in cognitive psychology is a distinction between normal and abnormal functioning. Many cognitive psychology courses emphasise the normal functioning of the human cognitive systems, but not because cognitive psychologists aren't interested in abnormal psychology. The reason is more because in order to understand how something goes wrong, you need to understand how it goes right. Sometimes the study of normal functioning helps psychologists to understand how a system can go wrong.

On the other hand, sometimes a clinical problem can inform people about how the system normally works. For example, a very rare condition known as *akinetopsia* (also known as motion blindness – see Chapter 21 for a case study) helped psychologists to understand that a distinct part of the brain handles the perception of visual motion compared to that of visual form. In other words, seeing and recognising an object occurs in one part of the brain, and perceiving that the same object is moving is handled by a different part.

Cognitive psychology can help people understand how different cognitive functions can go wrong, and also offer help in finding ways to treat or ameliorate a condition. Understanding cognitive processes and how they can have negative effects is at the root of the development of *cognitive behavioural therapy* (CBT), which shows people how to recognise negative or distorted thinking patterns and to modify them.

For example, in cases of *catastrophising* (where people turn small problems into major incidents) or the tendency to dwell on negative memories when depressed, the person can use CBT to recognise a developing negative thought process and nip it in the bud. (Check out *Cognitive Behavioural Therapy For Dummies* by Rhena Branch and Rob Willson [Wiley].)

Accepting that Cognitive Psychology Doesn't Have All the Answers

The short history of cognitive psychology has been tightly linked to the development of the digital computer. Therefore, as technology advances at an ever-increasing rate, the need for cognitive psychology and its potential usefulness to society increases. This is an exciting time to be involved in a growing field and new cognitive psychologists (like you?) can set forth and explore the burgeoning possibilities.

One caveat, however. Like other areas of psychology, cognitive psychology is an *empirical* science: it advances through the design of experiments and the collection of data – psychologists are finding out new things all the time. Studying it isn't just about learning the known 'facts' about human thought, but discovering the methods by which new discoveries may be made.

For this reason, throughout this book you see an emphasis on the methods and clever experimental designs used to establish the facts. Therefore, get into the habit of asking yourself not just *what* psychologists know but also *how* they know it. The methods used are at least as important as the findings.

Chapter 3

Improving Academic Performance with Cognitive Psychology

With this book, we aim to convince you that cognitive psychology is worth discovering and that it has many practical uses. In this chapter, we show how cognitive psychology led to improvements in how people teach and learn. If you use the skills and useful pointers that we describe, you can perform better when producing essays and taking exams. We present ways of improving the four aspects of cognition (from Chapter 2): perception and attention, memory, language, and thinking and reasoning.

It's true! These techniques really do work. In other chapters, we describe the psychological theories and scientific evidence for *why* they work, but for now we simply present a series of techniques to improve your cognition and help your academic progress.

Here are three crucial lessons to take from this chapter: the importance of practice; of recognising familiar problems in unfamiliar forms; and of using your higher-level thinking strategies to determine how you approach your work, plan your study and structure your written work.

Engaging Your Perception and Attention

The brain drives a lot of your abilities to sense, perceive and attend to the world, but you can also improve many of them by knowing about cognitive psychology. Here we give you some ideas on how to use knowledge about perception and attention to improve your performance in school and college.

Before we go into the specific details, one general rule is to be aware of your own *circadian rhythm* – the natural cycle of your body. Your brain and body work better at different times of the day, but everyone is different. Some people are best in the morning and some in the evening. One of your authors is a morning person, which means that his attention span is greatest around 10:30 a.m. Your other author is an evening person, and his attention span is greatest around 8:30 p.m. When you're aware of your own circadian rhythm, you can study when it's best for you.

Of course, schools often set exams in the mornings (dreadful for evening people). To ensure that you're in a suitable frame of mind for such exams, you can shift your body clock (in a similar manner to jet lag). Basically, wake up much earlier, so that the 9 a.m. exam occurs after you've been awake for some time and falls within your optimum attention time.

Massing your practice

Some experts are able to perceive something (typically an object, such as a chess board) they have extensive experience in perceiving using one eye fixation, looking only at the centre of an image. From this scan, they're able to remember, interpret and process more than mere novices. Chapter 5 has lots on improving your perception.

These experts have this ability because of *massed practice*, which is where a great deal of learning occurs in a short space of time. This method is in contrast with *distributed practice*, which involves short intervals of learning (the later section 'Storing for the long term' has more about distributed practice).

Typically, you need to do massed practice for approximately six hours a day for weeks, months or even years. Results consistently show that people who engage in massed practice perform better at perceptual and motor tasks than those who engage in other forms of practice.

Consider this example: if you play World of Warcraft for six hours solidly a day for a year, you'll be better at it than someone who plays it for one hour six times a day for a year. In other words, to improve perceptual and motor abilities, your practice must be consistent.

This technique works for perceptual and motor skills, such as playing sports, games (including chess) or music, but it doesn't work for learning maths or more intellectual subjects.

Capturing attention

One way to help engage attention on work is to develop a script (see Chapter 11) that ends with you studying.

A *script* is a chunk of behaviours that always occur together. You can create one by coming up with a routine. For one of your authors, it involves starting the computer up, logging onto Facebook, playing a silly game for 3 minutes 30 seconds (no more, no less), reading a news website and then starting work.

Focusing attention

You can improve your attention span and stay focused in a number of simple ways. For example, taking mild to moderate exercise 15 minutes before you attempt to learn, and drinking water, help to release the appropriate chemicals in your brain that aid learning and memory storage.

One obvious action is to turn off distractions, such as mobile phones and Facebook (though we struggle with both!). Also, remember that the average person has an attention span of around 40 minutes (though the figure depends on the task's complexity and how you're learning it). After this time, learning new information becomes harder. So, take breaks of about 15 minutes after studying for some 30 to 40 minutes.

Another key thing, as we describe in more detail in Chapter 7, is the ability to multitask. If the two tasks use different aspects of your working memory (see Chapter 8), you can do them both at the same time, as long as they're simple enough. But in most cases, performance on both tasks is much lower if you try to multitask than if you do one task at a time.

You can buy many apps designed to 'improve' your attention. At present, the research as to whether these work or not is highly mixed. You do find that people who practise one attentional task perform better at that attention task later, but does this ability generalise to other tasks or in studying? The answer is probably not.

Avoiding distraction

Knowing what distracts you means that you can learn how to avoid such distractions. A huge amount of research in ergonomics and human factors has explored these issues and the resounding result is (ta-da!) speech! That's it. Speech is the one thing above all else (and in fact it may be the only thing) that distracts people from working – whether it's speech from the TV, someone talking, the radio, a person on a telephone or whatever.

Researchers call this the *irrelevant speech effect*, and even something that sounds like speech can distract you. The reason is that speech is an unpredictable sound and yet it carries meaning and has superior access to memory. That's why open-plan offices are so bad for staff productivity if they have jobs that require focused attention. It's also one of the main reasons why speaking to someone on the phone while driving is incredibly dangerous.

To avoid this distraction, the best thing to do is study in an environment where you can avoid other people's speech. That can mean in silence or creating your own predictable noise, such as turning on music. Yes . . . one surprising device that focuses your attention is music and/or noise in general. Although rather counterintuitive and going against many people's opinion, you can filter out music that's very familiar – and if it's louder than any distracting speech, it prevents distraction.

So go ahead and pump up the volume, and if anyone argues say psychologists told you to. Of course, silence is also as effective, but then as soon as a speech-like noise sounds, it can distract you.

Improving Your Learning and Memory

An entire field is devoted to how best to learn and remember things: *educational psychology*. Here we review some of these techniques related to cognitive psychology. For studying and revision, most of the skills you want to know about concern remembering information, and so that's what we cover. Check out the chapters in Part III for loads more on the processes behind learning, memory and forgetting.

Most of the techniques we describe involve you actively processing the information or doing something to aid your memory. Learning is an active process, but some forms of activity help memory more than others. Sadly, simply listening to tapes of something while you sleep, or reading a book, doesn't provide you with the proper environment to learn. Instead, you need to engage with the material.

Working the memory

Most of the strategies that assist in learning information connect to working memory and involve combining new knowledge with existing knowledge. Here we give three examples of how you can do this in order to improve memory:

- ✔ **Chunking:** You group incoming information that's largely meaningless into small manageable chunks that are meaningful. We talk more about the concept of chunking in Chapter 8.

- ✔ **Levels of processing framework:** This technique comes from how you process information and suggests that information that's processed more deeply is more likely to be stored and therefore remembered (see Chapter 9 for more details).

- ✔ **Mnemonics:** Devices that aid learning by forming links between the lists of information to learn with something you already know. Mnemonics make the information more personally relevant and meaningful and so elaborate it during processing (refer to the preceding point). By making the mnemonic successful, you build more retrieval cues and links to memory. Studies show that memory scores are up to 77 per cent higher for people using mnemonics than for those who don't.

You can develop many different types of mnemonics:

  - Replace the words that you're trying to learn with something easier to learn (for example, Richard of York gave battle in vain, for the colours of the rainbow).

  - Replace the entire list of information to learn with a name (for example, the names of the US Great Lakes can make the name HOMES).

  - Put the lists to remember into a tune to form a song.

  - Use rhymes or draw pictures to remember information.

  - Create mental images to represent what you need to remember.

Storing for the long term

Many techniques claim to help people remember information for the long term. Here are just a couple that you can use in your studies and revision. They've been studied using research that explored people's ability to remember things following different types of learning.

Distributing practice

A consistent finding is that practice makes perfect. You can learn information from a textbook by reading it multiple times. But it's not as simple as that. You can study the same thing for hours and hours and then stop. Or you can study in short bursts. Which is better?

Results clearly show that distributing the practice is beneficial for academic learning (for perceptual and motor learning, massed practice is better – see the earlier 'Massing your practice' section). Distributing learning works best when you study in lots of bursts of study of less than one hour.

Testing what you know

One of the most intriguing findings is the *test effect*, which is where you study something for a short period and then test yourself on what you know. Research shows that you learn more than simply studying for the same amount of time. This testing seems to cause you to form new links in your memory with that information. You're building up the links between the information and retrieval cues needed to access that information. Read Chapter 9 for more on retrieval cues.

Test yourself on what you've learnt, correct any errors and test again.

Avoiding forgetting

Interference is when something you're learning or have learnt interferes with your stored knowledge or current learning (we discuss different types in Chapter 11). An example is when one of the authors foolishly tried to learn two languages at the same time. He failed completely, confusing the two.

You can easily avoid interference by ensuring that when learning two similar things, you employ different techniques to learn them. Don't learn two similar things in the same location or using the same style.

Retrieving information quicker

To get information from your head faster and so aid your exam performance, you can use techniques that improve your access to cues. Two specific skills can help:

✔ **Attempt to match the state and environment of learning to that of the test:** Evidence suggests that when you're retrieving information in the same condition as when you learnt it, your retrieval is better. This condition can be as simple as being in the same mood, in the same room, in the same seating position, wearing the same clothes, using the same pens (sounds a bit like a superstition, doesn't it?). Anything that can create an extra link between the retrieval situation and the learning situation helps you to retrieve information.

This method is less effective for recognition (and so don't use it for multiple choice exams). Also, don't rely on this method alone: you must have the information stored in your head to be able to retrieve it!

✔ **Relax your mind and think about other things:** When you calm down, a solution often presents itself. This skill stems from very recent research on *third-stream consciousness*, which is where solutions to problems, including retrieving memories, can come to mind precisely when you don't try to think about them.

Polishing Up Your Academic Reading and Writing Skills

Being a student involves a lot of reading. Many adults think that their reading ability is something that they acquire in childhood and is relatively fixed. But as with other cognitive skills, becoming an expert reader is a matter of practice.

Step one is to read as much and as often as possible.

Reading strategically

After you acquire the basic skills of reading printed words, you can further improve your reading skills by using *metacognitive strategies*: these refer to what you read, what order you read it in and how carefully you read. The word *cognition* refers to thinking, and so *metacognition* refers to thinking about thinking. Cognitive psychologists do this all the time, but everyone can benefit from thinking about how they think.

Reading the rules

Sometimes adults can have problems with reading because they haven't learnt the rules of the language. Research by cognitive psychologist Diane McGuinness shows that adults with poor reading skills often see a great improvement in their reading ability if they're taught with an intensive phonics-based programme – one that emphasises the correspondences between letters and sounds in the language. Chapter 2 has a little more on phonics.

This research suggests that an inability to read as an adult may be due to not having learnt the appropriate spelling-sound rules as a child.

If you're reading a novel, you start at the beginning and read every word until the last page. But this strategy isn't usually the best for academic reading. Instead, you can use a range of metacognitive strategies to help you get the most out of a text with the least effort.

Here's a process we recommend:

1. **Skim or preview the text.**

   Have a quick scan through the document, paying particular attention to any summary at the beginning, section headings and overall structure. Decide in advance what parts of a document are most important, what bits you can skim over and what bits you can ignore.

2. **Read with purpose.**

   Before you start reading, decide what you want to find out from the text. Setting goals for your reading helps you approach the text strategically.

3. **Make your reading personal.**

   When reading an idea, ask yourself what you think about the idea: do you agree with the author? Does what you're reading fit with your existing knowledge? How can the material help for your purpose, such as writing an essay or revising for an exam?

4. **Ask questions.**

   Question what you're reading and attempt to anticipate what would follow on.

5. **Translate into your own language.**

   Summarise ideas in your own words or explain them to a friend. To do so, you have to process the material more deeply, thinking about the meaning rather than just the words.

6. **Make it interesting!**

   Focus on the ideas in a text that interest you. If a passage is boring or technical, skim over it and come back to it later if necessary.

7. **Use context to make sense of ideas.**

   When children learn to speak, they make use of context to learn new words. If you don't know a word or phrase, try to guess what it means based on the parts of the text that you do understand.

8. **Make a note and come back to it.**

   If you need to read up on some concepts, note them down and look them up later instead of interrupting your reading.

9. **Keep the flow.**

   Skimming over bits you don't understand is usually better than constantly interrupting the flow of your reading. If children stopped listening every time they heard a word they didn't know, they'd never learn language. You may be surprised by how much you remember about a text when you stop trying to understand everything and just enjoy your reading.

10. **Read more!**

Practising strategic reading of academic books and research papers is the single best thing you can do to improve. Most cognitive psychology research is published in the form of papers, which follow a standard structure (see Chapter 22). With practice, you discover which bits to focus on and which bits you can skim over, depending on what you want to know.

Improving your writing

As a student of cognitive psychology, you're likely to have to write essays or research reports. Both have their own specific constraints.

The first rule of good writing is to understand the format. Read any guidelines you're given and make sure that you know the word limits. Writing has two basic stages: planning (when you decide what you're going to write and in what order) and writing the actual words. We deal with the planning stage in the later 'Planning systematically' section, but for now we consider the words.

Writing is an example of language production. As we discuss in Chapter 15, producing language involves your brain working through a sequence of stages starting with the semantic level, where you develop an idea that you want to express. Then you identify the elements of the sentence – such as subject, action and object – and translate the elements into words.

To speak a sentence, you need to convert the sequence of words into a representation of how they sound and then produce those sounds using a complex sequence of movements with your mouth and vocal chords – all without conscious effort. Well, your brain goes through this same process even when you don't speak out loud.

Thinking and speaking: It's all the same to me

When you're just working out mentally how to say what you want to say, tiny movements in your mouth and throat muscles reflect the full-size movements that would occur when speaking. Sensitive electrodes can detect this *sub-vocal speech*, which is how NASA was able to develop computer speech recognition software that allows you to communicate just by thinking a sentence rather than having to say it out loud.

If, like most people, you find spoken conversation easier than writing, you can help your writing by imagining that you're speaking out loud and focus on how your words 'sound'. Another useful trick is to imagine that you're explaining your ideas to a specific person or group of people that you know. Doing so enables you to bring into play your considerable existing experience of using language. You may not be an experienced writer but you are an expert at chatting to friends and family – when you imagine that you're doing this you can exploit a vast reservoir of existing knowledge in your brain.

Imagining that you're talking to friends is good for improving the fluency of your writing, but when writing essays and reports you need to take additional factors into account. One is the different style of language used in academic writing, and another is the more specific rules that you're required to follow, such as keeping to word limits or using a certain section heading structure.

You can do two things to improve these aspects of your writing:

- ✔ **Get as much experience of the appropriate style of writing as you can.** Read lots of research papers and text books in your subject to get a feel for the style of writing. Also, amass a large number of 'chunks' of material that you can use, such as specific ways to start a sentence.

- ✔ **Use your existing ability to modify your tone or work within constraints.** You probably use different language depending on whether you're talking to a friend, a grandparent or a stranger, so you're already used to modifying your language style for different contexts. Plus, most people have experience of working within tight word limits thanks to text messaging and Twitter.

The Manchester Phrasebank (www.phrasebank.manchester.ac.uk), a good source for academic writing style, lists many useful chunks of text.

Using Your Thinking Powers More Effectively

The *executive functions* of the brain guide your overall behaviour, including higher-level thinking skills such as problem solving, reasoning and decision-making (Part V of this book has lots more). This higher-level thinking is important in planning your study and the work you produce.

Using rational logic

Reading this book gives you a better understanding of the rules of logic and some of the common logical errors that people make. This knowledge can improve your ability to see the flaws in other people's arguments, as well as enhance your own ability to construct a rational argument. It also makes you aware of the steps that people go through when making or understanding an argument, which should help improve the structure of your academic writing.

Planning systematically

Planning each stage of a project makes sense, as does identifying the amount of work you need to do and what problems you're likely to face before you embark on a project.

Cognitive psychology uses the *state space approach* to planning (we cover it more fully in Chapter 17). In this approach, you plan a series of states between your current one and your goal state, considering alternative choices that you could make at each stage and how that's likely to affect the outcome. This technique can give you a good sense of how you need to direct your attention and spend your available time.

Creating and using sub-goals

Students sometimes panic because they see a piece of work as a single, indivisible whole that's too big to get their heads around.

Divide the task into sub-goals using *hierarchical decomposition*. Here, you break the problem down into a few smaller problems and then repeat the process to break the smaller problems into even smaller parts. Eventually you end up with a set of manageable problems that, when combined, solve the big problem. For example, when writing a research report, you can break the problem down into writing each section of the report and then break each section down to its paragraphs. Before you know it, the job's done!

The more experience you have with a problem, the more likely you are to recognise one that you know how to solve. Also, as you gain experience you recognise more of the sub-goals of a problem and have better ideas about how to solve them. Over time you build up a store of these chunks of experience and also learn how to deal with bigger and bigger problems.

Automating components

The more you practise any skill, the more you can deal with problems automatically. When you repeat a series of actions, the brain comes to recognise the pattern and creates a new procedure for carrying out the process without you having to think about it too much.

With lots of practice at writing essays or reports, you begin to be able to do more and more of the process automatically, which frees up your mental resources to deal with bigger problems.

Working backwards

When asked how he creates new jokes, the comedian Bill Bailey replied, 'I start with a laugh and work backwards'. This process isn't far from how people often solve problems.

In a process called *means-ends analysis*, people identify the goal and work out what they can do to achieve it: to get a laugh you need a punchline, to get a punchline you need a set-up and so on.

So when planning your next piece of academic work, start by identifying what goes into a top grade piece of work and then work backwards by finding the specific pieces that go into it. Doing so can help you break down the problem of writing your essay. Having a positive goal in mind also motivates you and focuses your attention on the most important aspects of the problem.

Developing a growth mindset

According to psychologist Carol Dweck of Stanford University, one of the most important factors affecting student performance is what she calls *mindset*. A person's mindset is another example of metacognition or thinking about thinking (we talk about this in the section 'Reading strategically' earlier in this chapter). According to Dweck, in general people have one of two main types of mindset:

✔ **Fixed mindset:** These individuals tend to think that people are born with certain abilities that remain relatively fixed throughout their lives. People with this mindset are likely to stick to things they're good at and avoid developing new skills in areas where they feel inexperienced. They value achievement over effort and often only like problems they can solve easily.

✔ **Growth mindset:** These people display almost the opposite approach – they think that people can get better through practice and so value effort over achievement. They often do much better at new problems, because they make an effort and aren't discouraged by their mistakes.

The exciting aspect about Dweck's work is that she shows that you can change people's mindset through simple interventions. Even just knowing about the concept tends to make people more likely to shift from a fixed mindset to a growth mindset.

Part II
Attending to the Subtleties of Perception

web extras

To test how your brain adapts as what your eyes see changes, go online to this part's free article at www.dummies.com/extras/cognitivepsychology.

In this part . . .

✔ Appreciate all the biological processes involved in perception. If you don't have the right information coming in, you can't decide on the correct course of action or reason and argue appropriately.

✔ See your amazing visual abilities in action – and how they can be fooled.

✔ Understand how you perceive objects of all sorts, particularly the special case of recognising faces.

✔ Pay attention to the concept of attention, one of the most vital abilities for human survival. Without it you'd be constantly overwhelmed and distracted.

Chapter 4

Perceiving the World around You

*B*efore you can learn, memorise or study anything, you need to perceive it. Sounds simple, but this process involves a number of biological processes that psychology textbooks often ignore and yet are fundamental to understanding the field (not to mention fun to look at!).

To understand cognition, and certainly to assess the cognitive psychology models that we describe throughout this book, you need to know what information the brain receives. For this reason, studying perception is vital for understanding cognitive psychology.

Although you have all sorts of senses, in this chapter we explore the eyes and how the brain uses the information they provide. We establish that seeing is a highly psychological process and affected by cognition. We demonstrate that seeing isn't always believing, by filling you in on some cool visual illusions that highlight how easily the human visual system can be tricked. Such illusions reveal important information about how people see and why they see the way they do.

Delving into Your Perception System

Everyone has the same basic biological set-up in order to sense the world: eyes, ears, nose and so on. But people don't see and hear things in exactly the same way, due to the psychological processes involved.

Two contrasting psychological approaches

Much of human behaviour is responding to the environment, and so *psychophysics* was devised to explore exactly how this occurs: in other words, to explore the limits of human perception. The main proponent of psychophysics research was Gustav Fechner, a German physicist, psychologist and philosopher. His logic was to find the minimum sensation to see a particular stimulus or to distinguish between two stimuli. The psychophysics approach treated humans as physical organisms and ignored things such as free will. Psychophysicists weren't interested in *how* people interpreted what they sensed – just that they did. Therefore, it's very objective and based solely on data.

An alternative school of thought primarily interested in the quality of people's perception was *structuralism*, attributed mostly to Wilhelm Wundt, a German physician, physiologist and philosopher. Wundt suggested that the mind represents the world as individual elements with many different cognitive processes that interact with each other. The mind takes what the body senses and creatively attempts to understand it based on its internal structure (see Chapter 10). Structuralists thought that the best way to research the human experience was analytic introspection. This approach requires a detailed verbal description of what's being seen or thought about and why this is happening. The data produced is highly subjective, based entirely on the individual's own opinions.

Psychophysics is still widely used, whereas structuralism is rarely taken seriously.

Two early schools of thought in psychology made the following important distinction between sensation and perception (see the nearby sidebar 'Two contrasting psychological approaches' for more details):

- **Sensation:** How the senses and brain detect and transmit information about the world
- **Perception:** What each person's consciousness 'sees' and responds to

Your brain sees the world differently to someone else's – and possibly in a way that isn't exactly correct – because it's always trying to make sense of the world in order to respond to it in the best way.

Sensing and perceiving the world is vitally important: you're constantly receiving sensory stimulation. Without such sensory information constantly streaming into your brain, you may not even be considered alive. If you're in a sensory deprivation chamber (used for meditation purposes), your brain creates sensations in the form of hallucinations. Without stimulation, people's brains create their own sensations!

Perception is critical to action. In order to do something, you need to perceive it. When you see a chocolate bar, you need to use all the information your eyes give you to reach out and pick it up. Then you use the combination of information from the eyes and fingers to open it so that you get the pleasure of the taste.

People use many different senses to understand the world: as well as vision, hearing, touch, taste and smell, you can also detect much more (such as balance and temperature). Although in this chapter we look only at vision, note that each sense gives you different information, with very little redundancy among them: information is generally only provided by one of the senses. That's not to say the senses are entirely separable, however: vision can affect taste, for example.

Seeing What's Going on in the World

The eye is one of the most amazing organs in the human body. It allows you to see in so many situations: from the bright sunlight on the deck of a cruise ship to a dimly lit nightclub. Even in these two widely different environments, your vision is sufficient for you to move around safely.

As these two examples suggest, the crucial element in seeing is light: it carries the information that you use to see the world and is extremely useful for sensation. Light interacts with many things that it touches, reflecting off some objects and being absorbed by others, and in this way providing information about what objects are. Fortunately, the world has lots of light: the sun (note, not *The Sun*!) produces a huge amount. To find out more details, check out the nearby sidebar 'Lighting up the world', which you can read, of course, due to light!

In this section we describe sight in physical terms: how the brain processes what the eyes see.

Positioning the eye

The eye is the device that detects the light carrying the information you need, for example to perceive objects.

Lighting up the world

Light is a form of electromagnetic radiation, which includes radio waves, infrared and ultraviolet. Electromagnetic radiation travels incredibly fast: at the speed of light, in fact. Therefore, light travelling from the teeth of a predator that's a few metres away reaches you virtually instantaneously, allowing you plenty of time to run away (you hope).

One important feature of light waves is their *wavelength*, which is the frequency with which light waves oscillate (think of sea waves crashing on the shore: if one crashes against the

shore very close to another, it has a short wavelength). Light with different wavelengths has slightly different properties. Crucially, only certain wavelengths of light are visible to humans and provide information about colour.

Light has one other important feature: *amplitude* (size of the wave). The bigger the amplitude, the more energy it contains. Again, think of sea waves. The size of the wave is the amplitude. Big waves that surfers ride are much more powerful than the little ones in which kiddies paddle.

Have you ever wondered why your eyes are placed where they are? Well, wonder no more. Certain animals have eyes on the sides of their head and others have them on the front, for very good reasons:

- Animals with two eyes facing forward have greater visual abilities for things in front of them, because light enters both eyes. Therefore, chasing other animals is easier for them, though they can't see much at right angles or more to the side of the head.

- Animals with eyes on the sides of their heads (such as rabbits) are able to see almost all the way around their bodies, with the exception of the very back. They're much less able to see fine detail in front of them. These animals are often prey and need to be on constant alert for animals that hunt them.

Like most apes, humans have eyes in the front of the head, helping them to see the fine detail necessary for hunting, foraging, stereovision and manual tasks, such as using tools to prise open impenetrable milk cartons.

Staring into the eye

The eye is a water-filled, jelly-like ball, with a black hole (it really is just a hole) at the front (the *pupil*) to allow light in. Behind the pupil is a lens (like those in specs) designed to focus the light coming in on the back of the eye (the *retina*), where the photoreceptors detect the light.

To let more light in when you move into the dark, the pupil widens. To reduce the amount of light coming into the eye (and prevent damage to the delicate parts of the eye beyond), the pupil constricts. Of course, pupil width can change in response to psychological factors too (such as when you see someone you fancy!).

Detecting light: Photoreceptors

The *photoreceptors* are at the back of the eye, behind layers of other stuff. They're distributed all over the retina, but with many more cones in the *fovea* (middle of vision) than in the *periphery* (edges of vision):

- **Cones:** Photoreceptors that respond in bright light and are good at colour detection (check out Chapter 5)
- **Rods:** Photoreceptors that respond in dim light and aren't great at colour detection (which is why detecting colour at night is harder)

This uneven distribution of photoreceptors means that the fovea is the place of maximum resolution. Seeing fine detail is much easier (has higher *visual acuity*) in the fovea and the periphery appears more blurry, which is why people move their eyes to look at important scenes.

The eye muscles are the busiest muscles in the human body. They move more than 100,000 times a day. In fact, eye movements are so important that without them you'd go blind.

Don't believe us? Check out Figure 4-1, which shows an example of what's called Troxler fading. Stare at the '+' in the centre and watch as the shading around the outside begins to fade away.

This effect happens because your brain works by comparing one retinal image with the next: with no difference, the brain thinks that nothing's present. The brain 'sees' by detecting differences between two scenes, and if you paralyse the eye muscles you see nothing at all. You require your eye muscles to see, even though they're not involved in the detection of light. The nearby sidebar 'Moving the eyes' has more about eye movements.

Responding to light: Centre-surround layout

In 1962, Nobel Prize winning neurophysiologists David Hubel and Torsten Wiesel discovered the interesting layout of visual cells beyond the retina (*retinal ganglion cells*). By shining a small bit of light onto each cell, and measuring the response that cell gave, they discovered what the cell responded to (its *receptive field*). They found that the cells have a donut-shaped layout (called the *centre-surround layout*). The centre responds to light being on, whereas the surround responds to light being off (you can have the opposite layout too).

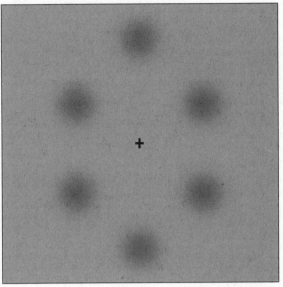

Figure 4-1:
Troxler
fading.

© John Wiley & Sons, Inc.

Moving the eyes

An entire research field is devoted to moving the eyes, because it's such a complex brain process. Several types of eye movements have been discovered, including:

✔ **Conjugate eye movements:** Where both eyes move together, such as when you follow an object from side to side when watching a tennis match.

✔ **Vergence eye movements:** Where the eyes move in different directions to each other, such as when you're watching things move closer to and farther away from your face. For example, if you put your finger directly in front of your face and bring it towards your nose, your eyes roll together and you go cross-eyed.

Your eyes can also move in two distinct patterns:

✔ **Smooth pursuit eye movements:** Identified by the smooth movement of the eyes, as when you're following an object.

✔ **Saccadic eye movements:** Far more common are these fast, bullet-like movements, jumping from scene to scene quickly between two items spaced apart (such as now, when you're reading).

These eye movement patterns reveal a great deal about what's important to a perceiver. If something is important, people look at it. If something attracts attention, people look at it. Patients with schizophrenia are unable to perform smooth pursuit eye movement tasks very well. In fact, the difficulty that patients have with this ability directly predicts the severity of their symptoms and how likely they are to relapse.

Eye movement is so important that no less than ten distinct parts of the brain are devoted to it. The most important is located in the frontal lobes farthest away from the rest of your visual processing (in the occipital lobe).

This layout ensures that you can see changes in light much more easily. It also helps you to see small things. If a small bit of light shines on the centre of an on-centre cell but doesn't touch the outer part, the cell responds a lot; however, if light shines across the whole cell (both on-centre and the off-surround parts), the cell doesn't fire. Light moving across a cell causes a small cellular response, except for the brief period when only the on-centre has light on it.

One of the consequences of the centre-surround layout is that sometimes you see things that aren't there. Consider the Hermann grid illusion in Figure 4-2: you should see illusory grey spots appearing in most of the white intersections. This effect occurs because at the intersections more light is on the off-surround than the on-centre of the cell's receptive field, causing the whole region to appear to have no light.

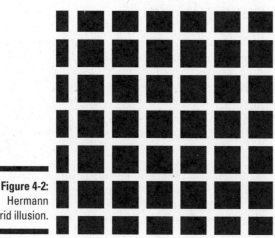

Figure 4-2: Hermann grid illusion.

© John Wiley & Sons, Inc.

The effect doesn't occur in the fovea, because the cells here respond to a smaller region (if you bring the book sufficiently close to your fovea, you get illusory dots in the intersections you're looking at as well).

Arranging the photoreceptors: Finding the blindspot

In the cells in the fovea, a small section in each eye doesn't have any receptor cells, which means that it can't see anything. This area is the *blindspot*, though you can't see a hole because the brain fills in the gaps.

To 'see' your blindspot, close your left eye and look at the '+' in Figure 4-3. Hold the book upright about 50 centimetres in front of you – you may need to move it forward or backward a little. Can you see what the other letter is? It disappears when it's in the blindspot. Your brain can't see the letter and so it fills in the region with whatever is around it.

Figure 4-3:
Seeing the
blindspot.

| + | | A |

© John Wiley & Sons, Inc.

This example demonstrates that vision is an active process and that the brain changes and distorts what you see. As a result, detecting whether you have visual problems is difficult, because your brain always tries to compensate. This filling-in is incredibly important. If you're crossing the road, a car can be in the blindspot and you don't see it. So, the road safety advice is right: always look, look away and look back again.

Organising the visual brain

The information from each eye leaves via an *optic nerve* (the blindspot in the preceding section exists because the information leaves the eye there and heads to the brain). Damage to the optic nerve means that you lose vision in one eye, because at a point (the *optic chiasm*) information from the two eyes mixes. Information representing the left of what's seen in each eye is sent to the right *optic tract* and information from the right of what's seen is sent to the left optic tract. If one optic tract is cut, you lose vision for one side of the world (called *hemianopia*).

Cells from the optic tract go to part of the brain called the *lateral geniculate nucleus* (LGN), which is arranged into six layers. Two layers are *magnocellular* and are sensitive to movement and the other four, *parvocellular*, layers are sensitive to colour and show high visual acuity.

Exploring primary vision

The neurons take visual information from the LGN to the *primary visual cortex* (area V1) of the brain in the occipital lobe. This is the first area of the brain that generates conscious visual experiences and is located at the very back of the head.

You can tell that this is the centre for vision, because if you stimulate cells (using brain stimulation or a hard strike!) in this part of the head you see something. If you hit the back of the head hard enough you see stars (like in cartoons) and this response comes from neural activity in the visual cortex (but don't try it!).

The primary visual cortex is said to be *retinotopically mapped*: it's like a map of the visual world – something that's next to something in space is processed by cells next to each other in the brain.

Some cells in the primary visual cortex are *simple cells* – the basic building blocks of vision. They detect and process simple shapes, such as edges or bars, but each cell processes only the edges in a particular orientation (a vertical bar detector doesn't 'see' a horizontal bar).

Simple cells exist for many different types of edges, bars and lines, with more cells for more frequently encountered edges. Humans have more cells for horizontal and vertical bars than for oblique angles. (Cats have cells for all orientations; perhaps that's why they often look at humans with superior disdain.) So, humans find detecting horizontal and vertical lines easier than those of other angles (the *oblique effect*). In other words, they have greater visual acuity for horizontal and vertical lines.

The oblique effect shows how experience affects the cells in the brain. For instance, people living in the rainforest or the North American plains don't display the same oblique effect: those in the rainforest have fewer horizontal cells and those in the plains have fewer vertical cells.

In the brain, the responses of several simple cells can be combined into a *complex cell*. A complex cell can process a vertical bar, but of any size and anywhere in the visual world. Farther into the brain, the responses of several complex cells can combine to form *hypercomplex cells*, which respond to even more complicated sets of patterns, such as a moving vertical bar.

By this simple process of adding up the responses of the cells, people create the entire world (this idea is the basis for some psychological models of perception; see Chapter 6). If you combine a series of simple cells representing curves of particular orientations, you can construct a hyper (or hyper-hyper) complex cell for faces. Indeed, Dave Perrett, a British neuroscientist, and colleagues have shown that some cells seem selectively to respond to faces.

Given this knowledge, perhaps a hypercomplex cell represents everything that you've seen, adding together the activation of many simple and complex cells representing the edges that make up the object. Therefore, you'd have a cell for every single thing you've ever seen – known as the *grandmother cell* argument: to see your grandmother, you need a cell that represents your grandmother. Indeed, brain imaging research shows cells that seem to respond only to Jennifer Aniston, which seems to indicate that the grandmother cell argument is valid.

But if this were the case, people would need many more neurons in their brains than they have. To address this major flaw in the argument, instead of each cell responding to a single thing, maybe a collection of cells together respond and some of these cells overlap with other objects.

Seeing farther into the brain

The primary visual cortex is associated with limited and basic visual processing. More detailed processing occurs in later brain areas. However, two main visual pathways appear to exist after area V1:

- **The 'what' pathway:** Designed to establish the identity of what you're seeing. It's described as the *temporal stream*, because it involves brain regions in the temporal lobes that process memory (see the chapters in Part III). It's also called the *dorsal stream*, because it rises over the top of the head (like a dorsal fin of a whale). The crucial brain regions involved in the 'what' pathway are areas such as V4 and V3, which process colour and shape, respectively. This stream is considered vision for perception.

- **The 'where' pathway:** Designed to establish where something is. It's more basic than the 'what' pathway: it simply signals the location and movement of something, but not what it is. This pathway is described as the *parietal stream*, because it goes to the parietal lobes, and sometimes the *ventral stream*, because it goes low through the base of the brain, closer to the stomach (*ventral* is stomach in Latin). It passes through area V5, which processes movement. This stream is considered vision for action.

The idea that the brain breaks up the world into many separate properties such as colour and form (known as *functional specialisation*) is the subject of extensive debate among psychologists. After the information is broken up, higher brain areas must then *bind* all the information together to form a complete representation (see Chapter 6).

Constructing What You See in the World

In the earlier section 'Arranging the photoreceptors: Finding the blindspot', we show how the brain changes what you see into what you perceive (which with the blindspot can be quite different to reality). Another example of how what you think you see isn't necessarily exactly truthful comes from *after-effects*: this is where the world appears different following prolonged exposure to a particular stimulus.

Stare at the fixation point between the gratings on the left of Figure 4-4 for about a minute. Then look to the fixation point between the gratings on the right. You should see an after-effect, where the top gratings seem narrower than the bottom gratings. Wait a while and look back at the gratings on the right. You can see that in reality they're the same size.

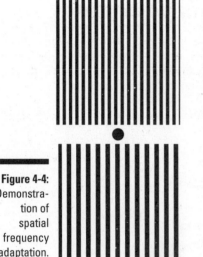

Figure 4-4: Demonstration of spatial frequency adaptation.

This exercise changes what you can perceive by *adaptation*: prolonged exposure to a particular stimulus affects the ability to see that stimulus later and is tied to the spatial frequencies we describe in Chapter 6. Looking at the gratings close together (high spatial frequency) *fatigues* (tires out) the cells in the brain that respond to them. Then when you look at other gratings, these cells no longer fire and so you see the world without these spatial frequencies. The same effect can exist for colour (see Chapter 5), brightness, tilt and even facial identity (see Chapter 6).

These examples highlight how perception is constructed by your existing knowledge. Psychologists have made a number of attempts to understand perception and we describe two major attempts here.

Directing perception

American psychologist James Gibson believed that perception was designed to respond to the visual world. This *direct perception* approach is similar to the idea that the sole purpose of perception is to help initiate some form of action.

Gibson believed that when people encounter objects, the way the objects are used is immediately brought to mind. Objects' uses are their *affordances*. So when someone encounters an apple, he perceives the process of eating; however, his psychological state affects the affordance. So if he's angry, he may perceive the affordance of using the apple as a projectile weapon, and throw it.

Resolving ambiguities in perception

Gibson's direct perception theory from the preceding section predicts that knowledge is available instantly when you perceive the world: the knowledge is about how an object may be used. But some objects have no use and yet knowledge is known to affect the perception.

One example is that of the ambiguous figure illusion: look at Figure 4-5 before reading on.

Figure 4-5:
The ambiguous figure.

Source: My Wife and My Mother-In-Law, W. E. Hill, 1915

People see either an old woman or a young woman. In fact, the perception of the two can change in front of your eyes – despite the fact that the visual input hasn't altered. This effect means that the brain must be involved at the first stage of visual processing.

If you still can't see the old or the young woman in Figure 4-5, the young woman is facing to the left looking upward. Her chin is the old woman's nose, because she's looking down to the left.

Illusions such as this one show that knowledge and context affect greatly what people see. In fact, knowledge and experience have quite amazing effects on perception: the more experience you have looking at something, the less you need to look at it to see it. Plus, experience of particular objects speeds up the brain's processing of them. For example, expert chess players can look at a chessboard and see the entire board with one glance at its centre, whereas novices need to look at each piece to have the same representation.

Following a World in Motion

Imagining a world without movement is almost impossible. Movement is one of the definitions of life and surely so is *perceiving* movement. Motion perception is fundamentally important for survival: imagine trying to cross a road without it! Plus, many other less obvious purposes lie behind your ability to perceive motion.

Being able to perceive movement helps people to detect things. If you're hunting your food in a forest, as we're sure you do most days, the slightest motion attracts your attention and helps you get your next meal – as well as help you avoid becoming somebody else's meal.

Motion perception also helps with figure-ground segregation (see Chapter 6) and can provide depth information: if you see something move, you know it's separate from the background as its own distinct entity. Motion perception also helps you orient yourself to the source of the motion and allows you to move yourself. Finally, motion perception can help you identify objects (check out Chapter 5). You know that a rabbit hops, so seeing a hopping motion helps you to establish that a rabbit's coming towards you and not a large, scary, bouncing rat.

In this section, we describe the intricate brain processes involved in detecting motion, including the involvement of optic flow. We demonstrate the importance to motion detection of timing, discuss the special role of biological motion and show how your motion perception can be easily fooled.

Perceiving motion

The question of how people perceive motion isn't as simple as it sounds. Consider these two distinct cases:

- **Retinal-movement system:** When you keep your eyes still and something moves in front of them. In one second, you see the object in one point in your retina. In the next instant, the object is in another position. How do you know it isn't two objects?

✔ **Head/eye-movement system:** When you move your eyes to keep an object in your fovea – in other words, you *track* the object using smooth pursuit eye movements (flip to the earlier section 'Detecting light: Photoreceptors').

A third case exists where you're moving and you have to move your eyes to keep the object still in vision. But here you don't perceive things moving, because you realise that you're moving yourself.

Scientists have devised two theories to explain how people achieve the incredible feat of motion detection:

✔ **Inflow theory:** Charles Scott Sherrington, a British neuroscientist, suggested that the brain keeps a record of how much people move their eyes. That is, the brain tells the eyes or head to move and then records how much movement occurred. This information is compared to the changes in the retinal image.

✔ **Outflow theory:** Hermann Ludwig Ferdinand von Helmholtz, a German physicist, suggested a subtly different approach. The brain plans to move the eyes (creating an *efferent signal*, which is a signal representing this plan) and compares this plan to what the retinal image displays.

So, how do these two theories cope with what has been observed in the real world? Both theories can easily explain *smooth tracking* (following an object smoothly with your eyes). Though no retinal motion occurs, both theories record that the object is moving, because the eye muscles are working (inflow) or the brain tells the eye muscles to work (outflow).

But if you poke your eye, you see movement (don't jab your finger in your eye – take our word for it). The muscles have moved, but the brain didn't tell them to move. So, the world should remain stationary according to inflow theory, because the muscles have moved and the brain should register the same thing as tracking. Yet you perceive motion, and so clearly inflow theory is wrong. Outflow theory suggests that the brain made no intention to move, and so because you saw motion, the eyes have moved (which is what happens).

Based on this and other evidence, outflow theory is more valid in explaining how people detect motion. But although it shows why your brain may perceive motion, it doesn't explain how the cells in the retina respond. To understand this aspect, you need some form of motion detector system.

A motion detector works by comparing the signal from two different receptors. It requires two receptive fields, a comparator cell and a time delay. A stimulus is caught on receptor A and then moves to receptor B. The comparator cell activates only if the activation at receptor B is delayed after the activation at receptor A by a short amount. This model is known as a *delay-and-compare detector* or a *Reichardt detector*.

Speed detection is possible by having comparator cells that respond to different levels of delay: a shorter delay means that something is moving faster; a longer delay means that something is moving slower.

Evidence suggests that motion detection is occurring in area V5 (otherwise known as MT) in the visual cortex. Cells in this part of the brain process motion in every direction – that is, each cell responds to motion in a particular direction.

Going with the optic flow

When you walk around, you often focus on a particular point (your intended destination). This *focus of expansion* appears motionless. The visual field around that point, however, appears to be expanding around it (getting bigger). This pattern occurs during *optic flow*, which is highly useful in determining direction of travel. On average, the error in predicted heading based on optic flow is very small. Although optic flow is useful, how it works isn't entirely clear.

In 1950, James Gibson suggested that people somehow use their entire visual field to make a judgement of direction from optic flow. In contrast, another theory says that you need only to focus on a single local element in the visual field that's normally stationary. Evidence points to the fact that judgements of direction can be made based on optic flow when no single stationary object exists, suggesting that the local theory is less valid than Gibson's global theory.

When you're on a train looking out the window, and a train in the platform next starts to pull out, often you can think that your train is the one moving (possibly out of a forlorn hope that your train will actually get you home on time!). This effect is an example of something called *induced motion*, but more specifically *vection* (or self-motion).

One method for showing vection is using an *optokinetic drum* (a rotating room). Participants are placed inside this rotating room, and they start to think the room is rotating, but for some reason they mistakenly believe they're the ones rotating and not the room. The reason is that the *vestibular system* (which signals balance) only signals changes. You're used to receiving a signal only at the beginning of motion. So, if you see the room move but you don't get a signal, your brain is confused but perceives that the room is moving. After a few seconds, your brain is no longer confused (it's just wrong), because it's receiving no input from the vestibular system, and so the room can't be moving, but *you* can be!

Vection has been linked to causing vomiting, because of the mismatch between what you're seeing and what's actually going on.

In 1976, British psychologists David Lee and JR Lishman used vection to show how movements of the environment can affect balance. They put toddlers (who had just learnt to stand up) in a room and waited until they stood. They then moved the walls slightly. The effect caused the toddlers to fall over. If they moved the wall in front of a toddler, the toddler fell backward. The toddlers mistakenly assumed that the wall was moving because they were moving, and so they leaned to compensate for it. A similar effect is used in IMAX cinemas.

Timing your move is everything

One of the important aspects of perceiving motion is being able to estimate when you may walk into something or catch a ball in the annual inter-faculty softball match. The time to contact (or to catch a ball) can be calculated by the rate of expansion of the object on the retina – as a ball comes toward you, it gets bigger on your retina. By calculating this rate, you can work out its time to contact. *Tau* (τ) is the measure of time to contact; it's equal to 1 divided by the rate of expansion.

Your brain uses this simple calculation when approaching an object or when an object approaches you. You need to know the final size of the object, however, before you can estimate time to contact: you can't prepare to catch something you don't know the size of, because you don't know what size on the retina it will be when it's in your hands.

In addition, experience dictates whether you take advantage of speed of approach and distance information. Sportspeople, who have more experience making judgements of approaching objects, tend to take more note of distance information than speed information.

Things get more complicated when you consider that people are often moving at the same time as the object they're going to make contact with. For example, when making an expert piece of fielding during a game of softball, you're running to catch a ball, and the information you have is an estimation of the *optical trajectory* of the ball.

One interesting result is that catching the ball on the run is easier than waiting for the ball to come to you. People running towards a ball in midflight can estimate its 'catchability' more accurately than people waiting for the ball to come to them. When moving toward the ball in midflight, accurate fielders run at a speed that allows the ratio of the height of the ball to the distance to be maintained at zero. This way, the fielder always arrives at the same time as the ball.

But this strategy only works when the ball is moving toward you. When, more commonly, it isn't coming directly toward you, fielders run in a curved path in order to keep the trajectory of the ball appearing straight. Nevertheless, they still get to the catching point at the same time as the ball, as opposed to getting to the catching point early and waiting.

Showing your animal nature: Biological motion

Motion helps people to extract three-dimensional information about an object. If it moves, its size changes on your retina and you can perceive its distance – known as *obtaining structure from motion*.

An example is when you can interpret a static image in a number of ways. Say that you see a shadow of a straight line – the object casting the shadow could be a piece of string or a hard stick. If the object is moved, you can gain information regarding its structure (you'd see a stick move in rigid ways, whereas a string would bounce).

A special case of obtaining structure from motion is the ability to obtain information about *biological motion*: movement from a living creature. It can be distinguished from mechanical motion, which is rigid and harsh (you know, the robot dance!). Biological motion is more fluid.

Biological motion is very important for humans to detect, providing them with information about predators (or dangers) or prey. This importance means that humans are experts at reading biological motion.

People can often recognise their close friends simply from their way of walking. Biological motion can also provide information about someone's age, gender and even sexuality.

The expert nature of biological motion is highlighted by the fact that if you reduce the amount of information to the bare minimum, people can still recognise biological motion. In 1975, Gunnar Johansson, a Swedish psychophysicist, used points of light attached to the joints of some people. He then asked them to move in particular ways. The people were recorded wearing all black on a black background leaving only the *point-light motion* visible. Without motion, people couldn't identify the point-light object stimulus, but as soon as the person moved the participants easily identified the stimulus.

In fact, people can readily recognise different types of movement from point-light displays – painting, doing push-ups, riding a bike, and they can lip-read. Participants can even recognise other people's gender from point-light displays. They can identify their friends, family members, and even dogs and cats, with this minimal information.

Furthermore, they can extract this information very quickly from point-light motion; participants can make these judgements in less than 200 milliseconds, suggesting that the process is fairly automatic. Humans aren't the only creatures able to do this – cats can identify other cats from point-light displays.

Autokinetic effect

An effect related to, though not technically part of, biological motion is when a single point of light is presented to participants in a completely darkened room. Participants often report seeing the point of light move by itself. This *autokinetic effect* is caused by eye-drift and the lack of supporting context to compare the position of the light to.

Point-light displays are used widely in films. Many computer generated characters (such as Gollum from *The Lord of the Rings*) were filmed with point-lights. This technique enables the computer animators to ensure that the computer-generated character moves in a realistic manner.

Biological information is so important that specialised brain regions may be devoted to processing it. Researchers have identified clusters of cells in the superior temporal sulcus that seem to be specially recruited when processing biological motion.

Seeing is believing: Apparent motion

The way cinemas display films is similar to the way in which the human visual system codes movement. In the cinema, a series of still images are presented at precisely 24 images per second. The speed of each frame means that audiences perceive a smooth apparent motion. This may seem strange, because the human visual system can detect flickering at this speed. But film projectors have shutters that open up to three times per frame, creating a flicker rate the visual system can't detect (nearly 75 frames per second).

Images are presented at this rate, because if the frames were presented much more slowly, you wouldn't perceive motion, just a series of still frames. If the frames were presented at a much greater rate, you wouldn't see motion, but everything simultaneously.

You can discover what determines how fast a frame rate people can detect with the delay-and-compare detector that we describe in the earlier 'Perceiving motion' section. If the image appears at receptor B sooner than the delay from receptor A allows, the image is perceived as happening at the same time. If the image appears at receptor B much longer after the delay, you perceive seeing two separate still images. Thus, the frame rate that people detect as motion is the same as the delay in their motion detectors.

Another form of apparent motion is quite fascinating. If you look at the hub cap of certain cars when in motion, it appears to be rotating either with the direction of the car's movement or in the opposite direction to the motion of the car (often called the *wagon-wheel effect*). When the wheel is moving slowly, your motion detectors detect frame 1 because the spokes are in one position. At frame 2, the spokes have moved a little, and your motion detectors assume that they've moved forward. But if the wheel is moving too quickly, by the time frame 2 happens, the spokes have moved so far around (more than 45 degrees) that you think the wheel is moving in the opposite direction!

Experiencing the motion after-effect

Prolonged fixation of a particular motion causes stationary objects to appear to move in the opposite direction. This after-effect is a fun illusion, sometimes called the *waterfall illusion*, because Robert Addams first described it while looking at a waterfall in Scotland. After staring at the waterfall for a minute or so, and then looking at the rocks, he reported that the rocks appeared to move in the opposite direction.

You can see a demonstration of this effect at `https://www.youtube.com/watch?v=OAVXHzAWS60` (be aware, it always works!). Stare at the motion for one minute, and then look at your own hand (or better still, the face of someone near you). The after-effect usually lasts only a few seconds, but it's quite challenging for your brain to interpret. Our students report things as weird as 'something crawling under the skin'. The brain has to interpret motion appearing where none should be. In fact, the things that you're looking at don't change position: they remain in the same place, but they're moving. This paradox can only be explained as the brain interpreting motion differently from the way it processes position.

This effect can be explained simply (for once!). When you look at something stationary (the rocks), your motion detectors are all active to the same degree (firing at a low baseline level). Because all motion detectors (for all directions) are firing equally, you see no motion. When you look at the motion (the waterfall), the detectors that respond to that motion (downward) are more active than all other directions (makes sense: you're looking at something moving downward, and so the downward cells are active). When you turn to see the stationary rocks, the downward cells are fatigued and so don't fire at all (firing less than the baseline rate). Therefore, you appear to see movement in the opposite direction, because the cells processing the opposite direction are relatively more active than the cells processing the motion.

This illusion reveals a number of important things about the visual system. Like colour, people process things in opposition. More accurately, they process direction relative to other directions. It also suggests that the baseline activity of the visual system isn't zero, which is important and suggests that your brain is always active. This always-on system may sound like a waste of energy, but psychologists have proposed that adaptation is adaptive! In other words, the process of adaptation helps your brain to function better, helping you to notice changes between different states.

Given that brain area V5 is active for processing motion, you may assume that this area is active for processing the after-effect (after all, it's motion!). Indeed, some researchers have found just that when experiencing the after-effect. Others have found that activation in V5 is reduced following adaptation to the motion. So, as so often in psychology, uncertainty remains about which part of the brain is responsible for the after-effect.

Chapter 5

Seeing How People See Depth and Colour

*I*f your vision is normal, imagining a world without the ability to perceive depth and colour is difficult. But for people who can't see these things, the problem can be highly debilitating.

How the human brain processes these aspects of the visual experience is quite remarkable. (To read about the basic biology of human perception and some theories about how people see the world around them, turn to Chapter 4.) As well as describing here how you see depth and perceive colours, we also include real-world examples and some fascinating illusions that fool your visual system. The world isn't what it appears to be!

Seeing the Third Dimension

Depth perception is vital – without it you wouldn't be able to cross the road, pick up things or even identify what things are. For cognitive psychologists, establishing how this awesome skill works is really important. For one reason, it highlights how the human mind influences how people see. For another, people need depth cues to know about things (and knowing is very cognitive). In this section, we introduce depth perception and review the various cues to depth.

Introducing depth perception

Being able to see in three dimensions (3-D) is critical. Without depth perception, you'd walk into lampposts, knock things over and not realise how far away a speeding car is. Just think of this example: you're sitting at a bar and you need to pick up your pint. Without depth perception, doing so would be hit or miss and you may end up spilling it – a tragedy!

People use depth perception to work out how far away things are from them – called *egocentric distance*. For example, you know that your laptop is a couple of feet in front of you when you're on Facebook, er, we mean writing a research paper. You also use depth perception to work out how far things are away from each other – called *object-relative distance*.

You can also use depth perception to help identify objects. For example, look at Figure 5-1. You can see a gorgeous chinchilla behind the wires of her cage, because depth perception allows you to tell the difference between the animal's grey fur and the metal of her cage.

Figure 5-1:
Can you see where the chinchilla ends and her cage begins?

The eye of the tiger: Monocular cues

A variety of cues signal depth. A common fallacy is that you need two eyes for depth perception, but as you can see from Figure 5-2, only two cues are based on *binocular* (two-eyed) vision. In fact, you can determine many depth cues using only one eye. These *monocular* cues are also known as *pictorial depth cues*, because you can obtain them from a simple 2-D image. When you look at a picture, having one eye is just as good as two eyes.

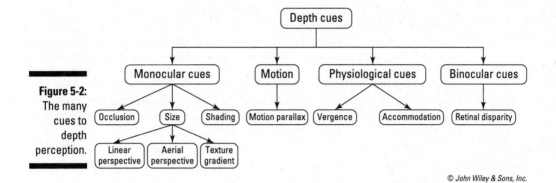

Figure 5-2: The many cues to depth perception.

Sizing objects up

The simplest cue to depth is size. Generally, the bigger something is, the closer it is to you. Simple . . . or maybe not. Consider looking at a cube in isolation. You can't tell how big it is without some other reference point. The cube can be any size, so you need something to compare it to.

You need a reference point only for ambiguous or unfamiliar objects. For example, if a rabbit appears 2 centimetres tall, you know that it's quite far away, because rabbits are larger than that. Therefore, size cues require familiarity with the object or a reference point.

Linear perspective is related to size cues. Think about walking down a straight road at night. As you look down the road, it appears to narrow, and the lamp-posts get closer together. Although you *see* this, you *perceive* that the road ahead is farther away from you. (Chapter 4 covers why seeing and perceiving aren't always the same thing in more detail.)

Figure 5-3 shows a variant of the *Ponzo illusion* (named after its creator, the Italian psychologist Mario Ponzo). In the figure, you perceive the top horizontal bar as larger than the bottom one, even though they're exactly the same size; linear perspective tells you that the two converging lines are in fact parallel. Therefore, the upper line must be bigger because it almost touches the perceived-to-be parallel lines whereas the bottom line doesn't.

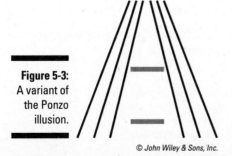

Figure 5-3: A variant of the Ponzo illusion.

Figure 5-4 shows the *Müller-Lyer illusion* (the German sociologist Franz Carl Müller-Lyer came up with it) – this illusion is similar to the Ponzo illusion and is potentially a result of implied depth perception. The line with the outward pointing arrows seems shorter than the arrow with the inward pointing arrows despite the fact that the lines are the same length. One hypothesis for this effect is that people are so used to seeing inward pointing arrows in the corners of rooms and outward pointing arrows on the exterior corners of buildings. Evidence shows that Western peoples are more susceptible to this illusion than pre-Stone age forest-dwelling peoples.

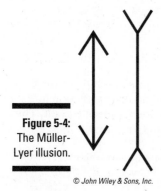

Figure 5-4:
The Müller-Lyer illusion.

© John Wiley & Sons, Inc.

In the real world, you can experience size depth illusions simply by looking at the moon (appropriately enough called the *moon illusion*). When it's high in the sky, it appears smaller than when it's close to the horizon.

Very similar to linear perspective are *texture gradients*. If you're on a pebbly beach and you look along it, the pebbles appear larger near your feet but smaller farther away from your feet. Again, that's the sensation – it's what you *see* – but the perception is that all the pebbles are the same size: the ones that *look* smaller are simply farther away.

Another important cue is *aerial perspective*: objects appear blurrier and more faded in the distance. If you look out across the countryside, distant hills are slightly blurry. So, you know that the blurrier an object, the farther away it probably is.

Covering objects partially

Occlusion (also known as *interposition*) is another simple cue to depth. People naturally believe that objects will be complete.

Making room for Frodo

All size cues can be linked together to form a highly compelling illusion known as the *Ames room* (check it out at: `https://www.youtube.com/watch?v=Ttd0YjXF0no`). To see an Ames room in action, watch the *The Lord of the Rings* films and pay close attention when Frodo is talking to Gandalf. Frodo (Elijah Wood) appears tiny in comparison to Gandalf (Ian McKellen). Now, Elijah Wood is no giant, but he's not *that* short. In fact, Wood is much farther away from the camera than McKellen, but the shape of the room causes viewers to perceive that he's smaller. The lines of the room aren't straight, even though that's what you perceive.

Figure 5-5a appears to show an illusory bar positioned over three circles. You don't perceive three incomplete circles though; you perceive a bar over the top. In fact, your brain responds in the same way to the illusory bar as to the real bar. These shapes are similar to the figures in Figure 5-5b, where a square appears to be placed over the top of the four circles.

Figure 5-5:
Are the circles complete or incomplete? a) you perceive a bar; b) you perceive a square.

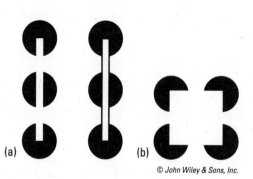

(a) (b)

© John Wiley & Sons, Inc.

The Necker cube (see Figure 5-6a) highlights occlusion nicely. When presented with a hexagonal shape with extra lines, people tend to perceive a cube: that is, 3-D is so important that it pops out from a 2-D image. However, the basic Necker cube is ambiguous: is the far-left vertical the back or front of the cube? Only when some of the sides are occluded (see Figures 5-6b and 5-6c) can you clearly work out the depth.

Figure 5-6: The Necker cube: a) ambiguous depth; b) and c) obvious depths.

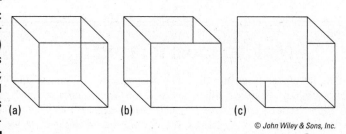

(a)   (b)   (c)

© John Wiley & Sons, Inc.

Transparency is a special case of occlusion, when one object covers another object but you can still see through it.

Occlusion is such a powerful cue to depth that it can override other cues. If you can manipulate an image so that the depth cues aren't consistent, occlusion is the one cue that people appear to follow most readily. Occlusion may even be processed by a special place in the brain, because some people can't see occlusion but can tell depth by other means.

The brain takes only 100 to 200 milliseconds (that's one-tenth to one-fifth of a second) to process occlusion. In other words, when presented with one of those part circles in the earlier Figure 5-5, your brain registers the bar over a circle in 100 milliseconds. Prior to this, however, your brain thinks of the shape as a single object.

Shading the world

People know that light comes from above, so when they see a shadow they assume that it's underneath something. Look at the pattern of dots and dimples in Figure 5-7. Those with light patches on top appear to be dots, whereas those with light sides on the bottom appear to be dimples.

Turn this book upside-down and watch the dots and dimples swap over. Now turn the book on its side – the dots and dimples may spontaneously swap and swap back. If you must, stand on your head to be sure. Whatever way you look at it, you know that light comes from above, which gives you an extra depth cue.

Flexing the eye muscles: Physiological cues

Six muscles control how each of your eyes move, and two muscles control the shape of the lens in the eye. These muscles change in tension depending on how far away an object is. Muscular movement of the eyes produces tiny electrical impulses that the brain can record and use to establish depth.

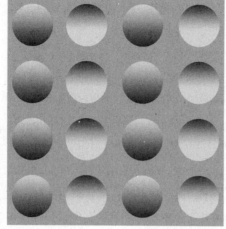

Figure 5-7: Shading provides depth information.

© John Wiley & Sons, Inc.

Accommodation happens when the muscles that control the lens by stretching the ligaments attached to the lens (which focuses incoming light) bend it sufficiently to deflect the light onto the back of the retina. When these muscles are relaxed, the lens is flat. Objects are about 3 metres away at this point. To bring a closer object into focus, the muscles have to relax, stretching the ligaments and allowing the lens to form its natural curved shape. These muscles can bend the lens sufficiently to bring an object 20 centimetres away into focus, but no nearer. So, accommodation is useful only for objects located between 20 centimetres and 3 metres from you.

Hold your finger directly in front of your face and slowly bring it closer to your nose: try to keep looking at it the whole time. To keep the image in your *fovea* (the middle part of each eye with the best resolution), you have to rotate your eyes (called *vergence movement*). You can probably feel your eyes begin to cross when your finger is about 10 centimetres away. Most people feel their eye muscles tense up. (Don't hold it for too long – otherwise, it hurts!)

The brain can use this tension as a measure of depth perception. Vergence movement can provide accurate depth perception up to about 6 metres:

- ✔ **Convergence:** Occurs when you have to roll your eyes inwards to see near objects.

- ✔ **Divergence:** Occurs when you have to roll your eyes outwards to see distant objects.

Using both eyes together: Binocular cues

Here we consider the depth cues involving two eyes. Your two eyes are in slightly different positions and so what they see is slightly different.

You can demonstrate that you have different images on each retina (like double vision) simply by holding a finger out in front of you and noting what object your finger is in front of. Close one eye and your finger appears to shift positions; close the other eye and the finger appears to shift again. This effect is called *retinal disparity*. People move their eyes inwards and outwards so that corresponding points in the scene fall onto the two foveas:

- ✓ **Horopter:** Region where no retinal disparity is present and you experience the singleness of vision. Points farther away or closer than the horopter fall onto non-corresponding parts of the two retinas, generating *disparity*. This disparity becomes greater, the farther in front or behind the horopter an object is.
- ✓ **Crossed disparity:** Images closer to you than the horopter.
- ✓ **Uncrossed disparity:** Images farther away than the horopter.

Normally your brain manages to form the two disparity images into a single image (called *fusion*). But if you suffer *diplopia* or are very drunk (we wouldn't know personally, of course), you have double vision.

The human brain can calculate the amount of disparity between the images of each retina. This ability is called *stereopsis*, and it gives people a measure of depth – the more crossed disparity, the closer the object is; the more uncrossed disparity, the farther away the object is.

Humans have cells in the visual cortex that respond when some form of retinal disparity exists. About 5–10 per cent of the population (including one of your authors) lack this ability. These people are *stereoblind* (unable to detect depth based on retinal disparity) and have to make use of all the other depth cues for accurate depth perception. This condition is often the result of a *strabismus*, a squint or lazy-eye, at an early age that prevents the development of these disparity cells.

You can induce depth perception experimentally with random-dot stereograms – created by neuroscientist and psychologist Béla Julesz in 1971. *Random-dot stereograms* are patterns of black and white dots, in which one dot is presented to the left eye and another dot is presented to the right eye. These patterns are identical, except that a portion of one of the dots is shifted in one direction. This set-up creates disparity and is perceived as being nearer or farther away than the rest of the stereogram.

3-D films and retinal disparity

Many 3-D films employ retinal disparity by recording the action with two cameras that have different filters overlaid. The two cameras are positioned in slightly different positions: one from the left eye position and one from the right eye position. In the 1950s, left cameras had a green filter and the right camera a red filter (technology has moved on since then). When you wear special glasses that cancel out the filters, you can see the depth, because you're fusing the images produced by the two camera angles into one internal mental image.

Alas, 3-D technology doesn't work for stereoblind people; at best, it makes them nauseous!

When you have no other cues available, you need to use two eyes for depth perception. To demonstrate, stand in front of a plain wall and close one eye. Hold your hands out with your forefingers pointing towards each other. Now try to make them touch. Most people find this quite difficult (not your stereoblind author!). Doing it with both eyes open is far easier.

On the move: Motion cues

Motion parallax is another form of depth perception based on a sort of retinal disparity (refer to the preceding section). *Motion parallax* is based on the fact that you have disparity due to movement.

Hold out your hand and raise two fingers – one behind the other. Staring straight on, you can't see the finger that's behind. However, if you move your head to the side, the back finger comes into view. The finger nearer to you should appear to move quicker than the finger that's farther away, because of retinal disparity.

Similarly, if you're on a train looking out the window and you keep your eyes fixed at a certain distance, objects near to you seem to move quickly in the direction opposite to your movement, whereas objects just beyond the fixation point appear to move in the same direction as you, slowly.

The human brain can calculate the relative speeds of the movement and use this information to work out how far away something is. This form of depth perception is incredibly powerful and widely used by animals for hunting.

Size constancy

If you look at a large oak tree from a very long distance and a small Bonsai tree close up, they cast the same size image on your retina: this image could be due to object size or distance. So, when someone walks towards you, the image on your retina gets bigger and your brain has to interpret whether the person is getting bigger or closer.

The brain employs Emmert's Law (the perceived size of an image is directly related to its perceived distance) to work out size and distance. For a particular image size on the retina, the perceived size of that object is directly proportional to the distance. That is, how big you think something is depends on how far away you think it is. Based on your knowledge of the size of objects, the context and so on, your judgements can be easily fooled. Several illusions – the Müller-Lyer and Ponzo illusions and the Ames room – highlight the potential breakdown of size constancy.

Given a familiar object, people are capable of working out how far away it is, because of size constancy. They can't judge the size of unfamiliar objects as well, however, because the scaling effects due to size constancy are unavailable.

Combining the depth cues

Given all the different cues to depth, you may be wondering how people use them to form an accurate representation of how far away something is from them. Psychologists haven't established precisely how this happens, but experts do know that the more cues to depth perception that exist, the more accurate the judgement of depth is going to be.

Evidence suggests that some depth cues are processed in specific parts of the brain. Some patients with a brain injury can't work out depth based on a particular cue but can use others, such as occlusion and retinal disparity.

Another way to view how the depth cues interact is to see what happens when the depth cues give conflicting information: for example, a huge mouse, partially occluded by a tiny elephant. Generally speaking, in this situation estimates of depth perception are very poor. The brain decides which cue is likely to be more reliable (how it does this is up to the individual brain) and uses that one cue at the expense of the others.

Living Life in Colour

Accurate colour perception can be the difference between life and death. Consider trying to find fruit nestled in trees if you can't see colour. Animals (including humans) also use colour to convey psychological states: certain frogs turn bright yellow or red to signal danger, humans give away more than they mean to by going red with anger (or embarrassment) and some monkeys change colour to indicate a readiness to mate. Without colour, poor Curious George would miss out terribly.

Colour perception has massive effects on other forms of perception too, such as affecting a human's sense of taste. Tests show that people dislike yellow strawberry milkshake even if the only difference between it and pink strawberry milkshake is the colour (people couldn't tell them apart with their eyes shut). Which is why food manufacturers add colouring to many foods – mushy peas would be yellow without the food colouring.

In this section, we describe colour and show that although your eyes are designed to process only three colours, you can see a whole myriad of them. We discuss two theories that explain how people see the range of colours in the colour spectrum: trichromacy theory and opponent processing. We also show how the perception of colour isn't as simple as identifying what the brain detects: colour perception is affected by knowledge as well.

Defining colour

Of course, colour makes the world look prettier, but what *is* it? Well, colour is simply the brain's response to light of different wavelengths. Light is a form of electromagnetic radiation, which includes gamma rays, X-rays, ultraviolet light, infrared light, microwaves and radio waves. Although some animals can perceive other wavelengths, the bit that humans see lies between ultraviolet and infrared – often called the *visible part of the spectrum*.

This visible part ranges from 400 to 740 nanometres. Light waves in the 400–500 nanometres range are purples; those in the 580–740 nanometres range are reds; and the rest of the rainbow colours lie in between.

Light waves don't contain colour, just a wavelength and intensity (or *luminance*). Colour is a response from the human brain and physiology (refer to Chapter 4).

Counting the colours: Trichromacy theory

Try to name as many colours as you possibly can in a minute. Perhaps ask a friend to do it, too. You probably name the 11 basic colours that anthropologist Brent Berlin and linguist Paul Kay identified in 1961, including red, green, blue, yellow, grey, brown and pink. If you're an artist, you may also list colours such as navy, indigo and violet. If you're a computer scientist, you may mention cyan and magenta. If you work for a paint company, you can probably come up with an infinite number of other colour names (such as applewood green or warming sunshine yellow!).

Three is the magic number

You may be surprised to discover that people have only three types of colour receptors (cones) in their eyes.

Think about how many colours you can see in dimly lit conditions. In the dark, all colours tend to look pretty much the same. People don't have colour vision in the dark, because the cones detect colour and they need more light to respond (refer to Chapter 4).

The three types of cones (*S* for short, *M* for medium and *L* for long) respond to different wavelengths of light. *Microspectrophotometry* (in which a small pinprick of light is shone on each photoreceptor and its electrical response is measured) shows to what wavelengths of light each cone type maximally responds. The *peak sensitivity* (the wavelength that causes the most amount of response) is as follows:

- ✔ **S-cones (420 nanometres):** Approximately blue-purple.
- ✔ **M-cones (530 nanometres):** Approximately yellow-green.
- ✔ **L-cones (560 nanometres):** Red.

In other words, when a light of wavelength 500 nanometres is shone on the eye, all three types of cones respond. The response is greater, however, for the M-cones than the S-cones and L-cones. So, you interpret the colour to be green. From three cones, you can see all colours.

Added to the direct physiological evidence for this *trichromacy theory* of colour vision is a lot of behavioural evidence. People can make every colour from mixing these three colours. This theory is often referred to as the *Young–Helmholtz theory*, after Thomas Young and Hermann von Helmholtz, the key researchers who developed it.

It's all in the genes

Recent evidence pinpoints the exact DNA responsible for these cones. The genes that control the cones are located on the X chromosome and other research has determined the cause for certain types of colour-blindness. People with colour-blindness (or, to be more accurate, colour deficiencies) usually have either a missing type of cone or an abnormal type of cone. Usually, they miss only one type of cone. Table 5-1 describes the types of colour deficiencies that experts have discovered.

Table 5-1	Types of Colour Deficiencies	
Name	*Cause*	*Consequence*
Dichromacies (only two types of functioning colour receptors)		
Protanopia	Missing L pigment	Confuses 520–700 nanometres (green to red)
Deuteranopia	Missing M pigment	Confuses 530–700 nanometres (yellow to red)
Tritanopia	Missing S pigment	Confuses 445–480 nanometres (blue)
Anomalous trichromacies (colour matches differ from normal)		
Protanomaly	Abnormal L pigment	Abnormal matches; poor discrimination
Deuteranomaly	Missing M pigment	Confuses 530–700 nanometres (yellow to red)

The cone types aren't evenly distributed in the retina, which means that people can detect certain colours more easily in the periphery than others. Specifically, no S-cones are in the fovea (the middle part of the eye) and so people are partially colour deficient in the fovea (because the fovea is so small, you never really notice). Also, many more M- and L-cones exist than S-cones. In fact, only 10 per cent of cones are S-cones; the rest are divided among the M-cones (30 per cent) and L-cones (60 per cent).

Colours in opposition: Adding more colours to the colour wheel

Although three cone types exist that respond to light of a particular wavelength (see the preceding section), people are clearly able to see many more colours. How is this possible? Well, experts aren't sure. One suggestion is that certain colours are processed in some form of opposition. We look at some evidence for this idea here. If you remain unconvinced after reading this section, check out the later one 'Categorical perception: Keeping colours straight' for more on the theory.

In 1878, Ewald Hering, a German physiologist, observed the existence of four (rather than three) primary colours that people only ever perceive in opposition (the *opponent-processing theory*). He suggested that blue and yellow are mutually exclusive and red and green are mutually exclusive in a similar way that black and white are mutually exclusive – that is, they're opposite sides of some sort of colour wheel or colour space.

Hering observed specifically that when describing colours, people never used the term 'bluey-yellow' but they did sometimes say 'yellowy-green' (the colour of a tennis ball). Likewise, they never said 'reddy-green'.

Enjoying the after-effect

More compelling evidence for the opponent-processing theory comes from something called the *colour after-effect*. Before reading on, look at the demonstration in Figure 1 in the Part II online article (at www.dummies.com/extras/cognitivepsychology). Stare at the black dot for 30 seconds and then the image swaps to a plain white screen. Most people report seeing something instead of the plain white.

Usually, during the prolonged exposure to the colour, you become adapted to it (similar to the adaptation experiments we describe in Chapter 4). When you look at a blank screen, you see the opposite colours where the colours used to be: when you adapt to red, the after-image appears green; when you stare at yellow, the after-image appears blue; and when you stare at black, the after-image appears white. Thus, the colours are processed in opposition.

You can prove that this effect isn't a computer trick, by adapting to the stimulus and then looking at a white wall: again you see the after-image. In fact, wherever you look, you see it. The after-image lasts for only a few seconds (though it returns when you blink), and it's usually weaker than the original image seen.

The explanation for the colour after-effect is virtually the same as the explanation for all after-effects: processing a particular colour for a period of time fatigues the cells that respond to that particular colour, but has no effect on cells for other colours. Thus, when you look at a plain white image, the 'opposite' colour is relatively more active than the actual colour.

Joining opposites

With this knowledge in mind, how do these opposite colours combine to form the plethora of colours that people can see? Figure 5-8 offers the coding system based on the opponent-processing theory. Basically, the system works out the ratio of activation coming from the S-cones relative to the other cones. Solid lines represent that maximum response signals the colour; dotted lines represent that minimum response signals the colour.

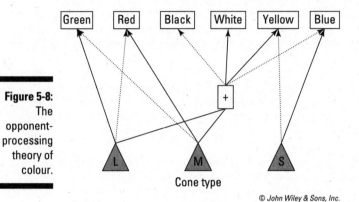

Figure 5-8:
The opponent-processing theory of colour.

Here's how the coding system works in practice. Three channels exist: one for red-green, one for blue-yellow and one for black-white:

✔ Luminance is signalled by adding the signal from the M- and L-cones.

✔ Red and green are signalled by directly comparing the relative activation from the M- and L-cones and ignoring all other signals.

✔ Blue and yellow are signalled by working out the ratio between the total of the M- and L-cones and the S-cones.

Table 5-2 describes how the primary colours are signalled with this system.

Table 5-2	Outputs from the Cones		
Colour to Achieve	*S-Cone Activity*	*M-Cone Activity*	*L-Cone Activity*
Black		Zero	Zero
White		Maximum	Maximum
Red		Maximum	Minimum
Green		Minimum	Maximum
Blue	Maximum	Minimum	Minimum
Yellow	Minimum	Maximum	Maximum

Processing colour

When you know how the cones combine to form the colour signals that get transferred to the brain, assessing how the brain then copes with this colour information becomes important. Until fairly recently, researchers assumed that the cortical area known as V4 processed colour information – because some patients with *achromatopsia* (an inability to perceive any colour) had damage typically only to area V4.

Researchers discovered new patients, however, with damage only to this particular brain region and yet who could still perceive colour. This discovery led to an investigation into what other brain regions may be involved in the perception of colour.

Research focused on an area called V8 (which happens to be right next to V4). V8 seems to process colour, but no patients with damage exclusively to V8 have been reported yet. One study showed that when people are looking at colour during an adaptation experiment, both areas V4 and V8 are activated. However, during the after-image (in which only illusory colour is perceived), only area V8 is activated.

So these brain regions seem to process colour differently, but exactly how isn't fully understood, yet . . .

Colour constancy: How colours remain the same

The light coming into your eye isn't always the same as the colour you perceive, and yet it often seems so. Colours appear the same under all light conditions, even though the sensory input is different. This effect, called *colour constancy*, was described by Edwin Land in 1977.

Imagine that you're getting ready to go out clubbing. You put on your favourite purple top and yellow trousers (yes, assume just for a moment that you have no dress sense!) and then look at yourself in the mirror under artificial light in your house. The colours seem clear. When you go out into the street and the orange glow of the street lights up your clothes, you still seem to be wearing purple and yellow. Then in the club, with a blue strobe light flashing, your clothes are the same: purple and yellow.

When you're outside, the orange glow means that everything entering your eye is some shade of orange. But you seem to be wearing colour filters over your eyes that change every colour by the same amount. So, your brain somehow filters out the glow and determines that the colour of your clothes hasn't changed.

How your brain does this is quite remarkable and not entirely understood. Here are three theories devised to explain colour constancy:

- ✔ **Adaptation:** When in an environment that has one particular colour, people adapt to it, which removes it from their perception.

- ✔ **Anchoring (retinex):** People find something that's supposed to be white, and then label everything from there (like creating a baseline).

- ✔ **Computations:** People identify one colour and then work through every colour boundary and compute what the colour must be from that boundary.

How does the brain represent colour constancy? Well, the higher visual areas are more responsive to context than the lower visual areas. So given the presence of cortical cells in the brain that respond to particular colours (for example, a blue cell that fires when S-cones are active), when all light is blue the S-cones are active even if the object would normally be yellow. The V1 area of the brain seems to respond as if the colour perceived were the colour sensed (no sign of colour constancy), but area V4 seems to respond as if the colour were the colour it would be under sunlight (following colour constancy principles). Hey, you didn't expect a definitive answer, did you?

Categorical perception: Keeping colours divided

Categorical perception is when two items can't be confused with each other – because people form a category, one thing is perceived as belonging to one category and can't belong to another category.

In the earlier section 'Colours in opposition: Adding more colours to the colour wheel', we describe the opponent-process theory of colour perception, which suggests only three categorical boundaries: between red and green, between blue and yellow, and between black and white. Blue and yellow, say, are therefore mutually exclusive – a yellow can never be confused with a blue. But this isn't what happens in the real world.

If you ask participants to name a series of colour stimuli, you tend to find more categories that aren't readily confused. Participants see a series of yellows that gradually become more and more green. They normally describe the colours as yellow, and then suddenly at a particular amount of green (a particular wavelength), they say the colours are green.

Think of a tennis ball. What colour is it? Most people say yellow or green. (Obviously, those of you who say yellow are right.) Only a few people automatically say yellowy-green. That is, a sharp distinction exists between what's considered yellow and what's considered green.

If you use *equiluminant stimuli* (ones that have the same level of brightness) and the whole colour spectrum, English-speaking people tend to describe the colours as being one of the following: purple, blue, green, yellow, orange or red. These are the *focal colours* that have distinct categories.

Using these stimuli, researchers presented new English-speaking participants with two colours (one after the other). The colours need to be very similar, and differ only by a few nanometres in wavelength. If they cross a category boundary (where the name changes), participants can tell them apart: known as *cross-category discrimination*. If the colours are from the same category (so that people would always describe them as one colour), participants have difficulty telling them apart: known as *within-category discrimination*.

In 1987, Stevan Harnad found that the hallmark of categorical perception is that cross-category discriminations are relatively easy and within-category discriminations are hard. In experiments, participants find the discrimination between a colour patch of 550 nanometres (yellow) and one of 555 nanometres (yellow) harder than the one between 550 nanometres (yellow) and 545 (green), even though the physical difference is the same.

Chapter 6

Recognising Objects and People

....

In This Chapter

▶ Isolating forms from each other and the backdrop

▶ Recognising objects as familiar

▶ Identifying people from their faces

....

*B*eing able to distinguish one object from another is vitally important. In fact, one of the most important purposes of vision is to recognise and identify things and people. This object-processing ability is surprisingly difficult. The world is made up of a constant stream of light entering the eye and your brain has to sort through this mass of information, detect edges and patterns, and from that decide what you see.

We explore three psychological aspects of recognising objects and people:

✓ **Figure-ground segregation:** To determine the form of something, your brain has to differentiate it from the background.

✓ **Recognition:** Whether you know the thing you're looking at: that is, whether you find it familiar.

✓ **Face recognition:** A special case of object recognition, because faces are so . . . well . . . special!

'Just Move a Bit, I Can't See the View!' Separating Figures from Background

In Chapter 4, we introduce the concept of simple, complex and hypercomplex cells: the brain acts as a supercomputer, working out what each of these cells say about a scene in front of you and whether an object is present. But even with many millions of hypercomplex cells, the fact that the brain can work out every single object is unfathomable.

A useful analogy of the steps involved in seeing a form is that of cooking: at the end of hours of cooking, you have a lovely meal made of many separate elements. Hundreds of processes are involved in turning the raw ingredients into the meal. Likewise, to see an object, hundreds of processes turn the many edges you see into an object.

We explore two key theories of how people group the basic building blocks so that they can see what's one object, what's a different object and what's in the background: spatial frequency and Gestalt principles.

Using spatial frequencies

Spatial frequency is basically a measure of how much fine detail something has. It's typically assessed using *gratings* (black and white bars; see Figure 4-4 – from Chapter 4 – and Figure 6-1). Wider gratings mean lower spatial frequency. Spatial frequency therefore refers to the rate of change in a pattern over a particular space.

Figure 6-1: Gratings used for the tilt illusion.

© John Wiley & Sons, Inc.

The whole world can be broken down into different spatial frequency information. If you look at a pretty meadow, you're looking at mostly low spatial frequencies. When looking at the grasses in the meadow, you're looking at higher spatial frequencies. If you look at the world and find one area with one spatial frequency and another area with a different spatial frequency, you can establish that they're different objects. So with Figure 6-1, you see the inner circle as a different object than the outer circle, because they're of a different spatial frequency.

Spatial frequency is a useful tool for detecting objects. But although people can see a wide range of spatial frequencies, some are too high or too low for them to detect. When the spatial frequency is too high, you don't see black and white lines, but instead a uniform grey colour.

The ability to perceive high spatial frequencies deteriorates with age: as you get older, you can see less high spatial frequency and less fine detail. Light is also important: you need more light to see the higher spatial frequencies, which is why reading in the dark is harder.

Recent experience also affects spatial frequency detection. Exposure can cause spatial frequency adaptation (as we discuss in Chapter 4). Reading for a prolonged period causes adaptation to high spatial frequencies and so can make seeing them after reading harder. That's why you should always take a break and go outdoors after studying to correct the after-effect (something we cover in Chapter 4).

Finally, context can affect how you see spatial frequencies. Again in Figure 6-1, notice how the centre gratings appear to be slanted to the right whereas actually they're vertical. This effect is called *the tilt illusion* – context makes the gratings look slanted.

Putting the world together: Gestaltism

In the early 1900s, a group of German psychologists, led by Max Wertheimer, proposed an alternative to the spatial frequency idea in the preceding section. This school of thought is called *Gestaltism*: an approach to perception in which things are grouped together (the word 'Gestalt' has entered modern speech to mean 'the whole').

A clear indication of how people perceive 'the whole' comes from using *hierarchical stimuli*, which are a whole stimulus made up of smaller elements such as *Navon letters* – a big global letter made up of smaller local ones (see Figure 6-2). Generally, people find it easier and quicker to identify the big letter than the small letters (the *global superiority effect*).

Some groups of people seem to see hierarchical stimuli differently to others. People with Williams' Syndrome are much less able to see the local letters. When asked to copy the letter, they only draw the large 'G' from Figure 6-2. People with autism show the opposite pattern and have difficulty seeing the large letter. When asked to copy the letter, they may only draw lots of little Xs in a random pattern.

```
              SSSSSSSS
              SSSSSSSSS
           SSSSS        SSS
           SSSS          SS
           SSSS
           SSSS
           SSSS
           SSSS
           SSSS    SSSSSS
           SSSS    SSSSSS
           SSSS      SSSS
           SSSS      SSSS
           SSSS      SSSS
           SSSS      SSSS
           SSSS      SSSS
           SSSSS    SSSSS
            SSSSSSSSSS
```

Figure 6-2:
A Navon
letter used
by one of
your authors
in his
research.

The global superiority effect shows that people naturally group things together. Gestaltists went about trying to identify what features dictated what would be grouped together. They came up with a set of principles or laws that people use to group the world together. The main law was that people group features according to the simplest pattern possible, called the *law of Prägnanz*.

Figure 6-3 highlights the main Gestalt principles:

- ✔ **Proximity:** You group together things that are closer together.

- ✔ **Similarity:** You group together things that look alike.

- ✔ **Closure:** You group things together to form a complete, closed object if possible.

- ✔ **Good continuation:** You cluster together things to form a path or string.

- ✔ **Uniform connectedness:** You link together anything that has a feature in common (for example, shape or colour).

- ✔ **Symmetry:** You group into one object patterns that are symmetrical.

Extra principles explain whether the grouping makes the figure or the background. Areas curving outwards, which are small, surrounded and symmetrical, are perceived as an object, whereas everything else is perceived as the background.

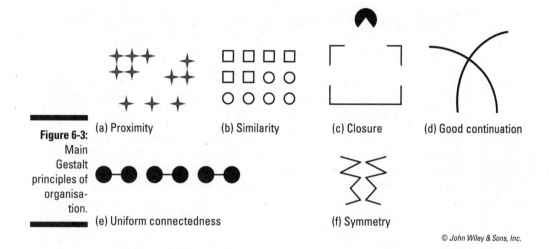

Figure 6-3: Main Gestalt principles of organisation.

(a) Proximity (b) Similarity (c) Closure (d) Good continuation

(e) Uniform connectedness (f) Symmetry

Brain imaging studies show that your brain uses specific parts of the brain for each of the Gestalt principles. It combines these features together, but makes use of uniform connectedness more readily than other features.

REMEMBER

One main issue with much of the Gestaltists's work, however, is that they used abstract patterns rather than anything in the real world. So their work lacks *ecological validity* (it may not apply to the real world).

'What's It Meant to Be?' Perceiving Patterns to Recognise Objects

The visual system breaks down what you're looking at into constituent parts and then groups them back together (see the preceding section). When this process is finished, higher-level parts of your brain can determine what the object is that you're looking at. We consider the three main approaches to object perception and recognition in this section: using shapes, sketches and views.

Recognition is subtly different from *identification*: the latter means that, in addition to finding an object familiar, you're able to name it.

Shaping up to recognise by components

American vision scientist Irving Biederman thought that when people see an object, they try to work out the components that make it up. Not in the same way as working out the simple edges that comprise a shape, though. He thought that every object people see in the world can be broken down into a few key three-dimensional forms called geons.

Geons are basic shapes that comprise every object, such as cubes, spheres, cylinders, cones and pyramids. Some art classes teach people to paint by breaking what they see into these simple shapes. To construct a cup, you need a cylinder with a curved cylinder attached to the handle.

Only 36 geons exist and they're sufficient to make all objects. When you see a new object, the idea is that you establish what geons are required to make it up and compare this group of geons to your stored knowledge about the geons needed to construct objects.

This theory solves one of the major problems in object perception: people find recognising objects easy even without being able to see the whole object and from different viewing angles. This ability is remarkable, because objects can look very different from different views. In Biederman's approach, people can easily distinguish geons from many different angles and so also recognise an object made up of geons at different angles.

Evidence also exists that the human brain has cells that respond only to these simple geons. The monkey *inferotemporal cortex* (part of the brain just below the temples) contains cells that respond to cylinders and nothing else, for example.

Biederman also provided a theory for what information is needed to construct a geon. His ideas are clearly based on the Gestalt approach (which we discuss in the preceding section). He suggested that *invariant* (unchanging) properties of geons distinguish them, as follows:

- ✔ **Curvature:** For example, cylinders have curvature.
- ✔ **Parallel:** For example, cubes have three sets of parallel edges.
- ✔ **Symmetry:** Most geons have some form of symmetry.
- ✔ **Cotermination:** Most geons have points where two edges finish.
- ✔ **Colinearity:** Points fall along a common line.

Although Biederman's theory has been highly influential, many people have difficulty accepting that every object can be broken down into the same geons. Consider, for example, a cup and a bucket. They're made of the same geons, just arranged slightly differently. The theory suggests that people should quite easily confuse them, but in practice they don't.

Sketching the world

David Marr, a British neuroscientist, suggested that images are subject to different computational processes, creating a series of sequential representations:

1. **The brain forms a *primal sketch*.**

   This two-dimensional line drawing provides information about edges, contours and blobs.

2. **The brain creates a *2½-D sketch*.**

   This image includes information regarding shading, texture, motion and depth cues. This sketch and the primal sketch produce images linked to one viewpoint.

3. **The brain produces a *3-D model*.**

   With this representation, people can view objects from many different angles to recognise them.

This model seems to be based on the physiological information produced by the visual areas of the brain involved in the first stages of processing. In this case, the primary visual cortex (refer to Chapter 4) produces information about edges and can be used to form the primal sketch. Later, areas in the brain produce information regarding colour, texture and so on. Further on in the brain, the inferotemporal cortex seems to combine all these sources of information.

Recognising based on views

The *view-based models* or *exemplar models* of recognition suggest that people store multiple representations of objects. Every time you see a chair, you store an image of it. Three-dimensional viewing is established by combining multiple views of the same object.

This recognition process is relatively simple. When you see an object, the brain produces a particular pattern of neural response (a certain set of cells are activated). This pattern of activation is stored and remembered. If you see something similar, the brain activates a similar pattern of cells. Depending on the similarity, you recognise the object or not.

A crucial aspect of this model is that the patterns of activation for the stored object and the newly seen one don't have to match exactly to give a recognition response. This is especially important, because sometimes part of an object is hidden.

Most objects have a natural agreed-upon viewpoint. For example, no one considers that looking down at the top of a car is a standard view, but a near front-on view probably is. If you ask people to name objects as quickly as possible, they're faster if the object is presented in a standard view than when it's viewed from a different viewpoint. The brain accesses the standard viewpoint more readily than other viewpoints.

Research also shows that when people learn about objects, they learn not only the way they look, but also the way they move. In other words, people attach motion to a stored image of certain objects. This means that the standard view of certain animals may include an element of motion. We talk move about movement perception in Chapter 4.

'Hey, I Know You!' Identifying Faces

Faces are the single most important visual stimulus in the human environment: it's one of the few undeniable facts in psychology. In your lifetime, you can recognise between 10,000 and 20,000 faces. You can easily discriminate between all faces (except identical twins) and recognise people, even if you haven't seen them in over 40 years. This ability is remarkable, because all faces share the same basic pattern: two eyes, side by side and over the nose and mouth. People must look at subtle and small information to tell faces apart.

When you see a face, you're bombarded with loads of information. A face can tell you someone's characteristics, including age, gender, ethnicity, emotional state, health status, name and occupation (if you know them), and intentions, as well as where the person's looking. Some people can even tell what others are saying from the way their lips move.

A face is the most important visual stimulus to new-born infants and the first thing that they see for a prolonged period. In the UK, standard practice is to ensure that the mother nurses her baby as soon after birth as possible and for the first few hours so the baby sees a face close-up.

Given their importance, a huge amount of research has tried to understand how people process faces, with much establishing that face recognition is 'special' in some way. This section explores the evidence by looking at research conducted on infants, psychological studies and some neuroscientific studies. We also describe the basic processes involved in face recognition and relate them to the models of object recognition in the earlier section '"What's It Meant to Be?" Perceiving Patterns to Recognise Objects'.

Testing the specialness of face recognition

To establish whether face recognition is 'special', we need to define the term. *Specialness*, in the psychological sense, means that the processing of faces is unique, different to that of objects and uses a special part of the brain. Face processing may also be innate.

The research that we describe in this section highlights that face recognition is very special indeed. People seem to show an early preference for faces, inverting faces makes them harder to recognise, certain brain structures are devoted to face processing, and certain disorders can affect face processing but nothing else.

This research doesn't explain *why* face recognition is different from object processing. Some psychologists believe that face recognition is innate, but no conclusive evidence exists for this idea. The best evidence suggests that because people encounter so many faces, they must learn to distinguish between them. To achieve this difficult task, people become experts at it, which means that part of the human brain becomes devoted to it. If this part gets damaged, people can lose this ability.

Seeing faces in new-borns

New-born infants, by their very nature, have very limited abilities (apart from crying!). This makes them difficult research participants (they can't respond by pressing buttons in a cognitive psychology experiment). So experimenters have to devise clever experiments to find out what new-borns can see.

Robert Fantz, an American developmental psychologist, conducted a number of elaborate studies investigating what infants can see. He developed the *visual preference paradigm* in 1958, in which he placed infants in a viewing chamber. They sat in front of two patterns in an otherwise plain room. The experimenter simply recorded which pattern the infant looked at more. If the infant looked at both patterns equally, he assumed that the infant couldn't tell the two patterns apart.

Fantz did many such experiments and found that infants prefer to look at patterns than plain screens. They prefer patterns with curvature, patterns with higher contrast (especially in the top half of the image), patterns with more features and patterns of a larger size.

Interestingly, infants prefer to look at patterns with features arranged to look like a face compared with patterns arranged differently. This discovery was followed up by Carolyn Goren, an American paediatric researcher, who tested new-born infants at around 9 *minutes* of age! The researchers showed the infants schematic drawings of faces, as well as drawings with the features of a face arranged randomly or vertically down the middle of the 'face' to the infants. They slowly moved the different faces and measured how much the infants followed them.

The infants followed the face stimulus more than the other stimuli, even though they were all made of the same features and so had the same level of complexity. The researchers believed that this finding suggests that face preference is innate, because the children were far too young to have had experience with faces (being 9 minutes old).

But other explanations also exist: new-born infants have seen blood vessels while in the womb, which leads them to be better able to see vertical striped patterns and make horizontal eye movements. Both help them to see faces.

Turning faces upside down

Behavioural evidence suggests that face recognition is different to object recognition in adults. Robert Yin, an American psychologist, conducted an elegant study that changed research in face recognition more than any other. He gave participants a series of faces to learn and then tested their recognition of those faces. The crucial manipulation he made was that some of the faces were upright and some were upside down.

Yin found that people are very good at recognising upright faces but very bad at recognising inverted faces. People aren't as good at recognising other kinds of objects, such as houses and aeroplanes, as faces, but turning them upside down doesn't make people much worse at recognition. The effect of inversion is therefore selective to faces. This *face-inversion effect* provides clear evidence that people process faces differently to objects – in fact, in a special way.

Perhaps, however, this ability is because people see more faces than any other object, instead of any innate or unique brain process. To examine this idea, researchers tested the face-inversion effect in children, but as many studies report children displaying face-inversion effects as don't. A lot of controversy exists on this point, but what's clear is that children show a smaller face-inversion effect than adults, suggesting that the ability is the result of experience.

Another way to check whether the face-inversion effect is due to experience or a special innate mechanism is to look at what happens when you invert other objects that people are expert at recognising. Unfortunately, no such stimulus exists for most people: can you think of another object that you've seen more of than faces? (If you can, please write to us: we'd love to do a study on it!)

Some people do look at categories of objects almost as much as faces. Susan Carey, an American psychologist, showed that dog-show judges who've been in the job for more than ten years display an inversion effect for pictures of dogs, in a similar way as other people do for faces.

Overall, evidence suggests that people process faces in a special way, but that this ability results from years of experience processing upright faces.

Considering the brain of the face

Another way to assess whether face recognition is processed in a special way is to look at the brains of people when they look at faces compared to other objects. In 1996, American neuroscientist Nancy Kanwisher found a bit of the brain called the *fusiform gyrus* that's more active when looking at faces than looking at flowers in about 75 per cent of tested people. Kanwisher and colleagues went on to show that the fusiform gyrus is more active when looking at upright faces than inverted faces, providing further evidence that this brain area is selectively used for processing faces.

As with all things psychological, however, other research caused a bit of an argument. Isabel Gauthier, another American neuroscientist, produced compelling evidence that the fusiform gyrus is in fact a part of the brain used for anything that people are experts at perceiving.

She trained people to learn to attach names to fairly weird shapes called Greebles (strange putty-like creatures with horns and noses). She found that the fusiform gyrus was active when processing these Greebles in those trained but not in those not trained.

If children show activity in their fusiform gyrus when they see faces, it would show that this brain region processes faces from birth, but if they don't the ability probably develops with experience. Well, clever psychologists have studied this ability and showed that the child's fusiform gyrus *doesn't* process faces until about the age of 9 years.

Electroencephalography (EEG, refer to Chapter 1) has shown a similar set of findings. A particular spike of electrical activity in the brain (called an *event-related potential*, or ERP) seems to occur when people see faces. It's called N170 (because it's negative electrically and occurs 170 milliseconds after the person sees a face). This shows that the human brain knows that a face is a face within one-fifth of a second and that something is special about faces. This brain response is delayed when people view inverted faces.

British neuroscientist Martin Eimer, however, along with Roxanne Itier, a Canadian neuroscientist, showed that this N170 brain response is due to the presence of the eyes. Faces without eyes produce delayed N170. Furthermore, people who are expert at recognising other types of objects (for example, car experts) seem to show an N170 to those objects. Again, this research seems to show that the brain processes faces in a special way, but that this ability is due to extensive experience with faces.

When it goes wrong: Not seeing faces

One approach to cognitive psychology is to look at people who have problems with a particular ability but not others (called a *dissociation*, as we describe in Chapter 1). If face recognition is special, some people shouldn't be able to do it . . . and indeed that's the case.

People suffering from the clinical disorder *prosopagnosia* have an inability to recognise faces, and yet can recognise all other objects perfectly fine. The condition often occurs because of a brain injury. Patients with prosopagnosia usually have damage to the occipital lobe and in particular the fusiform gyrus. When presented with faces of familiar people, they don't recognise them. They also can't learn new faces. Cases even exist of farmers with prosopagnosia for their cows, but who can recognise people properly!

People with this disorder often wake up in hospital with a loved-one nearby but can't recognise the person. Although, unfortunately, no cure exists for prosopagnosia, sufferers can devise compensation strategies. For instance, one person with prosopagnosia that we met always asks what clothes someone will be wearing and then can look out for that.

People with a related disorder *Capgras delusion* can recognise a face and yet believe that it's not the person they're seeing. For example, you may look at your mother but believe that she's a robot imposter.

Eminent British psychologist Hadyn Ellis and colleagues compared Capgras and prosopagnosia. They found that when people see faces they consciously recognise them and their skin increases in conductivity (the *skin galvanic response* used in TV programmes as a lie detector – it doesn't work in reality). The idea is that when you see someone familiar, your brain gives you a sense of familiarity and their identity.

When patients with prosopagnosia see a face, they don't have the conscious recollection of the face but do have the skin conductance response. When people with Capgras delusion see faces, they don't get the skin conductance response but do consciously recognise the face. Their brains are getting conflicting messages: the first is 'I don't know this person' and the second is 'they look like X'. The only logical explanation for the patient to make is that the person is an imposter.

This discovery is important, because many people with Capgras delusion used to be wrongly diagnosed with schizophrenia; in fact, their delusion makes sense (given the disconnected messages of the brain).

Modelling face recognition

The preceding section shows that face recognition appears to be different to object recognition, and so psychologists need a new set of models to account for it. They can't just use the models of object recognition we discuss in the earlier section '"What's It Meant to Be?"' Perceiving Patterns to Recognise Objects'.

Here, we look at three of the most influential theories in face processing: face-space, configural processing, and the interactive activation and competition model.

Facing spaces

Tim Valentine, a British psychologist with a delightful moustache, devised *face-space*. He thought that the best way to describe how people recognise faces was to plot it on a graph (we tried it – see Figure 6-4). Technically, this graph is called a multi-dimensional space, but we draw only two dimensions (axes).

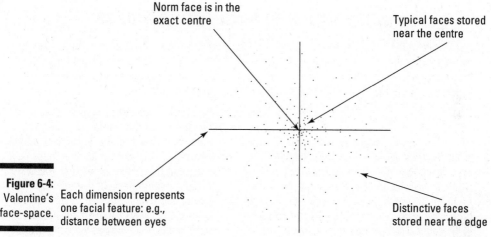

Norm face is in the exact centre

Typical faces stored near the centre

Distinctive faces stored near the edge

Each dimension represents one facial feature: e.g., distance between eyes

Figure 6-4: Valentine's face-space.

© John Wiley & Sons, Inc.

Each dimension of the space represents a facial feature that people use to recognise faces. Valentine hasn't specified exactly what features are used in this process, but eye-tracking evidence suggests at least one dimension for eyes. Estimations suggest that between 14 and 100 dimensions/features are used to recognise faces.

The most average face would exist in the centre. Every face is coded on its values relative to this average face. A face with huge eyes is stored at the opposite end of the space from a face with tiny eyes. Both faces are far from the centre and considered *distinctive*.

Recognition is done by matching the face currently being looked at with faces stored in this space. The two faces are recognised if they share enough of the features and can be confused when they're very close to each other in the space – which is why people don't confuse two distinctive faces.

This beautifully simple and highly influential model explains a lot of the data from face-recognition experiments (as well as data regarding the own-ethnicity bias that we describe in the nearby sidebar 'Research into own-group biases'). For example:

- ✔ Average faces are *categorised* as faces much faster than distinctive faces, because they look more like an average face.

- ✔ Distinctive faces are *recognised* faster than average faces, because no other faces are nearby in the space to confuse you.

REAL WORLD

Research into own-group biases

People are better at recognising faces of their own ethnicity than other ethnicities, which is the source of the unfortunate phrase 'they all look the same to me'. Psychological evidence can shine a light on this ability: all ethnic groups show the own-ethnicity bias.

We can dispel one common myth: faces of one ethnicity *aren't* more or less variable than your own. The fact is that the features that produce variability in one ethnicity may not be the same as in another ethnicity. For example, White people's eyes can be of many different colours, but in East Asian or Black people, the variety of eye colour is much less. In White people, the variability in the size and shape of the nose is much less than in East Asian or Black people. All ethnicities have the same variability, just not in the same features.

You may think that the own-ethnicity bias occurs because of racism, but no strong association has been detected between racism and the bias. The following two answers have been suggested for own-ethnicity bias:

- ✔ **Socio-cognitive account:** People immediately try to classify faces as being of their own group or of an out-group. They put effort into remembering an own-group face but much less (or none) if the face is from an out-group.

- ✔ **Perceptual expertise account:** Brains are designed to process faces that people encounter more frequently. You look at the features of someone's face that helps distinguish it from other faces and you learn through experience what those features are. Indeed, White British participants tend to look at the eyes more than Japanese participants, who look at the nose. Other-ethnicity faces are therefore stored using features that are less helpful in differentiating them. This account is especially important for people working in identity checkpoints, such as passport control. They're better at matching faces of their own ethnicity than another ethnicity.

Research has yet to discover a method for reducing the own-ethnicity bias.

Other own-group biases exist, such as biases for age, gender and sexuality.

Not dividing up faces: Configural processing

One of the models of object recognition suggests that people break the world up into separate features in order to recognise them (check out the earlier 'Shaping up to recognise by components' section). Applied to face perception, the model should show that faces are processed by combining a series of spheres, a cone and some cylinders. But the evidence is extremely clear: people don't process faces by breaking them down. Here, we present how psychologists know.

In Figure 6-5 we show the *Thatcher Illusion*, named after the first face this illusion was done to (we don't use Thatcher's face, thankfully). In this illusion, one of the two faces looks weird. If you turn the book around and look at the faces the right way up, you quickly see which one (try it out on your friends!).

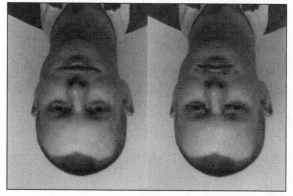

Figure 6-5: Thatcher Illusion.

© John Wiley & Sons, Inc.

Seeing that grotesqueness of the face is harder when it's upside down, because you process the upside-down face by breaking it into its constituent parts: none of them are odd. When the face is the right way up, however, you don't process the face by breaking it up. Instead, you look at the whole.

We show another demonstration in Figure 6-6: the *parts and wholes test*. If you try to learn the names of the faces presented at the top and then are asked to identify which nose belongs to one of the faces (say Tom), doing so is easier when it's in the context of the face. Therefore, again, people don't learn face parts in isolation.

If you still don't believe us, try the example in Figure 6-7. This shows the *composite face effect* devised by Andy Young, a British neuroscientist, and his team in 1987. Look at the face on the left first. It's made up of two faces: the top half of one and the bottom half of another. Can you identify them?

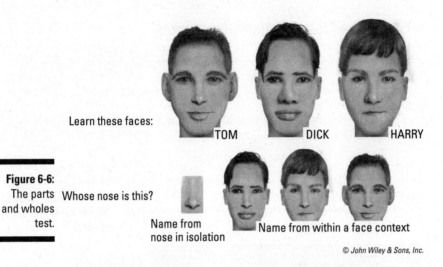

Learn these faces:

TOM   DICK   HARRY

Figure 6-6:
The parts and wholes test.

Whose nose is this?

Name from nose in isolation

Name from within a face context

© John Wiley & Sons, Inc.

Figure 6-7:
The composite face effect.

© John Wiley & Sons, Inc.

Most people find this task quite challenging. But if we separate out the two faces slightly, it becomes much easier (see the right part of Figure 6-7). This effect occurs because people tend to process faces as a whole stimulus rather than the sum of the parts. Put together, the face fuses to form a new identity and your brain struggles to separate the forms.

This phenomenon is called *configural* (or *holistic*) *processing*. The human brain seems to code the whole face in one lump instead of engaging in *featural processing*, where it would break up the face. When presented with an inverted face, people engage in featural processing.

Indeed, Bruno Rossion, a neuroscientist from Belgium, suggests that face processing is due to expertise at configural processing: when people are experts at processing faces, they look at the centre of the face and can take in all the information simultaneously. But people who aren't experts need to look at each individual feature in turn. Therefore, people with prosopagnosia (see the 'When it goes wrong: Not seeing faces' section earlier in this chapter) and children look at all features equally in a similar way that adults look at inverted faces.

Combining face processing: Structural model and interactive activation and competition model

The two models of face recognition we discuss so far in this section (face-space and configural processing) are notable, but they deal primarily with how people perceive faces. But faces give lots of information, not just about identity. To understand how these abilities interact, we turn to Vicki Bruce and Andy Young's model of face processing – the *structural model* of face recognition.

This model suggests that separate components exist for eight different things (see Figure 6-8):

- ✔ **Structural encoding:** A simple description of a face
- ✔ **Expression analysis:** Of other people's emotions
- ✔ **Facial speech analysis:** Of lip-reading
- ✔ **Direct visual processing:** Codes only facial information
- ✔ **Face-recognition units:** Represent the structural information of a known face
- ✔ **Person identity nodes:** Link all information specific to a known individual
- ✔ **Name generation:** Stores names separately
- ✔ **Cognitive system:** Stores other information, such as facts about someone, elsewhere

The *interactive activation and competition* model has superseded parts of the structural model. It more accurately represents the interactions between face-recognition units and semantic information in the above list. This model predicts that people can have deficits in emotion processing but intact face recognition, something that has indeed been observed. The model also predicts that name information can prime faces of known people: that is, if you present the name of someone familiar, you become faster at recognising the person from a picture.

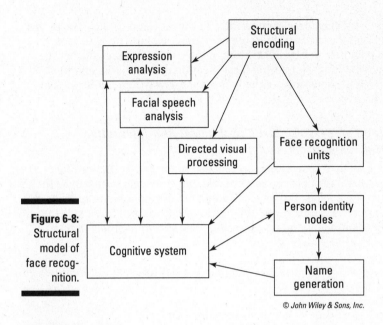

Figure 6-8:
Structural
model of
face recog-
nition.

Furthermore, this model highlights why you can get feelings of familiarity with faces, but without remembering the names: your face-recognition unit has become active (meaning that you recognise the person), but it hasn't activated the person identity node. This experience is certainly familiar to us and can be very embarrassing.

Note that you never recall someone's name without recalling other semantic information. Names are clearly more special.

Chapter 7

Atten-hut! Paying Attention to Attention

- -

In This Chapter

▶ Understanding how to grab someone's attention

▶ Controlling attention when you have it

▶ Digging into attention disorders

- -

Consider the environment around you while reading this book. We doubt that it's absolutely quiet. Most likely you can hear distractions (perhaps a TV, music, the sound of someone vacuuming). Yet, despite these distractions, you can remain (mostly) focused on what you're reading. The huge amount of sensory input that everyone is constantly receiving would be overwhelming if humans weren't able to block out some of it. The psychological mechanism of this filtering and focusing ability is attention.

Attention acts like a spotlight, a focusing device to bring to mind a particular stimulus. It also acts as a filter, blocking out distractions.

In this chapter, we describe the key features of what attracts attention, what doesn't attract attention (even when it probably should!) and how attention helps you search for things. We also discuss how to control attention, the mechanics of involuntary attention and some clinical disorders of attention.

'Hey, You!' Grabbing Attention

Understanding attention is essential in many areas of life. One group that relies on it to make a living are magicians.

In 2008, the prestigious journal *Nature Reviews Neuroscience* published an article by a number of magicians (including Teller of Penn and Teller fame) explaining how they use knowledge of human cognition to execute their tricks and how this knowledge can help cognitive psychologists understand how the brain works. One sure common skill is *misdirection* – guiding the audience's attention away from the real trick. Misdirection involves several aspects of attention that we define and discuss in this section:

- ✔ **Priming:** Where seeing one object or word (the *cue*) speeds up the processing of a second object or word

- ✔ **Inattentional blindness:** Where people don't spot or attend to something visually

- ✔ **Visual searching:** Where people have to search the visual environment for a particular object

In the vanishing ball illusion, the magician throws a ball in the air and catches it a few times. On the final throw, the ball seems to disappear in midair. In fact the magician palms the ball, but audience members don't notice because of inattentional blindness. The magician has misdirected them. To start, she primes the audience by really throwing the ball a number of times (so that people expect the same thing to happen again). Then on the final throw, she cues the audience to look where the ball should be by using the same hand movement and gazing at the imaginary ball – doing so guides the audience's attention to where she's looking, because people automatically follow one another's gaze.

Priming the pump

The simplest explanation for priming is that the presentation of something (an object or word) makes it easier for the brain to activate its stored representation for that something (object or word) later. So, if you hear the word *square*, you're quicker to respond to a square when you see it.

Expectation can also be used for priming. American psychologist Michael Posner developed a test called the *Posner cueing task*, which measures how the attention system responds to different cues.

Participants are presented with a *fixation cross* (a '+') in the middle of the screen. Then a cue appears, directing their attention to one or the other side of the fixation cross. A target appears, and participants have to respond to the target (for example, by saying what shape it is). The cue can be valid or invalid. On valid trials, the cue predicts the location of the target. On invalid trials, the cue doesn't predict the location of the target. Neutral trials, in which no cue exists, are also used.

The number of valid and neutral trials is always greater than invalid trials. So, the participants can expect that the cue is going to predict the target location. The results are that the valid cues speed up identification of the target, whereas invalid cues slow it down.

People's desires can also prime their attention. For example, alcoholics spot alcohol-related objects in a visual scene quicker than non-alcoholics.

Failing to notice the obvious

Inattentional blindness is a phenomenon in which people fail to notice or attend to something in their visual world. In 1998, psychologists Arien Mack and Irvin Rock carried out research showing that people can miss something right before their eyes when their attention is distracted.

Participants were presented with cross shapes and had to identify whether the horizontal bar was longer than the vertical bar. The crosses were on screen for only 200 milliseconds; participants were looking at a fixation cross, not looking directly at the cross shape. People were highly accurate at this task. But when researchers replaced the fixation point with a shape (a triangle, rectangle or cross), 86 per cent of participants didn't notice the change.

Change blindness is a related and more intriguing phenomenon. People often fail to notice changes to an image that seem really obvious when pointed out to them. Normally, when something moves or changes in front of people, the change grabs their attention because it changes their retinas (creating *transients*, cell responses to something new).

To produce change blindness, psychologists need to mask these transients. They can do so in several ways:

- **Blink:** If the image is changed during an eye blink, the change doesn't attract the person's attention.

- **Flicker:** The whole screen blanks out for a brief moment, hiding the location of the change.

- **Mud splash:** A number of shapes flash on the screen while the change occurs to distract the participant.

- **Slow change:** If something changes slowly enough, such as the colour of a wall, it doesn't attract people's attention.

Change blindness and inattentional blindness often occur in films, with people missing continuity errors or ignoring a camera operator in the shot. Scientific studies of continuity errors show that 90 per cent of people fail to notice them, even if they expect some changes. Change blindness may also be a reason for the type of road accidents in which a driver pulls out into the path of another vehicle because he 'looked, but failed to see'.

He's behind the door!

Research by American psychologists Daniel J. Simons and Mike Ambinder shows how inattentionally blind people can be and how little they're often paying attention. They carried out a study in which a stooge walks up to a passerby (the participant) and asks for directions. During the conversation, the couple is interrupted by builders carrying a door. The door obscures the stooge, who changes places with one of the men carrying the door. In 50 per cent of cases, the passerby continues to have a conversation with the new stooge, failing to detect the change in appearance (see a demonstration at `http://www.simonslab. com/videos.html`).

This experiment was repeated on students handing work to a secretary: the secretary ducks behind the counter and another secretary stands up. Even psychology students who know about this effect sometimes fail to notice the change!

Daniel J. Simons offers these explanations for change blindness:

- ✔ Your brain overwrites the first image with the second.
- ✔ After your brain stores the first image, you ignore the next one.
- ✔ You don't remember either image for long enough to compare them.
- ✔ Your brain stores both images but you don't consciously compare them.
- ✔ You don't expect changes, so your brain combines the two images mentally.

Another explanation is based on *inhibition of return*, which is where you don't look back at somewhere you've recently observed. Inhibition of return prevents you from getting stuck looking at one part of an image.

Change blindness typically occurs only for less central aspects of the visual scene and only for things that you don't expect to change (say, the face of someone you're talking to). So, part of the attentional system's role is to prepare you for what's likely to change. But the result is that it may not provide you with a true representation of the world.

Visual search: Looking for a needle in a haystack

The popular *Where's Wally* books (*Where's Waldo* in the US) involve trying to find the eponymous hero in a distinctive outfit in a cluttered scene. The task is difficult because the scene contains lots of other people and objects, and many of them share colours and features similar to the target. Cognitive psychologists use a more formal version of this task called the *visual search task* to understand the role of attention in vision.

In the visual search task, people are shown an image full of different shapes and they have to say whether a particular shape (the target) is present or absent. The researchers record the time taken for people to decide whether the target is present or absent. Before reading on, find the B in Figure 7-1a and the O in Figure 7-1b.

In both displays in Figure 7-1a, the B shares the same features (vertical and curved lines) as the distractors P, so it doesn't pop out. You have to check each item in turn, searching for the specific conjunction of features, so you take longer to find the target in the top image because of more distractors. In Figure 7-1b, the O is the only shape containing curved lines, so it pops out and the number of distractors has little effect.

```
P  P  P  P  P  P  P
P  P  P  P  P  P  P
P  P  P  P  P  P  P
P  P  P  P  P  P  P
P  P  P  P  P  P  P
P  B  P  P  P  P  P
P  P  P  P  P  P  P
```

```
X  X  X  X  X  X  X
X  X  X  X  X  X  X
X  X  X  X  X  O  X
X  X  X  X  X  X  X
X  X  X  X  X  X  X
X  X  X  X  X  X  X
X  X  X  X  X  X  X
```
(b)

```
    P
              P     B
              P
                        P
         P
```
(a)

Figure 7-1:
a) Find the
B; b) Find
the O.

By varying the number of other objects (distractors) and the similarity between the target and the distractors, psychologists can discover some interesting facts about visual search and attention:

✔ If the target is different from all the distractors in terms of a single, simple feature such as colour or shape (as in Figure 7-1b), it tends to pop out and the time taken to find the target stays the same when researchers increase the number of distractors. But to report that the target is absent takes longer and this time period increases with the number of distractors.

✔ In a *conjunction search* (searching for a target that shares elements with distracting items), the target doesn't have a unique single feature but a unique combination of features. Here the time to find a present target increases with each distractor added, and deciding that the target is absent takes about twice as long. Figure 7-2 shows the pattern of results for the two kinds of search (where the search item is present and the search item is absent) and different numbers of distractors.

Figure 7-2:
The average times for different types of search and different numbers of distractors in a visual search experiment.

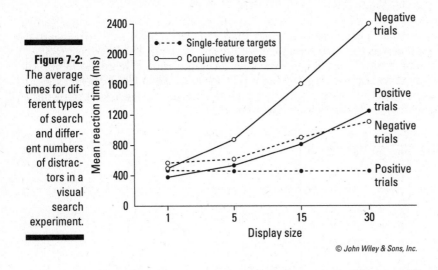

© *John Wiley & Sons, Inc.*

According to psychologist Anne Treisman's feature integration theory, attention is the 'glue' that binds the features together in visual search. In *pre-attentive search*, your visual system picks out features (such as colour, shape, size and movement). At this stage, if the target is the only item containing a certain feature, it pops out. But if the target depends on a conjunction of features, it doesn't pop out and you have to look for it, one item at a time. By attending to an object, you're able to 'glue' the different features together.

Pre-attentive search only allows you to process simple features, but it's fast – everyone processes all the features at the same time (in a *parallel search*). To use attention, you need to examine each object one at a time (a *serial search*), which is slower because you have to attend to each item in turn. On average, people have to examine about half the objects in a display before finding the target. But in order to say that the target is absent, they need to search exhaustively every item, which is why people take about twice as long to respond when the object isn't present.

The psychology of meditation

Meditation is an ancient art, but only recently have psychologists started to try to understand how it works and what it does. Two main types of meditation exist:

- ✔ **Focused attention meditation:** You focus on a particular thing and try to avoid distractions.

- ✔ **Open monitoring (OM) meditation:** You monitor your own conscious state.

One study shows that those who practise OM meditation avoid being distracted by irrelevant stimuli in experimental tasks. Another study comparing highly experienced Tibetan Buddhist meditators with novices found differences in the electrical activity in their brains – both in location and type of electrical waveform. This difference was present even when they weren't meditating, suggesting a longer-term effect on the organisation of their mental activity.

'Now Concentrate!' Controlling Attention

Implicit in the definition of attention is the idea that you can take control of your conscious experience. Attention shines like a spotlight on a stimulus (or stimuli). It raises awareness of key parts of the thing you're attending to while dimming others. It selects what reaches your consciousness.

Imagine, for example, that you're revising for a cognitive psychology exam (reading this book, of course, and writing notes), while the TV's on, someone's hollering about dinner and you're expecting a text message. Attention removes the distraction and focuses on the key task (revising) or tasks (revising and listening out for your mobile phone).

In this section, we cover how you choose (or not) what you attend to. We also describe what happens when you have multiple things to attend to at once and how difficult that is. Plus we explore what factors push your attentional capacity to the limit.

Investigating selective attention

The first thing your brain needs to do when studying is to select the relevant things to attend to: in other words, on what to put the attentional spotlight (or unidirectional microphone for sounds!). Here we look at how the brain selects information to attend to.

Classic studies of auditory attention use a *shadowing paradigm* (an experimental task in which participants must pay attention to sounds in one ear but ignore the other). Participants wear headphones and their task is to repeat what they hear. Simple, you say. But psychologists make things harder by presenting different messages to each ear (called the *dichotic listening task*): for example, the message '1, 2, 3' to one ear and '4, 5, 6' to the other ear. When asked to repeat what they hear, participants report hearing '1, 2, 3, 4, 5, 6'.

In other dichotic listening tasks, participants have to shadow one ear but ignore the other. They're then asked to recall information from the attended ear (in which the message was shadowed) and the unattended ear (the one they were supposed to ignore). Participants are nearly perfect at remembering information from the attended ear, but remember very little from the unattended ear. In fact, participants don't notice whether the language used in the unattended ear swaps from English to German or even if the same word is repeated several dozen times!

Participants do notice, however, if the gender of the speaker in the unattended ear changes. Furthermore, most participants are unaware of an instruction to stop the task in the unattended ear unless it's preceded by their name. Colin Cherry, a British cognitive psychologist, described this tendency as the *cocktail party effect* – even if you're attending to something else, you sometimes hear your name spoken.

Researchers Daniel Simons and Christopher Chabris report a similar effect in the visual domain. They present a video to participants in which two teams (one wearing white and one wearing black) pass balls between themselves. Participants were instructed to count the number of times the team in white passes the ball to each other and to ignore the team in black. During the video, a man in a gorilla suit walks into the middle of the screen, beats his chest and walks off. Less than half the participants noticed the gorilla (try the video out on your friends at `http://www.simonslab.com/videos.html`).

To explain why people don't notice things even when they're in plain sight (or sound!), Donald Broadbent, a British psychologist, proposed a filter theory of attention in the 1950s. His *early-selection theory* was based on the idea that attention acts as a filter shortly after the senses detect the stimulus. Low-level stimulus properties (such as volume or pitch) are then used to decide what's to be allowed through the filter. Basically, all unwanted sensory stimulation is sieved out.

Some researchers use the cocktail party effect to criticise the early-selection theory. Specifically, one study criticised the theory by giving mild electric shocks to participants every time a particular word was presented in the unattended ear. This formed a classical conditioning pairing of a word and a shock. When asked to recall the words, participants couldn't recall the word paired with the shock. But when shown the word, they had a higher *skin galvanic response* (their hands got a little sweatier), suggesting that they were mildly afraid of the word. This suggests that they had attended to and memorised the word, but not consciously.

Anne Triesman developed *the attenuation model* in which attention simply reduces the amount of information that can get through the filter. The early filter still blocks out unwanted stimulation, but allows information through that has certain physical properties. Diana Deutsch, British-American perceptual and cognitive psychologist, went further, and suggested that all information is processed and attention simply filters out the unwanted information and the semantic (meaning) level (known as *late selection*). We present these theories in Figure 7-3.

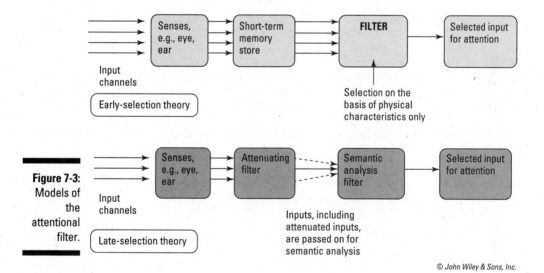

Figure 7-3: Models of the attentional filter.

© John Wiley & Sons, Inc.

 So which is more accurate: early selection or late selection? Experiments show that during highly demanding tasks, people filter out unwanted information as early as possible. For example, when driving along and having a conversation, the talking stops when you reach a busy junction: the attentional filter prevents distraction for a more demanding task. During easier tasks, however, you can employ late selection.

Getting your divided attention

No doubt you've tried *multitasking* (deliberately focusing on two tasks at the same time), perhaps having a conversation with someone while washing up. How well can you perform the tasks? What about when you're writing an essay and your roommate asks what you want for dinner? How do you swap from the first task to the second (known as *task switching*)? Many people finish the sentence they're writing before answering the question. Both multitasking and task switching are examples of *divided attention*.

In an experiment on multitasking, participants shadowed one list of words from one ear while ignoring a second list presented verbally or visually. The conditions for list 1 and list 2 were respectively: spoken words/spoken words; spoken words/visual words. Researchers tested recall for both lists and accuracy was higher for the spoken words/visual words condition than when the lists were matched across senses. The message is clear: you can divide attention across multiple tasks as long as they're dissimilar enough.

One suggestion for when tasks may interfere with each other stems from the *working memory model* of memory proposed by Alan Baddeley and Graham Hitch in 1976, which contains components for processing visual and verbal material. These two components can process information in isolation. A *central executive* (the control part of working memory) controls the processing in the two components. Tasks interfere with each other only if they're using the same component of working memory or when they're too difficult.

Pushing things to the limit

Although people can multitask a little (see the preceding section), limits apply. If you're in a room full of noisy people who're moving around and discussing what they watched on TV the night before, planning an essay in cognitive psychology is nearly impossible. You simply have too much sensory information to filter out.

One of the most useful explanations of a *limited capacity system* is that of *executive control* (a series of processes that allow for task switching, focusing; see Chapter 8). Here, working memory and the *central executive* or *episodic buffer* (another component of working memory that links short-term and long-term memory) work to plan people's strategy for completing tasks (see Chapter 8 for more on working memory).

Research shows that executive control allocates attentional resources from one task to another and inhibits automatic responses. Cognitive psychologists have found that executive control is strongly related to tests of inhibition. Executive control also correlates with intelligence, suggesting that more intelligent people can allocate their attention more appropriately than less intelligent people.

Switching from one task to another

In task switching, researchers have assumed that you have to wait to start the second task until you finish the first task. But an experiment in which participants are presented with two tasks concurrently highlights that this isn't entirely true. The first task is to identify whether a sound is high pitch or low pitch by saying 'high' or 'low'. The second task is to identify the spatial location of a square (left or right), by pressing the appropriate computer keyboard buttons. If you have to complete the first task before starting the second, the total time to do both tasks should be equal to the time taken to do task 1 plus the time taken to do task 2. However, the study found that the total time to do both tasks in this way is actually less. Nevertheless, reaction time to the second task is longer when following the first task than if the second task is presented alone.

The explanation for this effect is the *response-selection bottleneck model*:

The idea is simple: you can't think about how to respond to a particular task until you complete the response to the previous task. This model explains several other effects. You can vary the duration between the start of the first task and the start of the second task (known as the *stimulus onset asynchrony* or SOA), and it doesn't affect the overall time to react, provided that the SOA only lasts as long as the processing and thinking time for task 1 (known as the *psychological refractory period effect*). The logic is that the response has to be initiated for the first task before the decision-making process can begin for the second task.

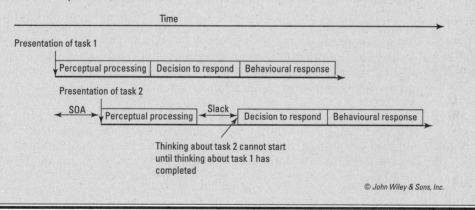

© *John Wiley & Sons, Inc.*

Running on Autopilot

Your attention can be under voluntary control – such as when you decide to ignore your ringing phone to carry on watching your favourite TV programme. But your attention can also be automatic – everyone has experienced their attention being drawn to something because of a loud noise or an unusual display. Sometimes, people simply work on 'autopilot' – for example, one of us (no names, no blame!) accidentally travelled to college one day instead of to an interview, because that was his normal morning routine and he was too sleepy to prevent the automatic behaviour.

In more serious examples, several aircraft pilots have landed aircraft having apparently 'forgotten' to deploy the landing gear, leading the plane to crash land. In many of these cases, the pilots simply went through the landing checklist on 'autopilot' without paying attention.

Psychologists have used a number of tools to investigate why this happens. In this section, we cover what factors can interfere with attention and make it worse. We also examine the important effects practice has on attention.

Interfering with attention

Automatic processing can adversely affect your attention. How many times does the letter *f* appear in the following sentence?

> Finished files are the result of years of scientific study combined with the experience of many years.

The most common answer is three but the correct answer is six. Many people seem to miss the 'f's when they occur in the word 'of'.

Words such as 'of', 'the' and 'to' play a functional role in language and appear in most texts. They tend to occur much more often than content words, and so people are more used to them and more practised at reading them, which means that they're more likely to ignore them. Like anything that's practised a lot, reading functional words becomes automatic.

The *Stroop effect* (named after John Stroop, the American psychologist who discovered it) is known as the 'gold standard' of automatic processing. The effect is simple: participants are presented with a series of colour words (for example, 'RED'). The word may be printed in the same colour as what the word means (a *congruent condition*) – for example, the word 'RED' printed in red ink – or in a different colour from its meaning (an *incongruent condition*) – for example, the word 'RED' printed in green ink. Participants have to name the colour the word is printed in.

Participants find the incongruent condition much harder and take longer to name the colours than with the congruent condition: reading is so automatic that psychologists assume that the word's meaning disrupts people's ability to name the colour.

The *Simon effect* is a similar example of automatic processing. Participants are presented with a display in which a symbol is on the left or the right side of the screen. They have to press a left button for one particular cue (for example, an '@') and a right button for a different cue (for example, a '#'). If the '@' appears on the left, the trial is considered to be congruent, whereas if it appears on the right, it's an incongruent trial (and vice versa for the '#'). Participants' reaction time to state that the symbol is present takes longer for the incongruent trials than the congruent ones, confirming that knowledge of spatial positions can interfere with attention.

Practising to make perfect

The nature of attention changes with experience and practice: experts not only focus on different aspects of the task, but also multitask better.

Driving is an obvious example. Novice drivers tend to pay more attention to the car in front of them and its position than expert drivers do. But the latter tend to pay more attention to cars to the side or at junctions (in positions where cars may do unexpected things, such as pull out suddenly).

One suggestion is that practice makes a task more automatic, and so it requires less attentional resources. Executive control is primarily needed to inhibit automatic processing or when automatic processes are unavailable. So, when a behaviour is well practised, it becomes habit and, as a result, you don't think about the action.

Consider playing the guitar: when you're learning a new chord, you have to look at your fingers to position them in the right place. But when you've practised enough, you simply change to that chord without looking at it.

Another simple aspect of how skill diminishes your awareness of the precise acts involved is through chunking (see Chapter 8 for more on this concept). *Chunking* is where you group items together to make remembering easier.

When you're learning the chord of C on the guitar, you have to do four steps: you need to position your forefinger on the b-string, your second finger on the d-string, your ring finger on the a-string, and then strum on all but the e-string. Eric Clapton, however, can chunk all these small aspects into one instruction: 'play the chord of C'. The cognitive resources to make four responses are simplified into making one response.

Belgium psychologist Bruno Rossion suggests that experts have a wider attentional spotlight, allowing them to see more of a stimuli in one glance than a novice.

When Things Go Wrong: Attention Disorders

Attention is crucial for human survival. Yet neuropsychological conditions exist in which the ability to attend is severely impaired. In this section, we take a look at two attention disorders: spatial neglect and attention deficit hyperactivity disorder.

Ignoring the left: Spatial neglect

Don't worry, despite the heading this section isn't going to get all political! *Spatial neglect* is a relatively common disorder of attention usually caused by damage to the right parietal lobe (a bit of the brain towards the side and back of the head). Patients suffering from spatial neglect appear not to see or attend to half of the visual field (usually the left side – the opposite side to the damage). That is, they can see only what's on the right side of an object.

Tests of spatial neglect include the following:

- **Cancellation tasks:** Patients are asked to cross out all the items, but they tend to cross out only those on one side (see Figure 7-4a).

- **Line bisection:** Patients are asked to mark the middle of the line, but they tend to mark the line to one side, as we show in Figure 7-4b.

- **Copying:** Patients are asked to copy an image, but they tend to copy only half of the image, as Figure 7-4c depicts.

In all cases, patients can't detect what's on the neglected side. Things can be so severe that patients even shave only one side of their face or eat half the food on their plate. Patients with spatial neglect can't visualise, imagine or even describe the neglected side of a place. In one study, a patient with neglect was asked to imagine and describe a famous square in Milan. The person described the features on the right-hand side of the square. When asked to imagine and describe the square from the opposite side, the person again described the right-hand side (the opposite side from before). Clearly, someone with neglect doesn't have a problem with perception, but attention.

Although patients with neglect seem unable to attend to one side, they're unconsciously aware of the neglected side. British neuropsychologists John Marshall and Peter Halligan conducted a study in which patient PS was given two pictures: house A was a normal line drawing (see Figure 7-4c); house B was identical, except that it had flames coming out of the upper window on the neglected side. PS was asked which house she preferred. On 15 out of 17 trials, PS chose the one without the flames but was unable to explain her preference.

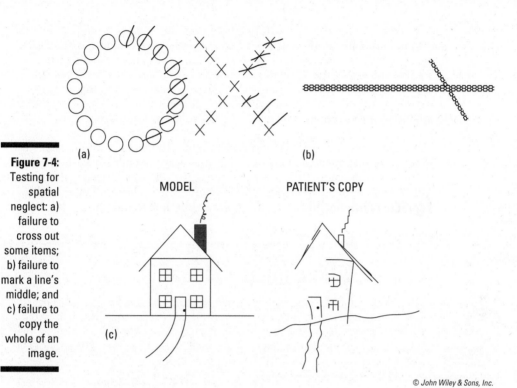

(a)

(b)

MODEL   PATIENT'S COPY

(c)

© *John Wiley & Sons, Inc.*

Figure 7-4: Testing for spatial neglect: a) failure to cross out some items; b) failure to mark a line's middle; and c) failure to copy the whole of an image.

Patients with neglect can also identify symmetry in the neglected side. These findings suggest that they do have some unconscious awareness of the neglected side. In other words, some things can enter people's minds without attention and without conscious awareness.

Having trouble paying attention: ADHD

Attention-deficit hyperactivity disorder (ADHD) is a common childhood psychological disorder. It occurs in 3–5 per cent of Western children and is characterised by an inability to focus or maintain attention for a long time, leading to restlessness and potentially aggression. Children with ADHD often interrupt others and are impatient.

Cognitive tests of children with ADHD usually involve *vigilance designs*, in which participants have to respond when they see a particular stimulus (for example, a square) among lots of other stimuli (for example, triangles). Each stimulus is presented one after another, with (crucially) the target stimulus presented very infrequently. Children with ADHD perform very badly at this type of task. They can easily name squares and triangles, however, showing that the disorder is one of sustaining attention.

Another experiment asks participants to respond with a button press when they see an X and a different key when they see an O. Children with ADHD perform well at this easy task. An instruction to stop the response when a sound is played at the same time as the X or O occurs on a few trials (the *stop-signal paradigm*). Children with ADHD are less likely to stop on these trials than other children, showing that children with ADHD have problems inhibiting their responses.

One treatment for ADHD is the stimulant methylphenidate, which makes the brain more responsive. The idea is that the brains of children with ADHD need more stimulation to show the same activation as children without ADHD. Methylphenidate makes children with ADHD perform better at the stop-signal experiment and makes them better able to inhibit.

Attending to the brain

The pre-frontal cortex is part of the brain at the front of the head and is critical for attention. It receives information from the parts of the brain associated with vision, hearing and feelings. The pre-frontal cortex of children with ADHD shows reduced blood flow. Also, people with damage to the pre-frontal cortex have problems with many tasks requiring attention. If asked to match two sounds, they perform much worse under distracting conditions than people without such damage.

The pre-frontal cortex has also been linked with inhibiting responses. Damage to this part of the brain causes people to have difficulty stopping responses to something: for example, if people with ADHD see something unusual, they may point it out even if they've been told not to. The pre-frontal cortex has also been linked with executive functioning.

The parietal lobe (towards the side and near the back of the head) has also been linked to attention. It shows higher activation during attentionally demanding tasks and also directs attention, priming parts of the brain to receive particular information. For example, if you have to look for your keys, attention can increase the activation in the visual areas of the brain.

Part III
Minding Your Memory

To find out what on Earth an executive function is (it has nothing to do with parties in the country's boardrooms), read the online article at www.dummies.com/extras/cognitivepsychology.

In this part . . .

- ✔ Remember that memory is central to cognitive psychology.

- ✔ Note the classic and most recent models of short- and long-term memory.

- ✔ Investigate how cognitive psychologists currently believe that the brain stores memory and knowledge.

- ✔ Read about the unfortunate process of forgetting, whether in typical conditions or more serious cases of amnesia.

Chapter 8

Where Did I Put My Keys? Short-Term Memory

*I*magine that you're on a night out. You bump into a beautiful person and because you're highly attractive yourself (obviously), you get talking and exchange phone numbers. Before mobile phones and their instant storage facility, you'd have to memorise the number before writing it down. To do so, most people rapidly repeat the numbers over and over again.

This technique is a classic example of using your *short-term memory* (STM for us lazy writers) – the memory for very recent things. Psychologists usually distinguish it from long-term memory (LTM, the subject of Chapter 9). (Although some memory models suggest no distinction between STM and LTM, relying instead on how strongly information is connected with other information, they're complex and not all that common.)

In this chapter, we discuss the evidence that STM and LTM are separate entities by describing the multi-store model of memory. We also look at how STM may operate and be used in terms of your working memory, which we relate to executive function and the ability to make important (even executive) decisions. Don't worry, we explain all these terms in this chapter to help you remember them – in the short term and the future!

Splitting Memory Up

Many psychologists in the early part of the 20th century believed that only one type of memory existed. They thought that memory was linked to learning, and after *associations* (links between different ideas in the brain) were learnt, they formed a permanent part of memory. The only differentiation these psychologists made was that at the beginning of learning, memory traces were weaker than later in learning.

One American philosopher, however, believed in two types of memory. William James proposed the following distinction:

- **Primary memory:** The contents of consciousness – what you're thinking about right now. If we ask you to imagine the most beautiful person in the world, primary memory contains the image of that person.

- **Secondary memory:** All your stored knowledge, most of which you aren't currently thinking about (such as what all the other people in the world look like!).

William James's distinction between two types of memory was largely ignored until American psychologists Richard Atkinson and Richard Shiffrin revisited it. They created the multi-store model of memory, which we discuss in this section – in particular, how it helps to shed light on STM.

Meeting the multi-store model of memory

The logic behind the *multi-store model* is that the brain rapidly encodes all the information that bombards your senses (the *environmental input*) into what's called a *sensory register*. A sensory register exists for each of the five senses:

- **Iconic memory:** Sight
- **Echoic memory:** Sound
- **Haptic memory:** Touch
- **Olfactory memory:** Smell
- **Gustatory memory:** Taste

The sensory registers contain an instant copy of the environmental input. They last for a short amount of time (less than a couple of seconds) – although different senses have different durations. The capacity of these registers is largely unlimited: they take an incredibly accurate snapshot of the environment for a very brief period of time. But their contents aren't available to your consciousness.

When you attend to something in the environment, it's transferred from the sensory register to the short-term memory store. This attention filters out unwanted information from the environment and focuses on the relevant things that are worth processing (refer to Chapter 7 for more details).

Figure 8-1 shows the multi-store model of memory and how the model distinguishes the sensory register, STM and LTM. The figure also details the processes involved in transferring information between these separate stores.

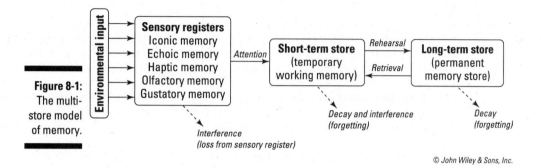

Figure 8-1:
The multi-store model
of memory.

© John Wiley & Sons, Inc.

The multi-store model developed from research concerning the primacy and recency effects:

✔ **Primacy effect:** Participants presented with lists of things to remember tend to remember all the items at the beginning of the list.

✔ **Recency effect:** Participants also tend to remember all the items at the end of the list.

Together, this pattern is called the *serial position curve*. Psychologists think that this tendency is because items at the end of the list are still in STM (and so easy to recall) and items at the beginning of the list have been transferred to LTM. But items in the middle of the list haven't been transferred into LTM and don't remain in STM, so they're forgotten.

The multi-store model is so popular that it's frequently referred to as the *modal* (as in typical or normal) model of memory.

Characterising STM

You can distinguish STM from the sensory stores easily, because it's available to your consciousness. Whatever you're thinking about right now is in your STM (we hope it's the words of the last two sentences; otherwise, you're daydreaming!). The STM is an ever-changing and updating stream of information, which means that it has a number of key characteristics regarding its capacity and duration.

Filling STM up

Short-term memory is the active part of memory and has a limited capacity: you can't store much information in your STM at any one time. This fact is obvious: how many things can you think about simultaneously? One? Two?

To answer this question, we turn to one of the founding fathers of cognitive psychology, George Miller. In 1956, he published one of the most influential research papers of all time. In an experiment you can try out on your friends, he presented word lists of different lengths to his participants and simply asked them to recall the words immediately after the last word was presented. He found that virtually all his participants were able to recall between five and nine items, leading him to conclude that the capacity of STM was the 'magic number seven plus or minus two items'.

Miller's experiments were quite easy and helped his participants remember; as a result, the magic number seven may be an over-estimate. Research also shows that when presented with long word lists, participants tend to recall only the last four items in the list (in addition to the first four). The more recent items in the list seem to replace the earlier ones in STM: in other words, items are displaced from STM. Along with more recent evidence, these results suggest that the actual capacity of STM is around four items.

What do we mean by an 'item'? You may think of an item as a single digit or single world, but is that true? Try remembering the following list and then after 30 seconds, write down as many letters as you possibly can:

NBCNASABBCAPAUKSTMLOLUSA

If Miller's magic number of seven plus or minus two is correct, you probably remember that many items. Now try again, but use the same list in Figure 8-2. Chances are that this time you remember the entire list.

Figure 8-2: Chunking improves memory.

The original list: NBCNASABBCAPAUKSTMLOLUSA

A chunked list: | NBC | NASA | BBC | APA | UK | STM | LOL | USA |

© John Wiley & Sons, Inc.

The improvement is because we *chunked* the items into meaningful groups. Therefore, your STM's capacity can be counted in the number of chunks rather than the number of individual items.

Waiting for STM

Another critical aspect is the duration of STM. How long can you keep items in your head? When a person you fancy gives you her number, how long before you start to forget the digits? Psychologists have tested this issue using word lists (yes, again!).

Researchers present a series of words and ask participants to recall them, either immediately after they're presented or after various delays. Participants' recall is better immediately. After 18–30 seconds, their memories for the words have all but disappeared, suggesting this as the duration of STM: information in it decays after about 30 seconds.

You can enhance the duration of memory with rehearsal. By repeating the items in your head over and over again, you engage in *maintenance rehearsal*, which allows the information to be held in your STM for longer. If you engage in *elaborative rehearsal* (see Chapter 9), the information transfers from STM to LTM. This tendency also relates to the primary and recency effects that we discuss in the earlier section 'Meeting the multi-store model of memory'.

Delaying recall eliminates the recency effect, because items in STM remain for only a very limited time. It also allows for other things to replace what's in STM (interference). Making participants count backwards when they're reading the word list (an example of *articulatory suppression*, where speaking at the same time as learning reduces memory) prevents them from rehearsing the information and so eliminates the primacy effect.

Putting Your Memory to Work

Most cognitive psychologists believe that your STM is much more than a simple short-term store of information; they think that it's *working* – doing something. Alan Baddeley and Graham Hitch, two British cognitive psychologists, devised one of the most widely accepted models of STM – the *working memory* model (see Figure 8-3).

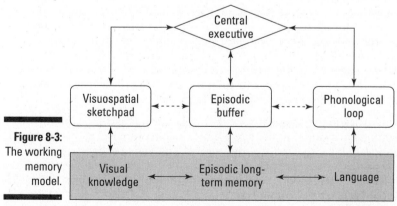

Figure 8-3: The working memory model.

© John Wiley & Sons, Inc.

The working memory model contains an attention-controlling central executive and three storage components: phonological loop, visuospatial sketchpad and episodic buffer. We describe each of these components, including how it may operate and the evidence that it exists, and how psychologists can measure a person's amount of working memory.

Storing and repeating sounds: The phonological loop

The *phonological loop* is often described as the mind's ear: it's how people are able to store and process sounds. Think of it as your inner voice (the voice that actually sounds good when you sing in the shower!).

Phonological loop basics

The phonological loop comprises two components:

- **A phonological store:** A very limited capacity store for sounds (usually associated with language)
- **An articulatory rehearsal mechanism:** A process where you verbally, but silently, repeat words that you've heard

Information stored in the phonological loop can only be held for a few seconds before decaying or fading away. Stored information can be displaced by new information as well. Therefore, the amount of information you can hold in your STM is limited.

Phonological loop in action

Two main sources of evidence back up that the phonological loop exists:

- **Phonological similarity effect:** A bit of a mouthful, but in essence it means that participants remember lists of words that sound the same (for example, 'man', 'cat', 'cap', 'map', 'can') far less accurately than lists of words that sound very different (for example, 'pit', 'day', 'cow', 'pen', 'sup'). This effect occurs whether the words are presented visually or verbally, suggesting that words must be *subvocalised* (silently repeated in your head) to gain access to memory: you have to say the words under your breath in order to store them.

  If you're asked to engage in articulatory suppression (for example, counting backwards) at the same time, the phonological similarity effect disappears for visually presented words. This result suggests that verbally presented words have direct access to the phonological store, but you have to say visually presented words aloud to gain access to the phonological store.

Measuring working memory

Psychologists have devised lots of tasks to measure working memory and its different components, usually involving presenting participants with lists of words and testing their memory for them. This approach, however, has the limitation of only being able to test verbal memory. Therefore, they devised many more tasks:

✔ *To measure the phonological loop*: The digit span task involves participants hearing a sequence of numbers and being asked to recall them. The number of digits presented increases until the participant fails at this task.

✔ *To measure the visuospatial sketchpad*: The Corsi block design test involves participants being presented with a series of coloured or patterned blocks in a particular

order. They're asked to remember the order in which the blocks were presented.

✔ *To measure the episodic buffer*: Researchers use many different visual search tasks involving binding together the stimuli to be found with single or multiple features.

✔ *To measure the central executive*: In the operation span test, participants have to remember a series of between two and eight presented words or letters. The participants are then given a mathematical puzzle to complete. Therefore, they have to complete two tasks at the same time. Their recall for the words or letters is then calculated.

✔ **Word length effect:** Participants remember lists of short words much more accurately than lists of long words (even if the number of words in the lists are the same), because the latter are too long and take up too much of the phonological loop's capacity.

Long-term memory and stored knowledge strongly influence the phonological loop. People can remember more words than non-words or words in another language when presented with lists to remember. Familiar sounds seem to be stored more easily in the phonological loop and so it must be connected to the LTM store (see the earlier Figure 8-1).

The phonological loop is crucial for learning new languages (as a child or as second-language learner). In your native language, you have sufficient experience with the speech sounds and words so that storing the words being said to you requires little effort. When learning new languages, however, you aren't familiar with the words and sounds and therefore you need to store more sounds in your phonological loop. The articulatory rehearsal system means that when you hear a new word, you try to say it under your breath. This rehearsal allows the word to be transferred into your LTM.

Some evidence suggests that the phonological store is located in part of the brain called the *left inferior parietal cortex*, which is just behind the left ear. The *left inferior frontal cortex* (just in front of the left ear) has been identified as the region associated with articulatory rehearsal.

Sketching and imagining: The visuospatial sketchpad

The *visuospatial sketchpad* is basically the same as the phonological loop of the preceding section, but for visually presented stimuli.

Visuospatial sketchpad basics

The made-up term for this component combines the two real words (visual and spatial) because it acts as a store and processing unit for visual images and spatial information, but deals with their memories separately:

- ✔ **Spatial memory:** Understanding where something is in the world – for example, being able to remember where the items are in your bedroom. Such spatial information can be provided visually or from other senses, including touch and sound, making this component of working memory *multimodal* (potentially involving many senses).

- ✔ **Visual memory:** Having an image of something, such as the face of someone you know.

The visuospatial sketchpad includes imagination: when you imagine your best friend's face, the image is brought to your visuospatial sketchpad.

Visuospatial sketchpad in action

The visual and spatial distinction is supported by the fact that the brain processes spatial information differently to image-only information (refer to Chapter 4). Combining spatial and visual information means that you can remember sequences of actions to learn motor skills: for example, learning a new computer game such as Super Mario Bros (that's new, right?) involves learning to click on the correct buttons in a particular sequence. You have to hold the spatial locations (where the Koopa Troopa is positioned relative to Mario), the temporal sequence (when the Koopa Troopa turns around ready for Mario to jump on his head) and the image (the entire platform) in your working memory at the same time. It's an amazingly complex process!

Evidence for the visuospatial sketchpad stems from data suggesting that completing two visual tasks at the same time is very difficult. For example, if participants have simply to watch a ball move around a screen, they perform much less accurately when they're asked to imagine a route around a university at the same time than when they're asked to remember words at the same time instead.

Considerable evidence suggests that the visuospatial sketchpad is separable from the phonological loop. Articulatory suppression (see the earlier 'Waiting for STM' section) has a much smaller effect on visual tasks than verbal tasks. Also, some patients have an intact phonological loop, as measured by the digit span task, but an impaired visuospatial sketchpad, as measured by the Corsi block design task (check out this chapter's earlier sidebar 'Measuring working memory'). Some patients have the reverse pattern (showing a double dissociation; refer to Chapter 1).

Two components of the visuospatial sketchpad parallel the phonological loop of the preceding section:

- **Visual cache:** A passive store of information, like a screen that captures the information you're thinking about. When you're mentally imagining something, the image stored is in the visual cache – like an artist's canvas.

- **Inner scribe:** The active part of the visuospatial sketchpad in which you plan movement. It's primarily involved in the storage of spatial information and the sequencing of actions. The inner scribe is easily disrupted by spatial movement and is the process by which images are drawn onto the visual cache. Think of it like being a painter.

Bringing long-term memories to mind: The episodic buffer

The *episodic buffer* links the working memory with LTM and is how information from memory (in any sense) is brought to conscious awareness. It's also a temporary store of information from LTM so that it can be used.

Episodic buffer basics

The episodic buffer links information to the other components of working memory so that they can process information more reliably. Linking LTM knowledge of language to the phonological loop allows you to interpret what people are saying much quicker than without this link.

Episodic buffer in action

The episodic buffer integrates or binds information into discrete episodes. The *binding* process is largely automatic and doesn't require a great deal of central executive processing (see the next section). It comes in two forms:

- **Static binding:** Links two sensory elements that tend to occur together, such as orange oranges (that is, the colour orange and the fruit!). Seeing the two features together frequently means that they become bound together as one concept.

> ✔ **Dynamic binding:** Much more attentionally demanding than static bind-
> ing, it involves combining rather arbitrary features and can be the basis
> of imagination. Therefore, dynamic binding can be of anything you want,
> even a pink orange with blue polka dots flying through a green sky with
> a purple sun (you get the idea!).

Given that the episodic buffer links all the other components of working
memory, it processes all different senses (*modalities*). It also has a limited
storage capacity and can combine or bind across senses as well as within
senses, and bind new information to information stored in LTM.

Introducing the managing director: The central executive

The *central executive* is the central processor of working memory. It's the
control unit that guides each of the other parts of working memory and is
often considered the driving force in attention (refer to Chapter 7 for more
on attention). Like a computer's central processor, it has a limited capacity:
it can devote resources to each of the subcomponents of working memory,
but only if it has spare resources. Its name (the central executive) reveals its
fundamental importance. Its functions are often called *executive functions*.

Central executive basics

The central executive is assumed to have three core functions:

> ✔ **To focus attention on a particular task:** The central executive ensures
> that complex tasks are focused on and distractions are ignored, such as
> reading a fascinating book on cognitive psychology and ignoring *TOWIE*
> on the TV! Your central executive puts its effort into reading, while
> blocking out other aspects of the environment (for more on this, check
> out the later section 'Focusing your attention').
>
> ✔ **To switch attention between different tasks:** Sometimes you need to
> switch quickly between tasks, such as cooking and when a child comes
> running in crying because he's been hurt. Your central executive keeps
> an eye on the information that has been blocked out, waiting for some-
> thing that requires attention to be focused on it (for more, attend to the
> later section 'Switching attention').
>
> ✔ **To divide attention between different tasks:** Sometimes you just have
> to do two things simultaneously, such as watching TV while doing your
> homework. Your central executive calculates how much of its resources
> can be allocated to one task and how much to another task (the later
> section 'Focusing your attention' has more details).

One way to explore the central executive is to use *dual-task procedures,* in which participants have to complete one task while being distracted with another task. If researchers can find a task that selectively disrupts one component of working memory but not others, they can find evidence for the existence of separable components.

In one experiment, psychologists measured people's performance while they (the participants, not the researchers!) played a game of chess during three different secondary tasks: articulatory suppression (affecting the phonological loop) and finger tapping (affecting the visuospatial sketchpad) didn't greatly affect chess; but trying to think of random numbers did because it's an executive process – like playing chess.

Central executive in action

Given the importance of the central executive's core functions, you may think it does a great deal. In fact, it's more a ragbag of processes. Some attempt has been made to unify the processes into a complex model of executive functioning (you've been warned!). This model is called the *supervisory attentional system* (see Figure 8-4).

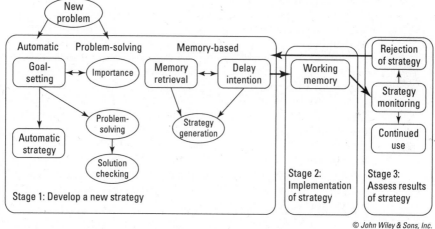

Figure 8-4: The three stages of the supervisory attentional system.

© John Wiley & Sons, Inc.

The supervisory attentional system is a model regarding how the central executive may be employed when presented with a new task to complete. Basically, the supervisory attentional system handles routine tasks, when things are more difficult, the executive system takes over. It has three stages, each containing different processes:

1. **Constructs new behavioural rules or schemas:** Subprocesses set goals and devise strategies to solve them. This process may involve automatic processing, problem-solving or retrieval from LTM.

2. **Implements the strategy:** The core process of working memory.

3. **Checks and verifies whether the strategies worked:** This assessing stage may result in continued use of the strategy or devising a new one, potentially using a different subprocess in Step 1. In other words, you can employ an automatic process, find that it doesn't work and generate a new strategy based on information from LTM.

Evidence firmly places the central executive's activity in the *dorsolateral pre-frontal cortex* (located near the base of the frontal part of the brain, just to the side of each eye).

Calculating your working memory

Short-term working memory is crucial. The ability to control your attention, focus on relevant things, engage in conversations with your friends, drive, play football, study and so on depends on working memory. Its involvement in conversation shows that even social psychology depends on it: you need to be able to focus on the right person to speak to, remember information relevant to a conversation, vocalise it and discuss it, while inhibiting irrelevant information.

Clearly, working memory is vital, which suggests that everyone has the ability. But in fact, people have significant individual differences in their working memory's capacity and ability. Psychologists use various tests to calculate a *working memory span* – a measure of how much working memory someone has. It correlates strongly with intelligence.

An example of the type of task that correlates with working memory span is the *antisaccade task*. In it, something appears on a screen. Participants are instructed to look at it or look at the opposite side of the screen. People instinctively look at the object that appears. Stopping (inhibiting) yourself looking at this object is quite difficult. Participants with higher working memory capacity are better able to perform this second condition than those with lower working memory capacity.

Working memory span changes with age. Working memory develops slowly through childhood, reaching a plateau during the mid-twenties, and declines in later adulthood. Importantly, working memory span predicts the ability to comprehend texts and therefore children's educational performance (even if the working memory test is done five years before the final exams!). It also correlates with reasoning tasks and even predicts performance by US Air Force pilots.

Working memory may be vitally important, but what does the working memory span actually measure? One suggestion is that it's based on the processing speed and the capacity of the neurons in the brain associated with working memory. Research shows that people with a higher working memory span seem to show smaller brain responses during complex tasks, suggesting that their neurons are more efficient than those with lower working memory spans.

Processing Your Memory – Executively

In the working memory model, the central executive is thought to control three executive tasks (see 'Introducing the managing director: The central executive' earlier in this chapter). Other executive abilities may also be related to working memory, but the evidence is mixed.

In this section, we review the entire array of executive processes and relate them to the most highly evolved part of the brain: the frontal lobes.

Focusing your attention

Executive attention involves focusing attention on a particular task or multiple tasks at hand. It's also vital for resolving conflicts (and we don't mean fights between warring children!). *Conflict resolution* in this case is when two potential competing responses exist for a particular task. One of your executive processes concerns deciding which of the potential competing responses needs to be undertaken.

Some examples may help here. Flip to Chapter 7 and read about the Stroop and the Simon effects (don't worry, we'll wait till you get back). In these tasks, the attentional system must focus on the relevant features of the task. Focusing requires a great deal of executive attention if it involves overriding an automatic process.

Imagine for some reason that you don't take the normal route to college or work. Your attentional system has to override the automatic route to your destination and allow you to go where you need to go (the doctors, perhaps).

To accomplish this aim, the executive system requires two processes:

- ✔ **A conflict monitor:** To identify a conflict between your goal and an automatic process (it's located in the *anterior cingulate*, which is part of the brain at the front, but about an inch or so from the skull).

- ✔ **An attention controller:** To direct the attentional resources to the relevant task features (it's located in the *dorsolateral prefrontal cortex*, which is part of the brain near the base of the frontal part of the brain, just to the side of each eye).

Executive attention is also vital for categorising objects. It acts as a link between the perceptual systems and the memory stores. Therefore, it's the part of the cognitive system responsible for consciousness.

Switching attention

Switching attention from one important task to another is an important executive function. Cognitive psychologists use the *switch task* to measure task switching. Participants are presented with a simple task, such as to press X when an odd number appears on the screen and Y when even numbers appear. Sometimes, and less frequently, the numbers are in red. In these cases, the participants must respond with the opposite keys to the ones they'd practised with. In these cases, participants take longer to respond.

This *switch cost* is due to the fact that when participants engage in a task, they develop a set of rules or strategies that they're applying. If the rules need to be changed suddenly, the participants' executive system needs to be engaged, which takes some time (up to about half a second).

Consider how the switch cost may affect pilots. They're engaged in landing a plane when, suddenly, an alarm goes off and they have to switch their attention from one demanding task to another and back again to ensure that they configure their plane appropriately. Taking an extra half second to react in such a case can be life-threatening.

Ignoring what's unimportant

Inhibition is one of the most important executive functions: not refusing to reveal your legs at the beach, but the ability to ignore irrelevant information. Response inhibition in particular is the ability to prevent an already prepared response from happening.

The Go/No-Go test is a simple task to measure response inhibition. Participants are presented with lots of one letter (say X) and are told to respond whenever they see it. They're also told not to respond if they see the letter Y. The test involves more Xs than Ys. Participants make errors in this task, often unintentionally responding to the Y.

A lack of inhibition has been implicated in a number of clinical disorders, including schizophrenia, attention deficit hyperactivity disorder and obsessive compulsive disorder. It's also involved in children's behaviour – when they simply act without considering their actions. The ability to inhibit develops slowly and isn't fully developed until a person's early twenties.

A great deal of debate revolves around whether inhibition is a single thing or whether many different types exist. Hundreds of different tasks can measure inhibition, however, and they don't all correlate with each other, which suggests the existence of different types of inhibition:

- ✔ **Motor inhibition:** Inhibition of a prepared motor response

- ✔ **Oculomotor inhibition:** Inhibition of eye movements

- ✔ **Cognitive interference:** Inhibition as a result of competing cognitive sources of information

- ✔ **Sustained attention:** Inhibition due to fixing too much attention on one task

Response inhibition is a special kind of attentional focus and involves additional brain areas being involved, including the *orbitofrontal cortex*, which is just below the dorsolateral prefrontal cortex.

Scheduling and planning

Certain types of planning are an executive function and can be a challenge. For example, when you cook a Sunday roast you have to ensure that the roast potatoes are ready at the same time as the beef joint, broccoli, stuffing and Yorkshire puddings (try to inhibit your drooling, please!).

Cognitive psychologists call planning, in this sense, *sequencing*, and you can examine it by giving participants a sequence of letters to remember. You test the participants on their memory for the letter that comes after the one they're presented with. This task requires them to remember the order of the presented letters. Participants find this task much more difficult than simply recognising whether a letter was in the list they'd seen.

The way in which people's executive processes code order is by binding or tagging order information to the item. In other words, when you're presented with a letter, you code the letter and the order in which it was presented.

Monitoring yourself

To ensure that you don't behave in an unusual way, like everyone else, you have to monitor your behaviour and speech. *Monitoring* is more complex than the other executive functions: it involves being aware of yourself, your performance and what the performance should be like. Plus, it's happening at the same time as the to-be-monitored process is occurring.

One test of monitoring is to give participants six objects. In the first trial, they point to one object. In the next trial, they must point to a different object. In the next, they point to a different one and so on. This task requires remembering (monitoring) what they've just done. Research shows that people with damage to their frontal lobes struggle at this task.

Another source of monitoring is looking for one's own errors. Whenever you're completing a task, such as writing a book, you're likely to make small errors, such as typographic or spelling mistakes (we made only two when writing this sentence!). The monitoring system constantly checks what you're doing and corrects the mistake by stopping the current task and instigating a corrective measure (such as reaching for the Delete button).

Some interesting evidence suggests that the brain is aware of its mistakes very soon after making them. A unique response measured by electroencephalography called *error-related negativity* occurs only 100 milliseconds (that's one-tenth of a second) after an error has been made, showing how quickly the brain detects errors.

Seeing where it all happens: The frontal lobes

Research reveals the role of your frontal lobes (of your brain, not your ears!) for most of the executive processes we describe in this section.

Your frontal lobes are part of a network of brain structures involved in attention and inhibition, which is known as the *parieto-frontal network*, because it involves the parietal cortex and the frontal lobes. These regions interact to produce the whole range of attention and inhibition effects that define executive processes.

Attention and inhibition must go hand-in-hand: focusing attention involves inhibiting irrelevant distraction around the to-be-focused item. This highlights how the network for executive functioning is so vast.

Extensive neuroimaging studies show that virtually all tasks that require executive processes activate the frontal lobes – which have also been implicated in personality.

When it goes wrong: Dysexecutive syndrome

Dysexecutive syndrome follows damage limited to a person's frontal lobes. Typically, damage to the frontal lobes doesn't affect memory or intelligence greatly, but it has severe effects on someone's mental functioning. People with damage to the frontal lobes typically don't display the executive processes that we describe in this chapter.

Someone with dysexecutive syndrome is unable to focus his attention. He's easily distracted and has difficulty holding conversations because he starts talking about anything that pops into his head. Dysexecutive syndrome is also associated with an inability to switch from one task to another easily. Sufferers are also unable to inhibit, which means that they can behave in ways that others consider rude: they don't stop themselves saying something offensive and may make up stories. Sequencing and planning are also almost completely devoid in someone with this syndrome. Given extensive training, simple rules and tasks can be completed, but any complex planning is impossible.

In addition, damage to the frontal lobes causes people to have limited awareness of their own condition: they can't monitor themselves. As a result they're unaware how they got dressed in the morning or how they shaved (they may not even do this without help). Someone with dysexecutive syndrome is also unlikely to initiate behaviours or plans.

Chapter 9

You Don't Remember Our Wedding Day? Long-Term Memory

In This Chapter

▶ Seeing how psychologists classify long-term memories

▶ Saving and retrieving memories

▶ Losing long-term memories

*Y*our memory is hugely impressive. Think about all the things you remember and know – even trying to remember the amount you know is impossible. You have skills, events, facts, words, people and so much more stored in your memory from a lifetime of experiences. In essence, this chapter is devoted to how your brain stores and accesses all this information.

Imagine that you're in an exam, answering a question on memory: how do you remember what to write? Although it seems to be a simple question, it really isn't. First, you have to access the memory, finding (we hope!) some stored memories. Second, you have to use your memory for writing and for finding words so that you can write an answer down.

Memory is much more complicated than you may think. It's not a simple passive store of information, but an active, continually changing collection of different processes.

In Chapter 8 we discuss the multi-store model of memory, the first part of which concerns short-term memory (STM). The second part of the model is long-term memory (LTM), which we cover here. Long-term memories are ones that you've stored in your head for quite a while.

Cognitive psychologists identify many types, classifications and processes involved in LTM. We look at how different types of processing lead to better memory storage, the different types of LTM, and how you store and retrieve memories. We also talk about when memory fails, as in cases where brain damage causes deficits in people's LTM.

Digging Deep: Levels of Processing Memories

When considering LTM you have to ask, how does the information get there? What processing allows you to remember information for a long time?

To help understand memory processes, Fergus Craik (a British cognitive psychologist) and Robert Lockhart (a Canadian psychologist) devised a novel approach in 1972. Most research up to that point had examined memory as a series of stages or components without looking at how things moved between stages. Craik and Lockhart specifically did and proposed the levels of processing framework of memory elaboration.

We call it a framework rather than a theory, because it's a descriptive model and doesn't make predictions about what exactly deep processing is. Nevertheless, it's a beautifully simple model that has stood the test of time and can be used to help you learn things.

With the *levels of processing framework*, the deeper people process something, the more likely they are to remember it. Deep processing is also known as elaborative processing, because it involves thinking around to-be-remembered information (in contrast to shallow, surface-level processing).

To highlight the difference, Craik and Lockhart asked participants to learn a series of words in three different ways:

- **Structural coding:** State whether the word was in italics or not.
- **Phonetic coding:** Consider whether it rhymed with another word or not.
- **Semantic coding:** Evaluate whether it can fit into a sentence or not.

They then gave the participants a memory test and found that people remembered the words processed semantically better than those processed phonetically and structurally. These results suggest that participants engaged in *elaborative rehearsal* when processing the word in a semantic manner, compared to *maintenance rehearsal* when a word is simply repeated.

Later, researchers found that when you process things in a personally meaningful way (you relate it to yourself, such as remembering a topic in a class because it's something you've experienced yourself), you're more likely to remember them than if they're processed semantically, suggesting a scale representing the depth of processing (check out Figure 9-1).

How can I remember the name of my new colleague, Scott?

Deepest processing	• **Personally relevant** • Has the same name as my favourite singer
Deep processing	• **Semantically meaning** • The name means 'Someone from Scotland'
Mid-level processing	• **Phonetic processing** • Rhymes with 'blot'
Shallow processing	• **Structural processing** • Has only one vowel

Figure 9-1:
Various depths of processing.

© *John Wiley & Sons, Inc.*

If you're trying to remember something, process it as deeply as possible. Instead of simply repeating it, make it semantically meaningful or personally relevant to you. This technique helps when you're trying to recall it.

Evidence suggests that these different depths of processing are processed by different parts of the brain. Shallow processing is often highly perceptual and is linked with brain areas associated with vision (the *occipital lobe* at the back of the head). Phonetic processing correlates with activity in the *auditory cortex*. Deeper, semantic processing involves more brain areas, including in the *frontal cortex* and the *temporal lobes*. Even more brain areas are active when you make something personally relevant (such as, the bilateral caudate in the basal ganglia – a brain area right in the middle).

Classifying Long-Term Memories

Psychologists commonly distinguish between the following two types of long-term memories:

- ✔ **Declarative (or explicit) memory:** Memory that you can declare or talk about. It's conscious memory of knowledge about yourself, your own life or all facts you've learnt over your life.

- ✔ **Non-declarative (or implicit) memory:** All other forms of memory that you can have. You can't talk about it (for example, describing how you kick a ball is difficult) and so it's considered unconscious.

'Let me tell you all about it!' Declarative memory

When psychologists talk about memory, they normally mean declarative memory, which they split into two types:

- ✔ **Episodic memory:** When someone asks you a question about something you've done

- ✔ **Semantic memory:** When someone asks you a fact about the world

In both cases, you're aware that you know something (even if you forget from time to time; see Chapter 11!). This division was first described by Endel Tulving, an Estonian-Canadian psychologist.

Remembering life events: Episodic memory

Episodic memory covers memory for events you've experienced. Tulving claimed that episodic memories have the following characteristics:

- ✔ Developed recently (in evolutionary terms)

- ✔ Develops later in life; that is, infants don't have it

- ✔ Earliest to be affected by ageing

- ✔ Easiest to be damaged by brain injury

You can differentiate episodic memory from *autobiographical memory*, which contains detailed information of events and experiences that have personal meaning. Autobiographical memory lasts a very long time whereas episodic memory is much more trivial and shorter-lasting.

One of the key pieces of evidence for the existence of episodic memory comes from neuropsychological studies on brain-damaged patients (check out Chapter 1). Hugo Spiers, a British neuroscientist, and colleagues reviewed 147 cases of *amnesia* (long-term memory loss) and found that episodic memory was damaged in all cases, but semantic memory was less often damaged.

People with no episodic memory can't remember things that they've done during the day, such as TV programmes they watch or conversations they have. But if they have normal semantic memory they can still function (children with no episodic memory can go to school, for example, and learn).

Typically, only damage to the hippocampus leads to episodic memory loss. The *hippocampus* is a small, sea-horse shaped structure of the brain in line with the ear. The area of the brain including the hippocampus is called the *medial temporal lobe*.

Remembering facts: Semantic memory

Semantic memory is your store of all the information that you've obtained throughout your life. The structure of semantic memory is open to much debate and discussion – so much so that we devote a whole chapter to it (Chapter 10). Here, we present some basic information about semantic memory and relate it to episodic memory.

One of the key differences between semantic and episodic memory is that semantic memory is much more conceptual: the knowledge is stored as concepts and not linked to any experience of obtaining them. For example, you may know that the Haǧia Sophia is in Istanbul, but the fact that you watched a TV programme about it yesterday is an episodic memory and that you visited it with your friend last January is an autobiographic memory.

Although some patients can have no episodic memory but an okay semantic memory, many people with amnesia have problems with both episodic and semantic memory. When the brain injury is bigger, including parts of the brain around the hippocampus (the *perirhinal* and *entorhinal cortices*), semantic memories are affected.

If these two types of memory really are different, some patients should show the opposite pattern (a double dissociation; see Chapter 1) of an okay episodic memory but no semantic memory. They do: sufferers of *semantic dementia* can't recall semantic information but generally have a working episodic memory (see Chapter 21 for a case study).

Semantic memories are usually stronger than episodic memories, because you've recalled them many times, whereas you don't recall episodic memories that frequently. Some episodic memories that you do recall a lot, such as childhood stories you tell people, are more similar to semantic memories and are often unaffected by hippocampal damage.

'But I don't know how I do it!' Non-declarative memory

Non-declarative memory is implicit: it's not available to your consciousness. You may well be able to remember your first swimming lesson (an episodic memory; see the preceding section) but if you try to describe how you swim, you wouldn't be able to describe verbally the exact process in detail (such as precisely which muscle to move exactly when).

Psychologists distinguish four types of non-declarative memory:

- ✔ **Procedural memory:** A memory for how to do things

- ✔ **Priming memory:** Repetition of information and where a recent event or thing influences your behaviour

- ✔ **Associative learning:** Conditioned behaviours, where you learn to link events or objects as being related

- ✔ **Non-associative learning:** Habits, where you learn behaviours and knowledge through experience

Remembering doing things: Procedural memory

You use *procedural memory* almost every single second of your life: in other words, you're almost always doing something that you've learnt. Procedural memory exists for every motor skill you have, such as writing, language learning, walking and playing sports.

One of the most important ways of investigating procedural memory is to look at how new skills can be learnt. Psychologists often train people on rather useless novel skills to study these processes. Examples include mirror tracing (learning to write by looking in a mirror – try it, it's very difficult), mirror reading and artificial grammar learning (see Chapter 14).

The first few times that people start learning these tasks, they probably rely on episodic and semantic memory (that is, declarative memory). For example, when you start to learn to drive a car, at first every single task is very difficult (checking mirrors, turning the wheel, controlling the gears, using the indicators and pressing the brake – just to make a right turn!).

But with practice, all these abilities are changed into a single procedural task, 'turning'. This process is similar to the chunking process we describe in Chapter 8: you chunk all the tasks into one. At this point, what you're doing can no longer be easily described and is therefore a procedural memory.

Evidence from neuropsychological studies of brain-injured patients with episodic and semantic memory problems shows that they have no problem with any of the skills they used to have; that is, their procedural memories.

Clive Wearing, a famous conductor and musician, developed amnesia as a result of a virus to the brain. Despite losing much of his episodic and semantic memory, he can still remember how to play music and conduct. In fact, he can learn new music and new skills (such as mirror writing), even though he has no memory of learning them. He's surprised every time he mirror writes because he believes that he has never done it before.

Further studies show that even severely amnesic patients can learn skills necessary for the real world, such as using new machinery and driving. Having an episodic memory of the learning experience is helpful (because you know that you've learnt it), but it's not vital.

Psychologists think that procedural memory is controlled by the *striatum*, a brain area just on top of the hippocampus. They can't conduct studies with patients with lost procedural memory but intact episodic and semantic memory, however, because those patients wouldn't be able to do anything and would be paralysed (though with no physical damage to the body).

Priming memory

Priming is a rapid form of unconscious learning. Both the following types mean that the repeated presentation of something affects the processing of it the second time:

- ✔ **Perceptual priming:** If you perceptual prime something, when you see it again, you process it faster.

- ✔ **Conceptual priming:** The same as perceptual priming, except that the two things need to be related conceptually rather than looking the same.

For example, presenting the word 'baby' makes people faster at recognising the word 'baby' (perceptual priming) and the word 'cot' (conceptual priming).

A lot of evidence shows that patients with amnesia have intact priming. In fact, the famous amnesic HM (see Chapter 21) had priming abilities of the same level as people without amnesia. Conceptual priming doesn't occur in patients with semantic dementia (again, check out Chapter 21), because they've lost their semantic memories, which are typically in the form of concepts (see the earlier 'Remembering facts: Semantic memory' section). But perceptual priming does exist in patients with semantic dementia.

Priming is known to activate the brain areas in the cortex associated with the thing being primed. So priming the word 'baby' causes all the brain regions associated with babies to become active for a short period of time. This extra bit of activity makes it relatively easy for additional information to activate them fully. Therefore, detecting these things for a few seconds is easier (known as *perceptual fluency*).

Conditioning memory: Associative learning

Some forms of learning exist even without conscious memory. Studies show that even patients with amnesia can be conditioned to learn a new behaviour:

- ✔ **Associative learning:** Where you learn to link two things together (such as the colour and shape of an orange and its flavour, or the library with the process of learning!). It's the basis of all simple learning – even babies can learn this way!

- ✔ **Conditioning:** Where you learn a behaviour through training and behaviour modification or by associating a stimulus with a behaviour (see the nearby sidebar 'Psychology as behaviour').

Children who don't have episodic memory can be conditioned to fear things: the most famous case is that of the 1-year old Little Albert. Whenever poor Albert played with a pet rat, John Watson, an American psychologist, made Albert afraid by making a loud noise behind him. Very soon Albert developed a fear of white rats (or indeed anything white and fluffy, including Santa Claus's beard). Later in his life, he retained this fear but had no episodic memories of the fear training.

Psychology as behaviour

In 1919, American psychologist John Watson created the approach known as behaviourism (see Chapter 1), which is concerned only with observable behaviour and all about the link between a stimulus and a response. Two forms of learning exist according to behaviourists:

- ✔ **Classical conditioning:** Russian physiologist Ivan Pavlov found that dogs learnt to associate two stimuli together – the sound of a trolley bringing food and the food itself. The dogs salivated to the food, but after learning the pairing, they salivated to the trolley noise.

- ✔ **Operant conditioning:** Particular behaviours are rewarded to increase the chances of the behaviour happening again (say, by giving food) or punished to reduce the behaviour (say, with a slap). So behaviours can be explained in simple stimulus–response pairings. For example, the simplest way to teach a child to tidy her room is to reward her after she tidies a bit (but don't do it too often; otherwise she may learn to clean obsessively!).

These forms of learning are thought to be associated with brain regions including the *cerebellum* (for operant conditioning) and the *amygdala* (for classical fear conditioning).

Learning habits: Non-associative learning

Learning behaviour can occur through simple processes such as habituation and sensitisation, both types of unconscious forms of learning:

✔ **Habituation:** When responses to a particular stimulus are reduced after prolonged exposure to that stimulus. For example, when you first put on your clothes, you're aware of the material rubbing on your body, but after a short while you're no longer aware of the sensation.

Habituation is seen in American developmental psychologist Robert Fantz's interesting studies on children's perceptions. He put infants into a viewing chamber and presented them with a stimulus (such as a checkerboard pattern). At first, the infants looked at the stimulus and then they got bored with it (*habituated* to it). If, after he replaced it with a new stimulus, infants showed renewed interest, the suggestion is that they can tell the difference between the two images.

✔ **Sensitisation:** Similar to habituation, but where repeated exposure to something causes participants to become overly responsive to it.

This occurs for especially irritating things. For example, the sound of your partner snoring is extremely irritating (especially when you're trying to sleep). Instead of getting used to this sound, it gets more and more annoying because you're becoming sensitive to the sound.

The information regarding the stimuli to which people become habituated or sensitised is stored in their memories. When they're presented with these stimuli, they simply react to them due to their brains' reflex pathways.

Processing long-term memory

Recently, Swiss psychologist Katharina Henke has come up with the *processing-based account* of LTM. Instead of dividing memory into systems, she suggests that different types of processing distinguish between different types of memories. Henke bases her theory on the idea that learning is achieved by forming associations (links between things). These links can be flexible (easily changed) or rigid (permanent structure). Accordingly, three processes are involved for memory: rapid processing of flexible associations done by the *hippocampus*; slow processing of fixed associations done by the *striatum*; and specialised rapid processing of things that are familiar or primed depending on the *parahippocampal gyrus*.

Storing and Recalling Long-Term Memories

Information needs to be stored appropriately to be in your LTM. In the earlier section 'Digging Deep: Levels of Processing Memory', we indicate that different processes help to store memories. But the levels of processing framework doesn't tell psychologists *how* memories are stored.

Also, after memories are stored in memory, you need to be able to use them (otherwise storing them is pointless). Memory may be like a warehouse stored full of knowledge, but that knowledge needs to be used from time to time. This process is called retrieval.

In this section, we investigate the active processes involved in storing information in and retrieving it from your memory. Of course, these processes concern recalling memories of things that happened in the past, but we also cover another type of memory: remembering for the future.

Consolidating memories

The process of storing memories in the brain is *consolidation*. Consolidation modifies the coded information from your perceptual system and binds (see Chapter 8) and combines all the features of what you're learning together. In other words, it fixes it into memory.

Consolidation takes a great deal of time, which means that the process of the successful storage of memories can be enhanced or made worse:

✔ **Enhancing consolidation:**

- Drugs that stimulate the central nervous system, administered after learning, enhance learning. Other naturally-occurring stimulants can also increase consolidation, including endorphins released following exercise.

- Sleeping after learning enhances the consolidation of procedural memories and, to a lesser extent, semantic memories (see the earlier section 'Remembering facts: Semantic memory' for more on these memories).

✔ **Reducing consolidation:**

- Electric shocks to the brain (up to 14 hours after learning)

- A lack of oxygen to the brain (caused by suffocation)

- Certain drugs (propranolol to treat post-traumatic stress disorder)

Consolidation has two stages:

1. **Stabilisation of the cells in the memory centres of the brain.** This process can take minutes or hours to complete.

2. **Reorganisation of the parts of the brain that store all your knowledge.** This process can take days, months or years to complete.

The reorganisation stage occurs in the hippocampus. As a result, the hippocampus is one of the most important structures in the brain for memory. It reorganises memories by activating all features of the memory at the same time and binds them together. The hippocampus can bind new information with existing information in memory by activating both at the same time. We illustrate this process in Figure 9-2.

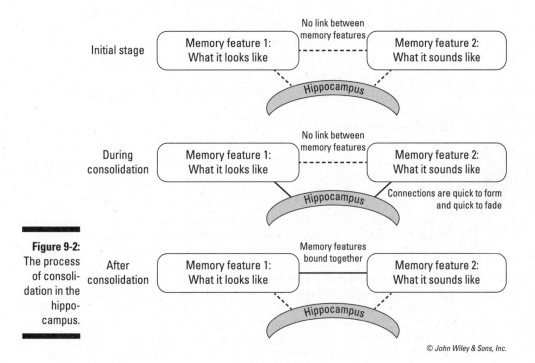

Figure 9-2: The process of consolidation in the hippocampus.

© John Wiley & Sons, Inc.

Retrieving memories

Your memory wouldn't be very good if all it could do was store information. It would be like a library without any visitors: quiet and dull. No, you need to retrieve information from memory as well. Interestingly, this area of cognitive psychology hasn't received as much attention by researchers as the storing of information.

We discuss three types of retrieval:

- **Active/conscious retrieval:** When you try consciously to bring the information to mind.

- **Non-deliberate/unintentional retrieval:** When things just spring into your mind.

- **Recognition:** Knowing that you've encountered something before.

Cognitive psychologists often investigate these three types using slightly different techniques (here we give examples of words, but these forms of retrieval are for all types of material):

- **Free recall to assess active, conscious retrieval:** Participants are asked to recall as many items as they can from a list of presented words.

- **Cued recall to assess non-deliberate retrieval:** Participants are given prompts to aid their remembering: for example, they're provided the preceding word in the word list and asked to recall the next word.

- **Recognition:** Participants are presented with a series of words and simply asked to identify whether they've seen a particular word before.

Conscious retrieval

Retrieval brings memories back into an active state and reinstates aspects of the past. In fact, retrieval changes a memory so that it goes through the process of consolidation (see the preceding section) again, meaning that it can be damaged and affected in the same way as if it were new learning.

Some psychologists call this process *reconsolidation*, because you reinstate the pattern of brain activation associated with when you learnt the information during retrieval. The only difference in the pattern of brain activation is that it starts from the cortex (where the memories are stored), moving to the hippocampus (where the memories are consolidated) and then to the sensory cortices (where the item was perceived), whereas during encoding, this pattern is in reverse.

Retrieval doesn't produce an identical pattern of brain activation to that seen during learning, because learning requires the involvement of a few more processes and because some information hasn't been stored properly. It may also represent memories changing while they're in your head.

Active retrieval is primarily directed by the frontal lobes in the brain. These areas control attention, thinking and deliberate behaviours. Patients with damage to the frontal lobes often have trouble retrieving information. Even when they can retrieve factual information, they can't remember how or when they learnt the fact itself (called *source amnesia*).

Unintentional retrieval

Sometimes you can't help but remember things, often when you're anxious or worried about something. Your mind wanders and you recall many events. All very annoying, and it can sometimes stop you sleeping.

This irritating tendency is down to the fact that retrieval of memories is dependent on *cues*: hints or clues that help lead to the memory. They can come from internal or external sources:

- **Context:** Memories are better retrieved when you're in the same place as where they were learnt.
- **State:** Memories are better retrieved when you're in the same physical condition as when you learnt the information. For example, researchers showed that if you learn a list of words after having smoked marijuana, you're better at recalling those words if you've just smoked marijuana.
- **Mnemonics:** If during learning, you link information to something you've already stored in your memory, you're better able to recall it.

Cues help retrieval because when you learn information, you don't simply encode the information. Instead, you're binding all the features of the information or event together in your memory: you're trying to form links between every aspect of the information to be learnt. So when you store the information in your brain, it's stored according to the information, the environmental context and the state you were in when you learnt it.

For successful retrieval, you try to access the stored memory, which requires you to find a route to the memory: the more cues to that memory, the easier the retrieval. The more you're able to reinstate the context of learning, the easier you find retrieving the information (called the *encoding specificity principle*; see Chapter 11 for more details).

Therefore, you sometimes retrieve information when you don't want to because the cues to that memory have become active. These cues then activate the memories attached to them. When you're anxious, all memories associated with anxiety become active and keep popping into your head.

Recognition

Recognition is the process of seeing something that you've seen before and knowing that you know it. For example, you may bump into someone when walking to school or work one day. She says 'hello' and you politely respond, knowing that you know the person but not remembering her name. This leads to that awkward conversation where you're trying to find out who she is without her realising that you have no idea of her name!

Recognition is central to memory because it's the unconscious process of establishing whether something is new to you (and needs to be treated with caution) or familiar. It differs from *recollection*, where you have a distinct episodic memory (which we discuss in the earlier section 'Remembering life events: Episodic memory') for something. Unlike recollection, recognition isn't based on retrieval cues, just on that sense of knowing something.

Cognitive psychologists can test episodic memory using the *remember/know* procedure. People are given a memory test in which they learn some words and later are shown more words and asked whether they saw the word before or not. If they did, they're asked whether they actually remember it (with an episodic memory attached) or if it's just familiar (a know response).

Recognition is different from recollection:

- ✔ Recognition is faster and less affected by context and state, because these cues to memory aren't needed.

- ✔ Failure to recognise something is usually because the item isn't stored in memory, whereas failure to remember something is due to a lack of an appropriate retrieval cue or because the item isn't stored in memory.

Travelling back to the future: Prospective memory

One type of memory is vital to your survival: *prospective memory*, which is remembering things for the future. Prospective memory concerns how people remember to do things, such as meeting that really hot guy at the cafe tomorrow afternoon. Therefore, it still involves retrieving memories but faces additional problems to recalling past events.

'I recognise that I remember you!'

Different brain regions are active when people are remembering things compared to when they're simply recognising them:

- ✔ **Hippocampus:** A small structure in the medial temporal lobes and the brain region typically associated with remembering. Patients with damage only to the hippocampus have problems remembering but no problems with recognition.

- ✔ **Perirhinal cortex:** Region of the brain surrounding the hippocampus that's associated with recognition judgements. Patients with damage to this area can't recognise things that should be familiar to them.

Cognitive psychologists have identified two types of prospective memory:

- ✔ **Time-based:** Remembering to do something at a given time
- ✔ **Event-based:** Remembering to do something when a particular event occurs

Event-based prospective memory is more reliable than the time-based type, because the event can serve as a cue to remember.

Prospective memory has five stages:

1. **Forming the intention to do something.**
2. **Monitoring the environment for a cue to the event (another event or a time cue).**
3. **Detecting the cue and retrieving the intention.**
4. **Recalling the intention.**
5. **Executing the intention.**

These stages contain all the possible chances for error as memories for the past, as well as the added component of a possible long retention interval between forming an intention to do something and when this intention is executed. This long delay can cause the intention to fade from memory or be interfered with (see Chapter 11 for all about forgetting).

Prospective memory has other differences to memory for the past as well:

- ✔ It's often about knowing *when* to do something rather than knowing *about* something.
- ✔ It's more reliant on internal rather than external cues and therefore more vulnerable (external cues are usually more useful aids to memory).

The vulnerability of prospective memory is highlighted in many tragic cases of plane crashes. Although they're extraordinarily rare, when they do occur failures of the pilot's prospective memory is often the cause. Prospective errors are more likely to occur when someone is interrupted from a task they have planned to do. Just think about how many times you plan to do something when you get to work, but you forget. The reason may be because you get distracted meeting someone and this distraction disrupts the cue.

Looking at When Memory Goes Wrong

People can't remember everything that happens to them. They often forget things such as when they were married or how old they are (though the latter may be deliberate in our cases!). We cover relatively minor disturbances in memory in Chapter 11, but more serious cases of memory loss also exist, as we describe in this section.

Two main forms of memory loss are associated with brain injury:

- ✔ **Anterograde amnesia:** People can't form new memories.
- ✔ **Retrograde amnesia:** People lose their existing memories.

These types of memory loss can be caused by head injury, severe alcoholism or viruses that damage parts of the medial temporal lobe. These cases typically damage episodic memories (memories of your own lifetime) and not semantic memory (memory for facts). Check out the earlier '"Let me tell you all about it!"' Declarative memory' section for more.

In this section we detail these two types of amnesia, providing examples and showing what cognitive psychologists have learnt from them.

Failing to form new memories

People with anterograde amnesia usually have their non-declarative memories intact (see '"But I don't know how I do it!"' Non-declarative memory' earlier in this chapter), so they can still learn new skills.

Think of the film *Memento*, where Guy Pearce's character has lost his ability to form new memories. His experiences quite accurately depict anterograde amnesia. He lives his life from one brief moment to the next, sometimes being unaware how he arrived somewhere and what he was doing.

Clive Wearing's pattern of anterograde amnesia is typical. Wearing (whom we introduce earlier in 'Remembering doing things: Procedural memory') describes his life as being in a constant state of feeling as if he has just woken up. With no continuity to his wakefulness, his only awareness is of what's in his attention at one particular moment. As soon as he's distracted, the effect is like being woken up. He can meet new people and become friendly with them, but at the next meeting he doesn't remember them.

Losing stored memories

Many films and TV programmes depict retrograde amnesia, in which characters are hit over the head and lose all memories of themselves (like *The Bourne Identity*).

If you're asked to recall ten events from your life where you were riding a bike, chances are that you'd remember events from throughout your life, emphasising recent ones but also including old events. But if someone with retrograde amnesia is asked, a completely different pattern emerges. The person would recall memories from much further back in her life and no recent events. This *temporal gradient* indicates that older memories are stored more strongly than more recent events (sometimes called *Ribot's law*).

Someone with retrograde amnesia could navigate around the place where she grew up as a child with no problem. But when asked to navigate around where she currently lives, she'd struggle.

Two main explanations suggest why this pattern of memory loss may exist:

- ✔ **Consolidation and reconsolidation of memories strengthens memories:** Every time a memory is reactivated, it becomes stronger, with more retrieval cues, and less susceptible to damage later on.

- ✔ **Semanticisation of episodic memories occurs:** Older memories are less emotional and 'episodic' than recent memories. In fact, older memories resemble semantic memories (which aren't damaged in amnesia). This suggests that older episodic memories have turned into semantic memories (we define these types of memories in the earlier '"Let me tell you all about it!"' Declarative memory' section).

Retrograde amnesia is caused by damage to the hippocampus and surrounding brain structures: the more damage to these areas, the more severe the memory loss. Another common cause of retrograde amnesia is Korsakoff's syndrome, which is caused by a deficiency in the vitamin thiamine (B1), usually due to chronic alcohol consumption.

Chapter 10

Knowing about Knowledge

*W*e'd like you to think about *One Direction* for a moment (a delight for some, a chore for others!). Whether you like the group or not, you've probably heard its songs, you may know some of the members' names and a few facts about them, and perhaps you can think of what they look like. All these aspects are called semantic knowledge.

As you can see, your brain can represent knowledge about the same item in various forms:

✔ **Fact:** You know that *One Direction* is a boy band created on *The X Factor*.

✔ **Visual:** You can easily picture the handsome features of your favourite band member.

✔ **Sound:** You can imagine the group's music.

✔ **Smell:** You know that the aroma of *One Direction*'s new fragrance 'Between Us' is alluring.

✔ **Touch:** You can remember that the texture of sandpaper is rough.

✔ **Taste:** You can recall the taste of your grandmother's roast dinners!

Note that you probably don't have direct knowledge of how the members of *One Direction* feel or taste – unless you know them very well!

Cognitive psychologists are interested in how you store and organise all the information you acquire, whether it's about *One Direction* or anything else. This chapter looks at two of the most important questions when thinking about knowledge: how does the brain represent this vast array of information and how does it know to link (or bind; see Chapters 8 and 9 on short- and long-term memory, respectively) all this information together?

Psychologists have developed many theories about how knowledge is stored. Here we discuss the idea of concepts and how they may be organised into hierarchies, hubs and spokes, schemas and scripts. We also look at a couple of theories of knowledge representation and at how cognitive psychologists think the brain represents knowledge.

Thinking of Knowledge as Concepts

Most cognitive psychologists think of knowledge as being stored in the form of *concepts*: abstract representations of categories. In order for this system to work, an individual needs to use the concepts consistently across time and be able to share them with different people. This ability is vitally important for communication: if people have different concepts for the same word, communication becomes impossible!

Concepts can be of anything for which you have a word and be of any level: for example, you can have a concept of people, a concept of boys, a concept of husbands in general and a concept of your particular husband.

Introducing the idea of concepts

You may be thinking of concepts as being like entries in a dictionary or an encyclopaedia. This interpretation of concepts is tempting, but overly simplistic. It works when you're asked questions in a pub quiz, but people rarely use concepts in exactly the same way every time in life.

Usually, you need to understand different aspects of a concept when you have different goals. In fact, concepts of objects must link to how they'll be used, which means that the brain has connections between the brain areas for concepts and the brain areas for movement and action.

Cognitive psychologists are extremely interested in the format by which the brain stores concepts and knowledge. In general, they identify four main formats for representations:

- ✔ **Images:** The brain can store some knowledge only in the form of images of the world (therefore in one *modality* or one format or sense). These images represent a particular moment in time and a particular area of the visual scene, like a photograph.

- ✔ **Feature records:** The brain stores some knowledge in terms of how useful combinations of features are. These features are all in the same modality. The idea is that creatures have representations of how useful a combination is. For example, a frog may detect motion of a small round object and combine these two meaningful features into the representation of an insect (a delicious snack).

✔ **Symbols:** Technically called *amodal symbols*. Representations of these types aren't restricted to one format. Instead they contain information about how other items may interact, including a list of all the properties that belong to a category. These properties are highly abstract. For example, to the frog, a fly has several features including its taste, sound, movement pattern and look.

✔ **Statistics:** Technically, *statistical patterns in neural nets*. This approach is very computational and is based on the idea that when a concept is active, a series of connected and related set of features are active and this pattern is the concept. Concepts are abstract entities that use information obtained across the different senses and which aren't tied to any particular modality.

Some debate exists about whether you can have concepts for things you don't have a word for (see Chapter 16). Most models of knowledge don't allow for representations of such things: they assume that you have to create a word for something first in order to represent it.

Ordering concepts: Hierarchies

After you realise that knowledge is stored as abstract concepts (see the preceding section), you need to establish how this information links together: such as, how does a concept of a person link to the concept of your husband? This issue contains two related problems: how do concepts at different levels link together and how do concepts at the same level link? Therefore, you need to consider the different levels of representation.

We look at two ways in which the brain may represent that knowledge: hierarchies in this section and the hub-and-spoke model in the next.

Look at Figure 10-1 and name the object before reading on.

When you're asked to identify something (label it), you tend to do so using different levels, which psychologists call a *hierarchy*:

✔ **General:** The top or *superordinate* level is general, vague and abstract and doesn't provide a great deal of specific information. For example, you may say that Figure 10-1 shows an 'animal'.

✔ **Basic:** This middle level is more informative than the general level. People find thinking of basic-level traits easier. For example, when shown Figure 10-1, many people go to the basic level and name it as a 'monkey' or more accurately an 'ape'.

✔ **Specific:** The bottom or *subordinate* level is specific to the object and highly informative. For example, you may label the creature in Figure 10-1 an 'orangutan' (or even 'Tuan' if you know its name!).

Figure 10-1:
How do you classify this object?

© John Wiley & Sons, Inc.

This hierarchy is similar to the way scientists classify living things in the natural world, starting with *Kingdom: Animalia* and going right down to the species level (*Pongo pygmaeus* in the case of the pictured orangutan).

People use concepts at every level depending on the context, but typically they use basic-level names. American psychologist Eleanor Rosch and colleagues conducted a study in which they showed a series of pictures, like the one in Figure 10-1, to participants and asked them to name the item in each picture. Rosch found that people used the basic-level names 1,595 times compared to 14 times for specific-level names and only once for general-category names. This shows a preference for the basic level.

With one type of object, everyone uses the specific level: faces. When you see a face of someone you know, you name the person (that is, use the specific level name) rather than say 'man' or 'person'.

Expertise also seems to affect the level you use. A primatologist (who studies monkeys) probably looks at Figure 10-1 and uses the specific level *(Bornean Orangutan)*. Mind you, instead of expertise, perhaps a better word is familiarity. If you present people with familiar buildings, they're faster to use specific-level names than basic-level names.

Naming tends to occur at the basic level, but it's not the fastest level for categorising objects. For speed, people tend to use the general category level, suggesting that it's the first level that comes to mind.

Wheeling away at the hub-and-spokes model

When you consider a concept, such as 'cheese', you may picture it, or think of its smell, taste or rubbery texture; that is, you can think of a concept in every sensory modality, not typically considered in the hierarchical approach. With this in mind, British neuroscientist Karalyn Patterson and colleagues proposed the hub-and-spoke model as an alternative to hierarchies.

The *hub-and-spoke model* is based on the idea of a bicycle wheel, with a central hub and spokes radiating out (see Figure 10-2). The hub represents the core aspects of the concept without any consideration of sensations. It links to each of the spokes, which are sense-specific representations. These spokes are linked to how you perceive and may use the concept.

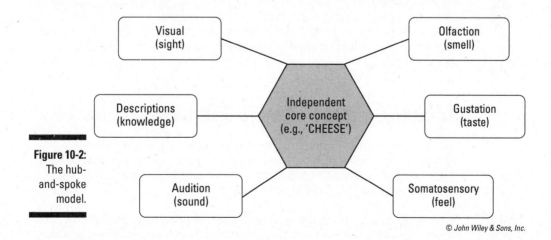

Figure 10-2: The hub-and-spoke model.

© John Wiley & Sons, Inc.

Organising Knowledge in Your Brain

As well as describing knowledge in terms of concepts (see the preceding section), you can also think about how knowledge is represented in another way. You can group or chunk concepts together (similar to the chunking we describe in Chapter 8).

When they're grouped together, cognitive psychologists call this way of representing knowledge a *schema*. If that concept refers to a way of behaving or acting, they refer to it as a *script*.

We describe these two forms of knowledge in this section, as well as discuss how people may represent spatial knowledge.

For example, some people may have a script for using a fast-food drive-through. The driver's schema involves knowing that he has to drive to the window, make the order, pay for it and drive somewhere else to collect the order. (We assume this is correct – we don't drive or haven't used a drive-through; we're writing this using a schema derived from watching American movies!) Having a schema or script is useful, because it enables the driver to know how to behave to achieve his goal (buying a burger) and what to expect. This has benefits in terms of processing, because the driver can use the same schema in many different contexts (any drive-through) without having to work out what to do from scratch each time.

Schemas are intricately involved in the way people store information. Without schemas, the world is a hugely confusing and bewildering place. For example, some brain-damaged patients have no problem with scripts but serious problems with concepts (they suffer from *semantic dementia*). Other patients, with damage to the brain's frontal lobes, have no problem with concepts but great difficulty planning and organising behaviour, suggesting that they don't have stored scripts.

Scheming your way to knowing

Schemas are large structures of knowledge, linking a group of concepts together to form knowledge about events or things. When a schema concerns events, cognitive psychologists call it a script (see the next section). When a schema is about a thing, they call it a *frame*.

Schemas integrate your existing knowledge and influence how future information is stored. Because schemas are based on existing knowledge, people have more difficulty recalling information that's inconsistent with their schemas. Remembering schematic information requires little effort, but information not in your schema is harder to remember and requires more effort to process.

For example, if you're presented with a picture of a room that has a slightly unexpected object in it and then are given a memory test, you tend not to remember that slightly unusual object (in fact you often 'remember' items that aren't in the room but are consistent with your schema for what should be in the room). If the object is highly unusual, however, it attracts your attention and is easier to remember.

Frederic Bartlett, a British psychologist, conducted what has become a classic study of the influence on schemas: the *War of the Ghosts* study. He gave his Cambridge students a Native-Canadian ghost story to read. He found that the students failed to remember information that was inconsistent with their existing schema (inconsistent with their culture).

 A stereotype is a special kind of schema that combines all the concepts relating to a particular group of people. Stereotypes are often negative and very rarely contain accurate statements. Stereotyping is usually tested by social psychologists, but the nearby sidebar 'Illusory correlations' gives an example of a cognitive psychological explanation about the formation of stereotypes – why they're inaccurate and the result of a lazy brain.

Illusory correlations

American psychologists David Hamilton and Richard Gifford found that the formation of stereotypes can be the result of *illusory correlations*. The human brain is lazy and forms connections based on minimal information. If one thing is unusual, people tend to assume that it's linked with something else that's unusual, irrespective of whether they're actually linked.

Hamilton and Gifford gave participants descriptions of behaviours performed by two groups. One group had more members than the other group. The behaviours described were good and bad and the researchers included more good than bad behaviours. Crucially, the proportion of good and bad behaviours was the same for both groups. However, the participants in the study rated the smaller group as committing the bad behaviours more. This correlation was provably wrong, and yet the participants felt convinced that it was true.

Many people hold negative attitudes toward minority groups, suspecting them of displaying more negative behaviours. In fact, people overestimate the amount of crime committed by minorities, because crime is distinctive by being infrequent and being a minority is also distinctive. Almost all statistics show that crime is much more likely to be committed by someone in a majority group than a minority group.

Scripting knowledge

Scripts are special kinds of schemas that are about how events are sequenced in time and how people should behave in a certain way if the right conditions apply. For example, going into a classroom, you sit behind a desk, get your pen and paper out, and wait (in silence!) for the teacher to arrive. (Are we hoping for too much here?)

A study conducted by American psychologists John Bransford and Marcia Johnson demonstrated how scripts help people organise knowledge. They gave participants a passage of text similar to the following one: it's a script of an activity, but which one?

> *It's a really frustrating task, but luckily you don't have to do it that often, though more often is better of course. First you have to get it out. You also need all the extra bits, because different bits are used for different things. When it's all ready you can begin, but not before you've made sure that there's nothing in your way: if there is you have to move it and it's better to do that at the start than partway through. If you don't you have to stop and move it and start it again. When you start you have to do it following the appropriate guidelines: this should be really simple – even a child can do it. You should do it thoroughly, making sure to cover every area. If you don't then it can be quite bad later on. You may need to change parts at different times, but that depends on you. When you've finished, you may have to remove the contents and then put it away.*

At first, participants have difficulty understanding or remembering elements of the passage unless they're given the title. But when they know the title they can remember almost all its elements and understanding becomes easy. This experiment shows that knowledge is stored as a group of concepts rather than each one being stored in isolation.

The script refers to vacuum cleaning. Test this passage out on your friends – see how much they can remember without and then with this label.

Finding your way around with routes

When considering knowledge, you often think of knowing facts or how to do things. *Routes* are important sets of knowledge that combine these two aspects. In order to walk from home to school (or somewhere more exciting, like the library!), you must know the route and the landmarks.

People need two types of knowledge of their environment:

- **Routes:** Specific paths from one place to another
- **Surveys:** Map-like knowledge of the environment (associated with more experience within an environment)

Knowledge of routes and surveys depends very much on the individual: it's egocentric. If you ask people to draw a map of their country, they over-exaggerate the distances between places closer to them.

When people think of their own cities, they focus on five main elements that develop based on their experience within the environment:

- **Paths:** Channels that people walk (you know, paths!)
- **Edges:** City boundaries, including walls
- **Districts:** Self-contained sections of cities
- **Nodes:** Important parts of an environment – focal points that are used, such as parks
- **Landmarks:** Important focal points of an environment that aren't use-able, such as historic monuments

Representing Items in Your Head

People often consider knowledge as a fixed construct, such as books in a library, and knowing how people incorporate new knowledge into their heads is certainly important. But knowledge is often used in *dynamic settings*: by which we mean that you often compare new information that you have to knowledge already stored.

In this section, we look at a few cognitive psychological theories that explore these ideas in a bit more detail. This approach to thinking about knowledge is primarily concerned with concrete objects (real things you can touch, such as, er, concrete).

Defining attributes

Simple models of knowledge use rules or definitions. Definition-based models work by finding *attributes* (features) that are common to particular objects. The attributes that are common then form a rule.

If you try to list the attributes of a fish, like most people you're likely to list a number of similar features.

People have a list of attributes in their brains for every kind of object. When you see something new, you list all the attributes and compare them to the ones stored in your knowledge.

Say that you think a fish is made of these attributes: scales, a fin, it swims, it lives in water. Now you see a newt. It looks like it has scales (but doesn't), swims (sometimes), lives in water (sometimes). If you haven't experienced it before, you may think it's a fish – until you obtain enough knowledge to separate the category of fish into fish and newts.

Similar to the object-perception models we describe in Chapter 6, the suggestion is that people break down objects into constituent parts to recognise them. Indeed, perception and knowledge researchers have come up with similar models (no wonder, because you can't have knowledge without an awareness for how things look, sound, feel and so on!).

The list of common attributes that link all fish are the features people use to define something as a fish. These common attributes must fit all examples in order for the category to work.

The common attributes that fit basic categories are more specific than those that fit general-level categories. Specific-level categories have detailed attributes that define them (see the earlier section 'Ordering concepts: Hierarchies' for more on the categories). These traits make them unique and different from the other objects in the basic category. For example, the goldfish has all the common attributes of a fish, but has the added distinctive trait that it's gold (well, orange).

Created definition rules must be specific enough to differentiate between similar types of objects, but not too specific. For example, imagine that you define a cat as a four-legged, hairy animal that purrs, and then you spot a Sphynx cat. It doesn't have hair, and so using that rule you may not think that it's a cat; but it really is (and cute in an alien-looking way!).

Rules tend to be processed in the frontal areas of the brain. Neuroscientists have shown that when categorising objects using rules, the frontal motor areas are more active than other areas of the brain.

Comparing to averages

Prototype theories are a different approach to think about how people store knowledge in the brain. (We consider a version of prototype theory when looking at how objects are recognised in Chapter 6.) The idea is that the brain stores an average example of something.

When you think of the average fish, you probably picture something like our description in the earlier 'Defining attributes' section (scales, fins and so on). You categorise quickly everything that's close to that image as a fish. When you're presented with something that looks dissimilar to that image, you don't think of it as a fish. Therefore, when you see an unusual fish type, such as the lionfish, classifying it at the general level as a fish is harder (though classifying it at the specific level and providing its name is easier, if you're familiar with that name, of course!).

This theory works nicely for objects that have prototypes, but it's problematic for more difficult concepts that may not have an average. For example, what's an average 'game'? The answer probably depends on whether you're sporty, like board games or are a gambler. Can you really find a prototype that accurately combines football, Monopoly and poker? Defining a set of attributes that links these three things is very difficult.

Examining exemplar theory

Possibly the simplest way of representing knowledge is to store memories of every individual category member: called *exemplars*. The logic is that every time you see an object of a particular category, you store a new representation of it.

For example, you see a black cat and add it to your exemplar store of cats. You then come across a white cat and also add it to your knowledge of cats. Now you know that cats can be black or white. With more and more exemplars stored, you have an accurate representation of a category.

Sufficient evidence exists that the brain stores exemplars of objects. Unfortunately, memories of exemplars can prevent people from correctly categorising objects. For example, many people have exemplars from seeing cheetahs; subsequently, categorising a leopard becomes more difficult, because of the similarities between the two species.

When storing exemplars, the sensory parts of the brain are used more than the memory sites of the brain.

Putting Aside Knowledge in Your Brain

A simple way of investigating how and where the brain stores concepts (in the sense of the earlier section 'Thinking of Knowledge as Concepts') is to measure the brain activity when people think about an object. We look at two such studies now.

Storing in modules

One set of theories suggests that modules in the brain store and process particular things. As we state in Chapter 1, the idea of modules is one of the core assumptions of cognitive neuropsychology. If it's true, different parts of the brain are responsible for storing different types of knowledge. In which case, you should be able to observe *category-specific deficits*, where someone has a brain injury that means that he loses knowledge of one type of concept but not others.

Some patients do indeed have difficulty identifying pictures of living things but display relatively preserved abilities to identify non-living things. The thought is that they have a category-specific knowledge deficit for living things but their knowledge of things such as tools is unaffected. Similar cases exist of people unable to name foods or kitchen utensils, but these are rarer than deficits in naming living things.

Another explanation for category-specific deficits suggests that the deficit is in terms of specific information use (that is, category-specific knowledge is really a loss of the most specific detailed level of knowledge). Living things may have more specific details than non-living things, which leads to the observed patterns.

Distributing knowledge

Most of the research on brain imaging when people are thinking about concepts shows quite a wide-ranging activation. Some simple results show that when people think about a physical object, the part of the brain associated with seeing is active. But when they think about an abstract concept (such as 'freedom') that 'seeing' part isn't active.

Similar results are obtained when people think about concepts involving action. If you think about a bicycle, the chances are that your brain activates the areas of the brain associated with movement. Whereas if you think about a stationary object (say a chair), the movement areas of the brain aren't active. Indeed, if the parts of the brain that process movement are temporarily switched off (using Transcranial Magnetic Stimulation), people have more difficulty thinking about moving.

Based on these findings, the hub-and-spoke model is quite plausible (see the earlier section 'Wheeling away at the hub-and-spokes model').

Karalyn Patterson suggests that the core of the concepts (the hubs) are stored in the anterior temporal lobes, which don't contain any sense or motor information. The sensory information (the spokes in the model) that relate to a concept are stored in the various sensory parts of the brain. The hubs integrate all the different types of knowledge. Other researchers, however, suggest the existence of a *convergence zone*, where part of the brain integrates all the sensory, conceptual and motor information about concepts. This may be located in the superior temporal sulcus.

Chapter 11

Discovering Why You Forget Things

....

In This Chapter

▶ Looking through the forgetting processes

▶ Forgetting deliberately

▶ Inventing false information

....

In Chapters 8, 9 and 10, we discuss your brain's impressive ability to store information (though, of course, all human beings are equally impressive!). People can't remember everything they learn, however, and in this chapter we look at the not-so-good part of memory – forgetting. Yes, like any episode of *Fawlty Towers*, it's devoted to things going wrong!

We describe some reasons and important theories behind why you forget certain things, including deliberately, and how researchers can mess with people's memories (all in the name of science, of course).

'It's on the Tip of My Tongue!' Forgetting Things

Clearly the human memory is impressive, and yet something stops people from being able to remember some important things.

If we ask you to list the names and birthdays of your grandparents, parents, aunts, uncles, brothers and sisters, chances are that you can remember some of them (we hope all the names!), but not every single one. This failure is despite the fact that you've been told them many times (one of us always has to be reminded to call his grandmother on her birthday every year, despite caring a lot!).

Here we discuss some of the reasons why people forget things:

- Not attending to information (as we discuss in Chapter 7)
- Not encoding information properly (see Chapters 5 and 8)
- Losing information from memory (through decay)
- Interfering with stored memories
- Not accessing the memory during retrieval

It's amazing that people remember as much as they do!

Paying insufficient attention

Obviously, if you don't attend to information appropriately, you can't remember it later. If you're not looking at something, you don't remember it; if you're distracted while learning, you don't remember it.

As we discuss in Chapter 7, attention is like a spotlight: what's in the spotlight receives the most amount of processing. Attention acts by focusing the brain's resources on something important enough to learn. When the attentional resources aren't directed well enough onto learning (through distraction, dividing the resources), learning simply isn't sufficient.

This idea suggests that you can't learn anything unless you pay appropriate attention to it. On the other hand, psychologists have shown that people can learn things implicitly, without conscious awareness or without the intention to learn.

Failing to encode properly

Even if you attend properly to the information (refer to the preceding section), you may not store it perfectly in your memory. You need to transfer the information from your working memory to long-term memory through a process of *rehearsal*. Rehearsing information requires effort and time to think about the item in question.

In Chapter 9, we describe how elaboration (deeply thinking and relating to existing knowledge) during encoding helps memory by making something more meaningful, distinctive and therefore more memorable. Sometimes, however, making things more meaningful isn't easy. When you're in a classroom trying to learn something that you don't really care about (obviously not cognitive psychology!) in order to pass an exam, you can struggle to make it personally relevant or meaningful.

One method that helps you to learn, apparently more than any other technique, is that of learning through testing (appropriately called the *testing effect*). That's why teachers love springing 'fun' surprise tests!

The logic is that when you learn something, every so often, you stop and test yourself to ensure that you've really learnt it. You may not remember much the first time, but by the second or third time you test yourself on the same information, you're better than you would've been by simply rereading it the same number of times. And the learning lasts a long time: by testing yourself multiple times, your memory becomes 50 per cent better for weeks after compared to rereading.

The science behind this process concerns what your brain is doing every time you access information. When you read something, your brain activates the knowledge store and adds information there. By reading something, and then reading it again, the knowledge may become better stored in your head (the memory trace is stronger). But memory isn't just about storing information, it's also about retrieving it. By testing yourself on your knowledge, you're activating the retrieval part of your brain too. As a result, you strengthen the retrieval pathway in your brain as well as the memory trace.

One thing that you may be doing when trying to remember things is creating links with existing knowledge (called *cues*). Retesting allows you to assess whether these cues are effective. If they aren't good cues, you create different ones. This creation of new cues provides more pathways to retrieval. You retest until you have the perfect cues to remember correctly every time. Additionally, more retrieval cues mean more routes to the memory and more chances to access the information.

This testing effect also exists because you have to put effort into remembering things. The more effort you make, the more likely you are to remember. Retesting also helps you to notice other aspects (such as context and other relationships between what you're trying to learn) that may help you learn more generally.

Decaying from memory

Even when you pay attention and encode information appropriately (as per the preceding two sections), it still may not remain in your head forever. Although we can easily remember our old school teachers' names and faces, no doubt we've lost a lot of what they taught us. One reason why people lose information from memory is through *decay*.

Hermann Ebbinghaus, a German psychologist, pioneered research on memory. He designed a series of studies where participants were presented with a set of nonsense *trigrams* (three letters that don't make a word). He asked people to try to remember them and tested their memory over various time intervals.

Ebbinghaus's results are clear: the rate of forgetting was fast and then slowed up (see Figure 11-1). This curve has been called the *Ebbinghaus curve*. The information people lost from memory was greater sooner after learning than days after learning.

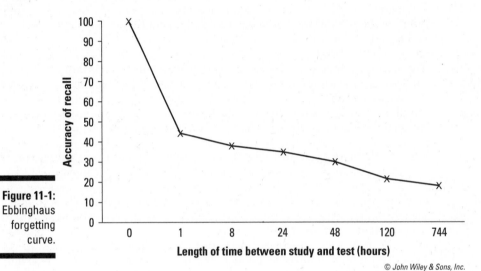

Figure 11-1:
Ebbinghaus
forgetting
curve.

© John Wiley & Sons, Inc.

One of the simplest explanations for this forgetting is that information simply fades or decays from memory. People may forget (and in particular forget more recent things faster) because they're constantly learning lots of trivial information.

Consider this: you don't need to remember exactly what you had for breakfast or what the strangers you passed on your way to college look like. It makes more sense for your mind to ignore this information (by not attending to it or forgetting it if you did attend to it).

Interfering with stored memories

Even if you attend to information, encode it properly and store it well enough to avoid decay, information in memory can still be made unavailable through *interference*: this is where other information that you have disrupts the stored memory.

Two kinds of interference effects exist:

- **Proactive interference:** Knowledge that you already have affects how you learn new information.
- **Retroactive interference:** New information that you receive disrupts stored knowledge.

Past information

Old knowledge can interfere with learning and storing new information.

We demonstrate a classic case of proactive interference through one of the author's grandparents. They'd lived in the same house for 50 years with the same kitchen layout for 20 of those years. When they came to replace some of the kitchen appliances, they (and one of the authors) found themselves putting food into the washing machine because the washing machine is now where the fridge used to be!

Proactive interference is caused by the same stimulus being associated with correct information and incorrect information. If the link between the stimulus and the incorrect information is very strong (because you've been putting food in the same place for 20 years) and the link between the stimulus and the correct information is weak (because you've only just moved the fridge), interference is more likely.

Automatic processing or habits have to be overwritten by new information. You can do so by ensuring that you use a narrow search through your memory: when searching your memory, you need to focus actively on specific and recent knowledge (only the recent times of putting food away) to ensure that you prevent interference from past knowledge.

Stored knowledge

Think of what your mother looked like ten years ago. You'll probably find this task more difficult than it sounds. You can easily picture how she looks now, but her current appearance interferes with your ability to think about how she used to look.

This retroactive interference is stronger if you currently live with your mother or you've only just moved out. If a long time has passed, you may find that remembering her a while ago is easier!

Similar to proactive interference, retroactive interference occurs because the correct information is hard to retrieve, but it's mainly because the incorrect information is easy to retrieve. It occurs more often when the two learning times are very similar. So if you're studying two related concepts, learning them in different ways and in different places is advisable.

Forgetting the cues

People can temporarily forget things when they fail to retrieve the information: they simply can't access it at that moment.

Endel Tulving (see Chapter 9) introduced the idea of *cue dependency* (where the activation of a memory requires a specific cue). You may experience this when you're asked a question such as, 'Which city held the Olympic Games in 2000?' The answer may not appear to mind straightaway, but if we were to give you a list (London, Paris, Sydney, Atlanta, Istanbul), you'd probably recognise the correct answer (Sydney). This is because you lacked the appropriate cue to remember the answer. When it was provided, you got the answer.

Tulving proposed the *encoding specificity principle*. The term is a bit of a mouthful, but essentially it means that you remember more when the information at retrieval most closely matches that of learning: in other words, when you store new knowledge, you also store information about how you learnt the information (the context).

So, to increase the chance of remembering, you retrieve the information in the same context as you learnt it. Context, in this case, refers to the place you learnt it, the emotional state you were in, the music playing in the background and all other environmental influences.

One of the most successful demonstrations of cue dependency and the encoding specificity principle is that of British cognitive psychologists David Godden and Alan Baddeley. They formed two groups of participants: one learnt a list of words in diving suits underwater, and another group learnt a list of words on the beach. Half of each group then attempted to recall the words in the same context and the other half attempted to recall the words in the opposite context. Recall was much greater when the context matched for learning and retrieving.

The same effect doesn't occur when participants are given a recognition test (where they're presented with lots of words and asked to identify the ones they've seen). This is probably because the recognition list provides sufficient cues to override those provided by the context.

Crucial to whether the cue helps memory is how much information it shares with the information to be remembered and whether it shares information with other bits of information. The cue must be as distinctive as possible and relate only to one thing to be remembered for it to be useful.

Often you can have the cue active in your mind but still not quite retrieve the thing to be remembered. This situation leaves you in an annoying position of being close to remembering something: the *tip of the tongue state*. This occurs because the memory is activated sufficiently for you to remember that you know the item, but not sufficiently to recall it. It can also occur because when trying to remember something, you activate different bits of potentially related information rather than directly activating the memory (that is, you're using the wrong cues to retrieval).

Intending to Forget

Most of the time, forgetting is the result of something going wrong. But in two situations forgetting can be intentional, whether deliberately (*motivated forgetting*) or unconsciously (*repression*).

Forgetting on purpose

Remembering everything isn't practical or useful for survival. If you could remember every single meal you've ever eaten, you'd have great difficulty sifting through all that knowledge to find whether you like the food on offer right now! Remembering only key examples makes more sense (such as your favourite foods and those you hate).

One way to ensure that you don't remember everything is not to pay attention to everything. However, if you do pay attention, you may need to forget something deliberately: called motivated forgetting.

 One way to study motivated forgetting is through a technique called *directed forgetting*. In the laboratory, you may be presented with a list of words and told to remember some (maybe written in one colour) and forget others (in another colour). You're then tested on your memory for all the words. Obviously, memory is worse for the items you were told to forget than the ones you were told to remember.

 One reason why you may not remember the items you were directed to forget is because you inhibit those items. *Inhibition* is the process where your brain tries to prevent itself being activated by the item. This suppression of unwanted information can occur by thinking about other things (*thought substitution*) and actively not thinking about the info.

 Research indicates that when you're told not to remember something, your brain activates the frontal part (used for controlling of intentions) and doesn't activate the hippocampus (responsible for memory).

Repressing memories

Sigmund Freud (remember him?), an Austrian psychoanalyst (we don't call him a psychologist despite the importance of his work), is famous for writing about repression. He claimed that people's unconscious minds blocked traumatic or painful memories from conscious memory.

Although repressing painful memories seems like a plausible idea, not a lot of scientific evidence exists for it. People claim to have recovered repressed memories as a result of therapy (including hypnosis; see Chapter 23), but research shows that 80 per cent of these 'recovered memories' are in fact fake and probably implanted by the therapist accidentally. When memories are recovered accidentally outside of therapy, they're much more likely to be true.

The mechanisms of repression aren't well understood, not least because researching verification of recovered memories is very difficult.

Alzheimer's disease

Alzheimer's is a relatively common disease that causes a serious deterioration in cognitive performance with age. It's caused by the brain tissue becoming destroyed and the connections between brain cells being damaged.

The earliest symptom of Alzheimer's is loss of short-term memory. Sufferers can't remember recent conversations and may also forget other unexpected things (such as the names of people they know well). Alzheimer's tends not to affect older memories as much as more recent ones. Some memory deficits, however, may be hidden due to *confabulation*, where sufferers unintentionally replace missing information in their memories with something they've created.

Later on, sufferers develop language problems (in particular with vocabulary) and their personality changes. The stages of the disease are similar to normal ageing, although people with Alzheimer's find their problems develop faster than someone not ageing.

Diagnosing Alzheimer's as early as possible is vital because, although no cure exists, medical staff can implement many techniques to delay the disease's progression, such as providing lots of mental exercises (like those developed and used by cognitive psychologists) and creating routines around the home.

Creating False Memories

Remembering can go wrong in several ways. You can make wrong associations, allow memories to be distorted and overshadow your memory verbally. If nothing else, this section suggests that you can't always trust your memory: it will play tricks on you!

Associating things incorrectly

Existing schemas (refer to Chapter 10) can cause people's memories to be mistaken. If you see something that doesn't fit with your schema, you may remember that information differently.

For example, a study conducted in 1947 involved showing white participants a picture of a white man with a razor next to a black man on a train. Sometime later the participants' memory for the event was tested: disturbingly, many white people 'remember' that the black man had the razor. This error is because of their schema that white people don't carry knives (which is blatantly incorrect).

More experimental evidence for how schemas can alter what you remember comes from the Deese-Roediger-McDermott paradigm (named after the researchers who first used it: American psychologists James Deese, Henry L. Roediger III and Kathleen McDermott).

In this research, participants are presented with lists of words that all belong to the same category (see Figure 11-2). Subsequently, the researchers test participants' recognition memory for the words. However, extra words are added to the recognition tests (called *lures*). The participants have to say whether each word was seen before. Crucially, one of the lure words is related in meaning to the words presented in the first list (a critical lure word).

The results show that participants often 'remember' seeing the critical lure word, which indicates that their memories have been tricked into seeing an extra word that wasn't present.

People make this mistake because they aren't very good at remembering everything; instead, they tend to remember the gist of things. So when presented with a series of related words, they find the context that links all the words, which is probably a stored schema. When they come to recall the words, they simply activate their schema and recall all the words in it – and make an error.

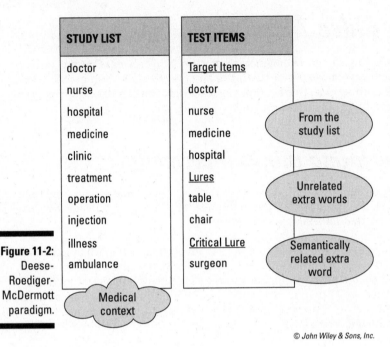

Figure 11-2:
Deese-
Roediger-
McDermott
paradigm.

Distorting memory

Much of the material in this chapter and in Chapter 12 (on eye-witness memory) shows just how easily you can change people's memories for events by later on adding new information.

One particular demonstration comes from Micah Edelson, an Israeli neuroscientist, and his colleagues. They had participants watch a video and later recall it. They then told the participants that other people had remembered the video differently to them. In a subsequent memory test, the participants recalled part of the video differently from the first time, incorporating this extra information.

This behaviour is partly because people's memories are reactivated when they try to remember something (check out the reconsolidation theory from Chapter 9). The new information can then mingle with the existing information. People mistakenly think that the new information is accurately part of the existing memory when really it isn't. Later, the memory becomes a combination of all the information.

Another example of memory distortions comes from *cryptomnesia* (unconscious plagiarism), which is due to failing to remember the source of one's own memory. For example, George Harrison's best-selling song 'My Sweet Lord' turned out to be a rip-off of a song called 'He's So Fine' that he'd heard years previously but forgotten all about. People are much better at remembering information than remembering where that information came from.

Talking things through: Verbal overshadowing

Although not strictly forgetting in the traditional sense, the verbal overshadowing effect does cause errors in memory (and we couldn't find a better place to cover it in this book!).

The *verbal overshadowing effect* (found in 1991 by Jonathan Schooler, an American psychologist) is when you're asked to describe an event and the mere act of doing so affects the accuracy of how you remember the event. Typically, *verbalising* (describing an event verbally) makes you much less accurate at recalling it later, particularly with faces, which are far less accurately recognised after they've been described.

This issue is particularly problematic for police procedures. Suppose that you witness a crime and go to the police to give a statement. They ask you to give a verbal description of the perpetrator. You describe the person as well as you possibly can. All seems perfectly fine, except for the verbal overshadowing effect. The fact is that, simply by asking you to describe a face, the police are making it less likely that you'll accurately recognise the face during a line-up.

This effect occurs because the way people see things isn't easily describable. Their verbal descriptions are nowhere near as colourful or as vivid as what they see. They lose information in their descriptions.

Part of the problem is that people may describe a single distinctive feature rather than process a face as a whole (which, as we show in Chapter 6, is what people are supposed to do). As a result, they don't process everything. In other words, their descriptions of crime scenes should be limited to the pertinent points, such as the colours of the clothes that someone was wearing.

Chapter 12

Memorising in the Real World

In This Chapter

▶ Remembering things about yourself

▶ Recalling distinct events

▶ Witnessing crimes

Chapters 8 to 11 are mainly about memory research conducted in a laboratory. Nothing's wrong with that (we've made careers out of it – if we remember rightly!), but you always have to question whether such studies adequately represent what happens in the real world. That is, can the results be repeated (replicated) and do they have ecological validity (something we discuss in Chapter 1)?

In this chapter, we look at three important areas where you need memory in the real world: remembering events in your life, recalling distinct events (*flashbulb memories*) and eyewitness memory. Never has the *For Dummies* Remember icon been more important than here!

Remembering Yourself and Your Life

You're unlikely to get far if you can't remember your own life and history: in fact, you probably wouldn't be yourself without a memory of yourself, because your memories affect how your personality develops and even your self-identity. Cognitive psychologists call this *autobiographical memory*. It's different to episodic memory (see Chapter 9), because it's much more personally significant – the memories are vivid, complex and longer lasting.

Autobiographical memories are some of the most important types of memories. People use them to identify themselves, often by telling stories about themselves to other people, which creates social bonds. But when they talk about their autobiographical memories, are they talking about memories from across their lives equally? And does everyone talk about them in the same way?

In this section, we address these two fascinating questions, and we describe how cognitive psychologists can measure autobiographical memories.

Measuring the accuracy of your autobiographical memories

You may think that measuring autobiographical memories is easy, but for cognitive psychologists it really isn't.

Recall as many memories as you can from when you were 7 years old and then as many as possible from when you were 10. No doubt you're able to reel off lots of stories and tot them up. That's fine, but you're only counting up the numbers.

Cognitive psychologists are interested not only in how many memories you can recall, but also how accurate they are. How can we find out whether your memories are accurate or not? We could ask your parents to come into the laboratory to verify the memory, but that just isn't practical (and what about the complicating factor of the accuracy of their memories of distant events?). So what do we do?

Well, some clever British cognitive psychologists (kudos to Michael Koppelman, Barbara Wilson and Alan Baddeley) came up with one approach, called the *autobiographical memory interview*. This test involves interviewing participants and asking them to provide memories from three different periods of their lives (childhood, young adulthood and recent events). The test is divided into two parts:

- ✔ **Part 1:** Provides a specific memory in response to a cue relating to, for example, something that happened at school.
- ✔ **Part 2:** Provides more factual information about things that happened in the past (such as the name of a school attended).

Two people then look at the interview transcript and rate each memory for how vivid and specific it is (such as giving the exact time and date when something happened). This appraisal allows for a reliable assessment of the quality and nature of memories across the lifespan. Accurate memories are likely to be more specific and vivid.

Thinking about what you remember – and why

Here we look at whether you recall autobiographical memories equally across your lifetime.

Try to recall as many memories as you can in two minutes and then note down from what period in your life they're from. Do the same exercise with a 25- and a 75-year-old person. From when do all three of you recall most and least memories?

Most people tend not to recall any memories from before the age of 3 and very few prior to the age of 6 (known as *childhood amnesia*). They do recall more memories from between 15 and 30 (the *reminiscence bump*, which is fortunately not as unsightly as it sounds). This pattern tends to happen for all people, no matter how old they are (unless you're under 15!). So why do these things happen?

Childhood amnesia

Cognitive psychologists have come up with a number of theories, though no definitive answers, for why no one can remember memories from before the age of about 3 years:

- Children don't have a developed sense of self (who they are in relation to the rest of the world) until about 3 years of age, which means that they can't form memories about the self until some time after they learn to recognise themselves in a mirror.

- Given that people tend to talk about themselves a lot, perhaps autobiographical memories are stored using words and language. Children don't develop sufficient language until about 3 years and so can't have autobiographical memories. The lack of language prevents them developing sufficient retrieval cues (see Chapter 10).

- In our opinion, the most convincing theory is *neurogenesis*, which is based on evidence about what exists in the brain. The part of the brain most important for memories in adulthood (the hippocampus) simply isn't developed in children. It develops much slower than other parts of the brain, and so it can't really store memories until about 3 years of age and isn't fully working until 6 years of age.

Young-adult super memory!

Most likely, people remember more memories between 15 and 30 years of age than all other ages because the sense of self, language and the brain are fully developed by this age; plus, the decline in the hippocampus associated with age doesn't start to occur until much older than 30 years.

One additional theory for this 'super memory' is based on the idea of the *life script*. Most people experience common, significant and culturally defined events. Lots of people go to university and live alone for the first time, start a career, get married (some more than others!) and have children. Most of these events tend to occur between the ages of 15 and 30. Socially-derived scripts exist for these events and so they're easier to remember, because they're ingrained into people from a young age. Indeed, when children think about the future, they think in terms of such life-script events.

Wondering whether all autobiographical memories are the same

When you think about autobiographical memories, you immediately realise that they aren't all the same. They're not all in the same detail and of the same level of vividness.

Mood affects autobiographical memory. Typically, people remember positive life-script events (which we discuss in the preceding section), such as getting married. Tim Dalgleish, a British neuroscientist, and colleagues show that people suffering from depression tend to recall many more negative life-script events than those without depression.

When the memory is from also affects how people recall it. You may think that people would recall older memories (more remote memories) less well than more recent ones. But in fact research from the 19th century found that some older memories are much more accurately recalled than recent ones (known as Ribot's law, see Chapter 9). However, the way they're recalled is very different.

You've recalled older memories more times than recent ones and told them to people more often than recent memories. Therefore, these older memories have stronger memory traces. They're also less likely to be lost due to brain injury (which is why many people with amnesia can still recall things from the past better than recent events).

In fact, the older memories become a lot more like *semantic memories* (facts about the world) in how you recall and discuss them. As a result, you describe them in a more emotionless and plain way, whereas you remember more recent events with emotion and feeling (check out Chapter 9 for more on this process, called *semanticisation*).

Flashing Back in Time

Some events just stick in the mind. We know this statement sounds colloquial rather than scientific, but in fact it's apparently true.

What were you doing when you heard about the attacks on the World Trade Center (the event known as 9/11)? We expect that you have a pretty clear recollection.

Many people can remember this event very well, certainly if they were more than 6 years old at the time (check out the earlier 'Childhood amnesia' section for why). These so-called flashbulb memories are typically very vivid, clear and distinctive.

Flashbulb memories are like a special kind of autobiographical memory (see the 'Remembering Yourself and Your Life' section earlier in this chapter), because they're extremely long-lasting and apply to an external event. If the event in question actually happened to you, you may get flashbacks to the event because of its traumatic nature.

Flashbulb memories are usually for a few very distinct events in your lifetime. Classically studied events include JFK's assassination, the moon landing, the space shuttle Challenger exploding, Princess Diana's death and 9/11.

Originally, cognitive psychologists thought that flashbulb memories were extremely accurate and consistent over time, but extensive research shows that they tend to be very easy to distort. For example, many people report seeing the first plane hit the World Trade Center live on TV, whereas the video footage of this happening wasn't released until sometime after the event. Furthermore, the consistency of people's flashbulb memories is questionable. People's memories tend to remain consistent for the facts that are repeated on TV, but for other aspects the memories get distorted.

No evidence suggests that flashbulb memories are any different to other distinctive autobiographical memories.

Being an Eyewitness

One of the most important moments when memory is required is for eyewitness testimony (though remembering to record the latest episode of *Doctor Who* comes close, naturally!). If you're ever unfortunate enough to witness a crime taking place, you're highly likely to have to recall the event and maybe identify the perpetrator.

The police and law courts frequently ask eyewitnesses to testify about what they saw, because juries believe eyewitnesses more than fingerprint evidence, evidence from polygraphs and handwriting analysis. In fact, juries believe 70 per cent of eyewitness testimonies, and this value doesn't depend on whether the eyewitness is accurate or inaccurate. Even if an eyewitness is proved wrong in court, juries still believe the person 44 per cent of the time!

These figures seem worrying, but it gets worse. Whenever reviews have been conducted on wrongful imprisonments, eyewitness error has been the main contributory factor. The Devlin Report, published in the UK in 1976, suggested that courts shouldn't rely on eyewitnesses, and yet recent statistics reveal that 90 per cent of all wrongful convictions are based on eyewitness testimony alone. Check out the nearby sidebar 'Stop! Who goes there?' for some experiments conducted on this issue.

Given these rather damning statistics, cognitive psychologists were asked to find out why people are so inaccurate in their eyewitness accounts and whether anything can be done about it. They discovered a number of reasons (see Figure 12-1), which we look at in this section, along with the very few techniques that can reduce eyewitness error.

Figure 12-1:
Reasons for eyewitness error based on the cognitive-processing stages from Chapter 1 (perceiving information, storing information in memory and then retrieving it).

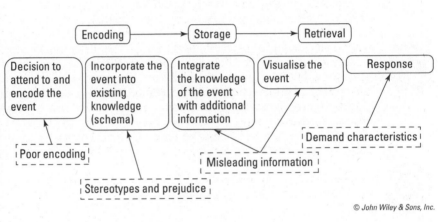

© John Wiley & Sons, Inc.

Stop! Who goes there?

Experimental studies confirm the worryingly unreliable nature of eyewitness testimony. Robert Buckhout, an Australian psychologist, has conducted many ingenious studies in this area. In 1975, he showed a video of a crime on a TV programme and then presented a line-up. He asked people to ring in with their thoughts as to the culprit's identity. Only 14.1 per cent of people got the right answer.

Buckhout followed this experience up in a more realistic manner. He staged a robbery at the start of one of his classes. The culprit ran off. The next week, he presented his students with a line-up of potential suspects. He found that accuracy was slightly better, at 40 per cent. However, 40 per cent chose someone who was in the room, but not the perpetrator, and 20 per cent chose someone random.

Making eyewitness errors

Here we review some of the main theories behind why so many people are wrong in eyewitness scenarios. Also, Chapters 8 to 11 describe a number of theories on memory that you may want to consider in relation to eyewitness mistakes.

Using schemas

In Chapter 10, we describe how people use their stored knowledge (in the form of *schemas*) to interpret and understand events. This is especially true in eyewitness research. When people are presented with ambiguous information, they interpret it within their schema.

In 2003, Australian psychologists Michelle Tucker and Neil Brewer showed a group of participants a simulated video of a bank robbery. The participants remembered things that are consistent with the 'script' of a bank robbery (such as the perpetrators wearing balaclavas) more accurately than things that aren't. Furthermore, ambiguous information was interpreted as being part of the schema: for example, even though the gender of the robbers was obscured, the participants referred to them as men.

Transferring identities

Australian psychologist Donald Thompson reported the case of a particularly unpleasant attack on a woman in 1988. The woman identified Thompson as the person who'd attacked her. She was very confident in this identification. But Thompson was taking part in a live television debate at the time of the attack with the chief of police. He wasn't the attacker.

The victim believed that he was her attacker because, apparently, the TV had been on during the attack and she'd unconsciously transferred the identity of the attacker onto someone else.

This process of *unconscious transference* may be a defence mechanism that protects people by allowing them to separate their consciousness from the event during an attack.

Misinforming witnesses

Participants' own knowledge can interfere with their memories for events, but so can the way the information is presented to them. Even changing a single word in questioning can make a person 'remember' seeing something that wasn't there. This observation is especially important, because after witnessing a crime, people are questioned about it. They also repeat what they 'saw' to several people and probably end up seeing reports about it on TV as well.

Elizabeth Loftus, an American psychologist, has conducted a number of studies on this *misinformation effect*: where information presented to witnesses after the event alters their memory of it. One of the classic studies involved researchers showing participants a video of a car crash. Loftus asked two groups of participants the same question in a slightly different way:

✔ One group was asked: 'How fast were the cars going when they smashed into each other?'

✔ The other group was asked: 'How fast were the cars going when they hit each other?'

Participants reported that the cars were going 7 miles per hour faster when the verb 'smashed' was used than when 'hit' was used.

A week later, the same participants were asked whether they saw any broken glass (none was present). Thirty-two per cent of participants who'd heard the word 'smashed' reported seeing broken glass compared to 14 per cent who'd seen the question with the verb 'hit'. Twelve per cent of participants (who were asked nothing) reported seeing broken glass (presumably because it was consistent with their car-crash schema).

So why does this effect occur? As we describe in Chapters 9 and 11, a process of reconsolidation occurs every time you access a memory and this makes the memory for the event flexible and changeable.

Being anxious

Something that laboratory studies often fail to replicate is the anxiety of witnessing a real crime. One of the most anxiety-inducing events that people can experience is when a weapon is used.

Psychological studies consistently show that people's eyes and attention are drawn to a weapon. Called *weapon focus*, this tendency impairs people's memory for the rest of the scene they're witnessing.

Of course, crime itself produces anxiety. To explore how anxiety makes people remember things, Tim Valentine, a British cognitive psychologist, and his colleagues conducted a fantastic study at the London Dungeon, a museum dedicated to the horrible history of London. The participants went through the Horror Labyrinth at the museum, where they encountered somebody dressed in a scary costume. At the end of their visit, the participants' stress levels were measured, as was their recognition for the person they saw. The more-anxious participants were less accurate at identifying the person.

Identifying criminals

One of the most important things an eyewitness can do is attempt to identify the perpetrator of a crime. Yet people aren't very good at it.

In the studies we describe here, the chances of participants recognising people have been made higher by matching the age and ethnicity of the witness to the suspect – something that doesn't happen often in the real world. Research shows (see Chapter 6) that people are much less accurate at recognising the faces of other ages and ethnicities.

Matching faces to photographs

People need to match faces to photographs at identity checkpoints, such as passport control. This activity should be straightforward: after all, you have a picture and a person standing before you. But in fact it's a difficult task to achieve. People are very bad at spotting that the person standing before them doesn't match the card they're holding, despite being careful and vigilant.

British psychologists Graham Pike, Richard Kemp and Nicky Towell conducted a study in a large supermarket. They sent participants into the store to buy products using credit cards bearing photographs. The checkout staff members were aware of the study and questioned users of photographic credits more than they normally would. Four different types of card were used:

- **Type 1:** Card with the correct identity, with a recent photograph
- **Type 2:** Card with the correct identity, with an old photograph
- **Type 3:** Card with a different, but similar-looking, person
- **Type 4:** Card with a different and not similar-looking person

The study found that the type 1 cards (with the correct person with a recent photo) were rejected 7 per cent of the time – probably because the checkout staff were trying to be very vigilant. They rejected the correct person with the old photo (type 2 card) 14 per cent of the time, which means that sometimes the staff couldn't tell that a photograph more than six months old matched the person standing before them.

Slightly worse for advocates of identity cards is that staff matched the wrong similar person (type 3 card) 50 per cent of the time and the wrong, dissimilar person (type 4 card) 34 per cent of the time. Oops barely covers it! The fact is that people were very bad at spotting that the person standing before them didn't match the card they were holding, despite being careful and vigilant.

Creating Photofits

Witnesses are often asked to construct E-fits (formerly Photofits) of the suspect despite the fact that, repeatedly, psychological studies show that people aren't very good at constructing them.

British psychologist Hadyn Ellis and colleagues asked participants to create Photofits using the full police guidelines. They then showed the constructed Photofits to other people to see whether they were able to identify them. Accuracy in Photofit identification ranges from around 4 per cent (in Ellis's study) to 12.5 per cent (in more recent work). When the Photofits are of familiar people, accuracy increases to 25 per cent.

These low figures are likely to be because people recognise faces as a whole rather than as lots of broken-up features (check out Chapter 6 for more). Unfortunately, most systems the police use to produce facial composites (such as Photofit and E-fit) require building faces from a set of separate features.

Improving eyewitness testimony

In essence, the preceding sections show that eyewitness testimony is pretty bad. So, we'd better earn our wages and make it better. Unfortunately, doing so is a bit of a problem, and cognitive psychologists haven't progressed as far as they would've liked.

Here we present two aspects where psychologists have improved eyewitness memory: line-up presentation and the cognitive interview.

Choosing better line-ups

In a line-up, the police present a witness with a series of faces and ask them to choose the perpetrator. The police use many different forms of line-ups, and they can be face-to-face, via video line-up or going through a photo album:

- ✔ **Simultaneous:** The faces are presented all at once with the witness taking a decision after seeing them all.

- ✔ **Sequential:** The faces are presented in turn and the witness decides after each one.

- ✔ **Target-present:** The faces include the suspected perpetrator.

- ✔ **Target-absent:** The faces don't include the suspected perpetrator.

Sequential line-ups (which the UK police use as standard) are generally better than simultaneous line-ups (despite these being more common in the media!). This is mostly because when the line-ups don't contain the target, witnesses choose someone wrongfully 32 per cent of the time in sequential line-ups compared to 54 per cent of the time in simultaneous line-ups. Therefore, if you're ever in a line-up and you're innocent, you'd prefer that the line-up is sequential!

Nevertheless, when the target is present in a line-up, witnesses choose that person 52 per cent of the time from simultaneous line-ups compared to 44 per cent of the time from sequential ones. So, if you're in a line-up and you're guilty, you'd prefer a sequential line-up (to increase your chances of getting off).

On balance, sequential line-ups are better, because although more correct selections are made with simultaneous line-ups (by 8 per cent), wrongful selection of an innocent person occurs 22 per cent less often than with simultaneous line-ups.

Another crucial aspect of line-ups is the instructions given. Research shows that if the person running the line-up knows who the suspect is, the witness is more likely to choose that person. The line-up organiser unconsciously (you hope) gives off subtle cues to indicate the suspect.

Interviewing cognitively

One way to improve eyewitness testimony is to try and extract the best information, such as with the *Enhanced Cognitive Interview* (ECI). This requires the interviewer to ensure that the witness adheres to five rules:

- Imagining mentally the environment in which the crime took place
- Encouraging the witness to report every tiny detail he can (even irrelevant ones)
- Describing the event in different orders
- Describing the event from different viewpoints (imagining viewing it from different angles)
- Creating a rapport between the interviewer and witness

This approach aids recall: people report more information than with normal questioning, although researchers do see a small increase in recall of incorrect information compared to a standard interview. The ECI also doesn't prevent the effect of misleading information being added during questioning.

The police tend to use the first two rules more than the others in order to save time. In fact, only the first rule of the ECI is absolutely vital for improving a witness's recall.

The ECI probably assists witness recall because the mental reinstatement gets the witness to think of the context and all the possible cues that relate to the memory. This is based on the cue-dependent retrieval we describe in Chapter 9 and cue-dependent forgetting from – oh, where is it? Oh yes – Chapter 11.

Part IV
Communicating What Your Brain Thinks about Language

Check out www.dummies.com/cheatsheet/cognitivepsychology for a quick, handy guide to the core cognitive psychology ideas.

In this part . . .

- ✔ Think about whether language is a unique ability to humans.

- ✔ Look at the structure of language, from the smallest to the largest parts.

- ✔ Consider some of the problems that your brain has decoding language in all its subtle forms.

- ✔ Ask yourself whether language influences the way you think and whether the language you speak changes what you perceive.

Chapter 13

Communicating the Extraordinary Nature of Language

L anguage was one of the first areas that cognitive psychologists studied, and it's still one of the most important. Here's why:

✔ Language cuts across all areas of study, gathering in perception and attention, long- and short-term memory, thinking and decision-making.

✔ Language was an area in which cognitive psychology could prove itself against rival approaches. Behaviourists had tried to explain language as they would any other behaviour, using learned associations between observable events. But cognitive psychologists demonstrated that, perhaps more than any other human behaviour, people can understand language only in terms of the mental machinery that makes it possible.

✔ Language is an extremely intricate mechanism. Cognitive psychologists like to understand how things work inside the human brain and language gives them something to sink their teeth into.

Some cognitive psychologists see language as being unique to humans. In this chapter, we discuss whether language is indeed what sets humans apart from other animals, covering what makes human language so unusual and how people learn it under normal and extreme circumstances.

Monkey Business: Looking at Language in the Animal Kingdom

People often see language as the one thing that makes humans special – gather round and stare at the amazing talking ape! But humans seem to distinguish themselves from other species in many ways (for example, by having an awareness of their own mortality and appreciating beauty in art). Therefore, you may ask whether humans are special because they have language or whether they have language because they're special.

One important question to consider is whether language is specific to humans or whether other species have similar abilities too. In this section, we look at different animal communication systems, not only to understand language in all its forms, but also to get a better idea of what makes human language special. We investigate the languages animals use to communicate, describe how people recognise unfamiliar languages and explore teaching language to other species.

Investigating how animals communicate

Many people argue that other animals are clearly capable of communicating with one another and so nothing's special about language.

Cognitive psychologists don't dispute the fact that animals are capable of communication, but they do make a distinction between different forms of communication, the relative complexity involved and the kinds of messages that can be transmitted.

Here, we consider three examples of the huge variety of communication systems in the animal kingdom and try to get a picture of perhaps why they aren't as powerful as human language. We show that bees and vervet monkeys produce meaning without much variety and that birds produce variety without much meaning. Only humans seem to communicate in a way that has both variety and meaning.

Through human language, people can communicate any meaning. For example, someone can translate this book into any human language (such as Italian, Mandarin Chinese or American Sign Language) without losing any of the main ideas. But, as far as we know, it can't be translated into any of the known animal communications systems – they just don't have the ability to convey new concepts.

Calling all monkeys

Vervet monkeys have several distinct calls to warn other members of the group of the presence of predators – they use different calls for different predators. So when vervets see a snake, they make a specific call that causes the other monkeys to climb into trees. But if they see an eagle, they make a different noise that causes the others to shield themselves from aerial attack.

Vervet calls were one of the first examples of a non-human vocal language to be discerned and created quite a stir in the scientific community – here was evidence of another species using what appeared to be a language. But, despite extensive studies of vervets, little evidence has been found that vervets are capable of going beyond a simple repertoire of alarm calls.

Singing to the birds

Many species of bird appear to produce an almost endlessly varied repertoire of songs, which seem much more varied than the vervet's simple set of calls.

In the countryside you can hear a variety of birds making recognisable vocalisations, which differ remarkably in their complexity. At one extreme is the cuckoo's simple and repetitive call – so simple that clockmakers imitated the sound in cuckoo clocks hundreds of years ago with fairly simple mechanisms. At the other extreme is the blackbird, which seems to produce a constantly varying and interesting stream of short melodies. You'd struggle to find any repetition or obvious pattern in its song, almost as though it's being judged on its originality or creativity – which may well be the case.

To the cognitive psychologist, the cuckoo call suggests a simple underlying cognitive process, but the variety in the blackbird's song suggests that something more interesting is going on in its bird brain.

Despite the apparent variety of some birdsong, scientists aren't sure that the different songs have different meanings in the same way that the vervet monkeys' calls do. Although the birds produce a lot of variety, they don't seem to be communicating different meanings. Scientists may be wrong, but to the best of their knowledge only two main messages are communicated by birdsong: 'I'm fit so don't mess with me' and 'I'm attractive so reproduce with me'. Perhaps complexity and variety enhance the power of these messages, but they don't seem to transmit different meanings as human language does.

Dancing with the bees

Research has unearthed a less familiar form of communication, which bees use to communicate the location of food sources to other members of a beehive. (The 'language' of bees is well understood because of some clever experiments by Austrian ethologist Karl von Frisch.)

Bees communicate through a special 'dance', which they perform on the vertical wall of the hive. They repeat a series of figure-of-eight movements, waggling their abdomens at different speeds. The angle, speeds and waggles of this dance communicate the direction and distance to food sources, and the other bees follow these instructions.

The precise details of a bee's dance can vary considerably and signal many subtle distinctions in direction and distance, but the language is restricted to a specific set of information. In a sense, it's more like filling in a form with certain standard pieces of information rather than producing sentences.

The bee dance seems very clever but only communicates the direction and distance of food. Bees can only answer one question – 'Where's the food?' They don't seem to be able to make small talk or gossip (but we leave you to decide whether that makes them inferior to humans or not!).

Recognising other languages (in sea and space)

You may object to the main point of the preceding section – that animal communication lacks the power of human language to express novel ideas. How do psychologists know that this point is correct? The short answer is, they don't.

A majority of people who study language and animal communication hold the view that human language is special. But others disagree, and argue that humans can't rule out the intelligence of a system that they don't understand.

Aliens and dolphins

This debate raises the question of how humans can recognise an intelligent communication from an unknown source. Interestingly, people studying earth-bound communication, such as from whales and dolphins, and those interested in detecting potential signals from aliens (such as The Search for Extra-Terrestrial Intelligence [SETI] Institute [www.seti.org], which scans space for radio signals and analyses them for signs of intelligence), face the same problem: how do people know when a signal is intelligent? What are the hallmarks of language?

In *So Long, and Thanks for All the Fish*, science-fiction author Douglas Adams presents dolphins as the true intelligent species on Earth. This idea has been played with for a long time: the inspirational cosmologist Carl Sagan said, 'It is of interest to note that while some dolphins are reported to have learned English – up to 50 words used in correct context – no human being has been reported to have learned dolphinese'.

Patterns in human language

If humans can't be sure whether other species aren't communicating in languages as sophisticated as their own, how can they expect to recognise intelligent communication? What should they be looking for – whether in animals or extra-terrestrials?

Well, some interesting patterns exist in human language. In the 1930s, George Zipf noticed that if people take a large sample of text and count how often different words occur in it, and then rank the words from most frequent to least frequent and draw a graph of the frequencies, they get a graph with a distinctive curve (like the one in Figure 13-1).

Figure 13-1: The Zipf curve. This graph is based on a set of English works of literature but you'd expect to get a very similar pattern for any reasonably large sample of English words.

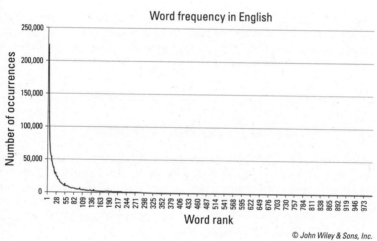

Word frequency in English

© John Wiley & Sons, Inc.

This shape is an example of something called a *power law* (a relationship between two variables where as one variable increases, the other changes by the amount to a certain power). Such patterns occur in many natural phenomena, but seeing it in language is interesting. The curve may suggest that people analysing signals from outer space or from other species need to look for distinctive statistical patterns in language.

Unfortunately, because many other natural phenomena follow this pattern, spotting a signal that exhibits this pattern doesn't mean that it's intelligent. Also, just because something doesn't follow this pattern, it doesn't mean that it's not an intelligent signal.

The patterns in language occur because of repetition – in every language, a small number of sounds occur very frequently and a large number of sounds occur very infrequently. English speakers spend a lot of time saying the word 'the' but relatively little time saying 'pterodactyl'!

In modern communication systems such as third-generation mobile phones, engineers put a lot of effort into removing this repetition to pack more information into a signal. The result is signals with no obvious patterns. So perhaps any sufficiently advanced signal would be indistinguishable from background noise – unless humans knew the code.

Another way of looking at this problem is this: how can humans devise a way of communicating with other species? This problem faces scientists who are interested in sending signals to other potential alien civilisations (see the nearby sidebar 'The Arecibo message') and people trying to teach animals to use language (check out the following section).

You may want to think about to what extent someone or something has to be human to understand, or learn, a human language. Is it just a question of being sufficiently intelligent, or do humans have a specific brain make-up that means that only they can use human language?

The Arecibo message

Scientists devised the *Arecibo message* to beam out towards nearby stars in the hope that, if aliens are listening out for intelligent life in the universe, they'd recognise the message as the unmistakeable sign of intelligence. The designers had to think about what kinds of meaning would make sense to a completely alien way of thinking, thousands of light years away in space and thousands of years away in time.

They settled on a number of concepts from mathematics, physics, biology and astronomy, which they considered may have some universal meaning. For example, prime numbers are prime numbers whatever language you speak, and the basic elements are the same and have the same atomic number throughout the universe, and so these concepts may be likely to be understood. The following illustration shows a visual representation of the Arecibo message that was transmitted as a series of binary pulses of radio waves. From top to bottom, the

Arecibo message shows the first ten numbers, the atomic numbers of three common elements, information on DNA, a figure of a human, an image of the solar system and an image of the Arecibo radio telescope.

© John Wiley & Sons, Inc.

Humans may never know whether the designers of the Arecibo message were successful.

Teaching language to other species

Some researchers believe that humans aren't special, but that language is: in other words, human culture invented language, and it enabled people to make massive advances. According to this view, the main difference between humans and apes is that humans have a more advanced culture. If humans can teach apes their special language skills, apes should then be able to demonstrate intelligence too. Starting in the 1960s, a number of researchers set out to train different species to communicate using human languages, or at least something akin to human languages.

One example project started in 1970 by Herbert Terrace tried to teach language to a chimpanzee called Nim Chimpsky (a play on the name of famous linguist Noam Chomsky). As with similar projects, Nim was raised in a context intended to be as similar as possible to a human child, though because chimpanzees lack human vocal capabilities, Nim was taught American Sign Language.

Although Nim learned to produce some interesting sentences, the complexity of his language never reached that achieved by a typical 4-year-old human child. As with other attempts to teach languages to other species, the linguistic achievement seemed to plateau at a stage equivalent to a young child and never went beyond it.

Also, questions remain about the creativity of the language displayed by such animals. For example, if a chimp combines the signs for 'water' and 'bird' when she sees a duck in a lake, is this a genuine sign of linguistic creativity (creating the phrase 'water bird') or just lucky coincidence (producing separate signs for 'water' and 'bird' in succession but not in a genuinely creative way)?

In more recent years, researchers have taught various forms of language to other species, including dolphins and grey parrots, with some degree of success. Other species do seem to be able to go beyond the simple fixed systems displayed by vervets (see the earlier section 'Investigating how animals communicate'), but they don't seem, so far, to have achieved the complexity that human children reach by the age of about 5.

Discovering What Makes Human Language Special

In this section, we describe the features of communication and demonstrate that human language potentially uniquely employs them all. We also present a theory of language that suggests all humans have an innate ability to learn grammatical structures. We show the importance of creativity in language and potentially in all human cognition.

Getting specific on what sets human language apart: Hockett's design features

In the 1960s, American linguist Charles Hockett proposed a set of design features for human language, to try and define what, if anything, makes it special or even unique.

The following list details what he came up with. As you read through it, consider to what extent these features are exclusive to human language and to what extent they're necessary for it.

- ✔ **Vocal auditory channel:** Language uses voices and sounds and by doing so frees you to do other tasks (such as moving), but it isn't essential, as sign language demonstrates.

- ✔ **Broadcast transmission and directional reception:** When you speak to a whole surrounding group, they all perceive you as the speaker.

- ✔ **Rapid fading:** A sound dies out quickly and allows you to say something else – which is different, say, from communicating by scent.

- ✔ **Interchangeability:** Any member of the species can say anything – unlike mating displays by animals, in which only sexual animals send certain signals in order to attract a mate.

- ✔ **Complete feedback:** You're aware of exactly what you're saying.

- ✔ **Specialisation:** You use specialised organs for speech – the vocal apparatus doesn't serve other purposes.

- ✔ **Semanticity:** Speech has meaning – the sounds you make refer to things, unlike, for example, birdsong (see the earlier 'Investigating how animals communicate' section).

- ✔ **Arbitrariness:** You use sounds as symbols to refer to things – for example, no relationship exists between the word 'dog' and the animal it represents, except for people who've learned the connection.

- ✔ **Discreteness:** Words and speech sounds have separate and distinct meanings. You don't blend sounds like you blend paints: for example, 'dog' and 'fog' are very different words with a sharp distinction between them. Also, people speak one word at a time and each word is perceived as distinct and non-overlapping.

✔ **Displacement:** You can use language to refer to things that are distant in space or time (or even completely imaginary). Contrast that with pointing, which has to indicate something present.

✔ **Openness or creativity:** You have the ability to say new things. You can invent sentences that have never been said before and create new phrases or words to refer to new developments.

✔ **Tradition:** Language is passed on to new generations in a culture.

✔ **Duality of patterning:** You can combine units of sound with no meaning in themselves in different ways to produce different meaning – the letters 'g', 'o' and 'd' can spell 'dog' or 'god'.

✔ **Prevarication:** You can say things that are untrue (though of course, *For Dummies*'s readers never tell porkies!).

✔ **Reflexiveness:** Language can be used to refer to itself – such as 'I was only joking', 'Don't shoot the messenger', 'This sentence is false'.

✔ **Learnability:** Human infants learn whichever language they grow up with. Many animal communication systems are innate rather than learned.

You may think that forms of animal communication meet each of these requirements – but human communication meets them all. None of these design features are unique to human language, but (at least probably) no single animal communication system exhibits all these features.

A system of language: According to Noam Chomsky

A defining moment in the history of psychology was the publication, in 1957, of a book titled *Syntactic Structures* by a young professor of linguistics at the Massachusetts Institute of Technology, Noam Chomsky. Chomsky has since become one of the most famous, and most cited, thinkers of all time. In a nutshell, he said that human language is governed by rules that are internalised in people's minds. Although they aren't aware of these rules, whenever they produce a sentence they show evidence of using them.

So when you learn a language (especially as a child learning your native language), you don't learn a set of words or phrases or sentences but a whole system, which enables you to produce and comprehend an infinite number of different possible sentences. No one teaches you these rules – somehow you just figure them out.

Chomsky believes that this system is quite different to any other forms of animal communication. The idea is that humans have an innate language centre in their brain that contains the basic structures of language (the syntax and grammar). Animal communication, on the other hand, isn't governed by such complex grammatical structures.

Infinite creativity: Writing the world's longest sentence, and making it longer

Language is a discrete, combinatorial system – it involves definite units that people can combine in many ways (but not mix, blur or blend) to produce a huge amount of variety.

Steven Pinker points out that *The Guinness Book of World Records* has an entry for the longest sentence. But, he demonstrates, coming up with an even longer sentence is easy: you just write a sentence that includes this longest sentence, for example, 'The longest sentence is. . . .'

Some nursery rhymes use this idea, such as 'This is the house that Jack built', which begins:

> This is the house that Jack built!
>
> This is the malt that lay in the house that Jack built.
>
> This is the rat that ate the malt
>
> That lay in the house that Jack built.

It ends:

> This is the farmer sowing his corn
>
> That kept the cock that crowed in the morn
>
> That waked the priest all shaven and shorn
>
> That married the man all tattered and torn
>
> That kissed the maiden all forlorn
>
> That milked the cow with the crumpled horn
>
> That tossed the dog that worried the cat

That killed the rat that ate the malt

That lay in the house that Jack built!

The last verse is all one sentence consisting of 'This is . . .' followed by a single phrase beginning with 'the farmer . . .'.

Chomsky also argued that human languages have a feature called recursion, which makes them much more powerful than simple word-chain devices. *Recursion* allows someone to talk about a thing that contains a thing of the same type – for example, English has noun phrases such as 'the man' to refer to a specific person or thing. But you can make the phrase more complicated, such as 'the man in the room', and take it further as 'the man in the room under the stairs' or 'the man in the room under the stairs in the old house' or 'the man in the room under the stairs in the old house on the hill'.

In theory, no limit exists to how far you can go with this process – though, in practice, you're limited by memory, breath and the patience of your listener. This distinction between what you can do in theory and what you can do in practice is termed the *competence-performance* distinction.

Relating language to other human skills

Other skills may have similar mental roots to language. Humans aren't just better at using language – they can do many other things that seem to leave other species behind. For example, the same creativity that humans exhibit in language is also manifested in the arts, technology and understanding.

In 1951, the neuroscientist Karl Lashley wrote an influential paper about the problem of *serial order* (how the order of information presented affects memory). He argued that many skills have a hierarchical structure. In language, people build sentences out of phrases, phrases out of words and words out of basic sounds. Similarly, composers make songs out of verses and choruses and each of those is made of short bars of music, which are, in turn, made from individual notes. This breaking down into units of decreasing size can be applied to behaviours as diverse as dancing, playing video games or understanding historical events.

Perhaps language isn't what makes humans special; maybe it's some more general capacity for creative thought that enables them to excel at a whole variety of skills including, but not limited to, language.

'Uggh. Mama. Me Want Be Psychologist!' Developing Language Skills

Language research contains a key argument about how humans acquire language. On the one hand, some theorists believe that language is innate. This notion is based on the idea that the human brain has evolved to be able to process language. On the other hand, some researchers believe that experience is required in order to develop language and that it's learnt through behaviour modification.

The American philosopher Willard Van Orman Quine gave the example of an explorer coming upon a tribe who speak an unknown language. A tribesman points at a rabbit and says 'gavagai'. What does he mean? The explorer may assume that the word means rabbit – seems simple enough. But perhaps 'gavagai' is the name of a particular pet rabbit, or it may refer to any animal, or perhaps the concepts of 'running away', 'scared' or even 'lunch'. Language is flexible, and it allows people to express a huge variety of meanings. So how does a person who doesn't know the language ever make sense of what it all means?

In this section, we walk you through the stages of language acquisition in children and the problems they face, cover how adults learn additional languages and consider how language is learned in extreme or unusual circumstances.

Picking up language skills in childhood

Children face problems when acquiring language, and they make mistakes. One suggestion is that they have constraints on what they're able to learn. For example, young children don't like to learn two words with exactly the same meaning. They also seem to assume a certain level of generality:

- ✔ **Over-generalising:** They may think that a word has a wider meaning than it does, for example, wanting to use 'Fido' to refer to all dogs or even all mammals.

- ✔ **Under-generalising:** They may assume a narrower meaning, such as using the word 'dog' only to refer to their own pet dog and no others.

Children also show further biases in their language acquisition:

- ✔ **Whole object assumption:** A new word is likely to refer to a whole object (for example, rabbit) rather than part of it (for example, ear).

- ✔ **Taxonomic constraint:** When dealing with new words, children assume different labels for objects (for example, poodle – dog – animal). If a child already knows 'dog' and 'animal', she's likely to assume that 'poodle' is a type of dog.

- ✔ **Mutual exclusivity:** Every word has a different meaning – British-born American linguist Eve Clark calls this the *principle of contrast*. If a child already knows the word 'elephant' and someone points at an elephant and says 'trunk' the child believes that the word refers to part of the elephant, where the person is pointing.

To demonstrate the above biases, psychologists examined what happens if children hear a new word referring to an object. Researchers found that the way in which children interpret the word depends on whether they already know a name for the object. If the object is unfamiliar, they interpret the word as being a name for the whole object, but if the object is familiar they interpret the word as referring to some noticeable part of the object.

Children learn new words at a phenomenal rate – they acquire about ten words per day, on average around the ages of 3 to 4 years, which suggests that they must be keeping track of a huge amount of information.

Following the stages of language acquisition in children

Although, of course, different patterns and rates of learning exist, language acquisition seems to go through a series of stages:

1. **Babbling (6–8 months):** Babies produce a string of consonant-vowel sequences. The frequency with which certain speech sounds occur reflects the language to which they're exposed, suggesting that they're modifying speech to fit language.

2. **One-word (9–18 months):** Children begin to use single words or parts of words, often to name objects, such as 'mummy', 'milk', 'cup'.

3. **Two-word (18–24 months):** Children show the first signs of syntax or grammar as they begin to produce pairs of words in different combinations such as 'more milk', 'daddy gone'.

4. **Early multi-word (24–30 months):** Children begin to produce utterances containing three or more words, but the language is often *telegraphic* – it tends to include only the most meaningful words, and it lacks the grammatical function of words and affixes such as 'ing' and 'ed'. For example, 'me go toilet', 'mummy put shoe'.

5. **Later multi-word (30 months on):** Children begin using full grammatical sentences, although they still make errors, such as 'I goed to the shops'.

Learning languages in later life

Adults have difficulty learning languages whereas children seem to do so effortlessly, leading some psychologists to argue for a critical period for language acquisition, an idea you can interpret in two different ways:

- ✔ Humans are specifically programmed genetically to learn language in the first few years of life.

- ✔ Brain development imposes a more general limit on language acquisition ability beyond a certain age.

Noam Chomsky proposed that language develops a bit like a biological organ – it follows a genetically defined programme that unfolds in a specific way and within a specific time frame. Others believe that language development is affected by more general issues and that the difficulty in learning language in later life is because the brain is less malleable. According to this view, the building blocks of language normally occur when the brain is developing rapidly and is able to adapt and change rapidly, known as *synaptic plasticity*.

Speaking more than one language

An interesting but not unusual case is when children learn more than one language. Estimates suggest that a majority of the world's children grow up in environments in which two or more common languages exist and so bilingualism is more normal than monolingualism.

An interesting feature of children learning two languages is that initially they seem to treat it as one language – learning only one word for each object. But they seem to reach a point of sudden realisation when they begin happily to accept two words for everything.

Another interesting feature of bilingualism is a phenomenon called *code-switching*, in which a bilingual speaker switches between two languages in a single sentence. This switching isn't random but seems to follow something called the *equivalence constraint* – a switch can only occur at a point where it doesn't break the grammatical rules of either language. For example, a

French/English speaker is unlikely to say 'a car americaine' or 'une American voiture', because the phrases are wrong in both languages. But the switch 'J'ai acheté an American car' (I bought an American car) is possible because English and French share the rule that a verb is followed by its object.

Considering language development in extreme circumstances

Cognitive psychologists like to test theories using experiments that alter the conditions under which a phenomenon occurs, to see its effect. For obvious reasons (they can't take a random group of children and raise them without language for ethical reasons), they can't interfere with the process of language acquisition to see what factors matter. But throughout history some unusual, often unpleasant, events have occurred in which circumstances affected children's learning. These extreme situations can provide some insight into the extremes of the human ability to learn language.

Genie: A case of extreme neglect

Some evidence seems to back up the idea that children have a critical period in language acquisition.

Genie was a child raised under conditions of extreme neglect until the age of 13 years. After being discovered, she was given intensive help, including language tuition, but her language never progressed into the fluent style of language normally acquired by relatively young children. Although possibly evidence for a 'critical period', researchers can't be sure that Genie's problems with language acquisition weren't just down to the age she started learning or a side effect of her more general neglect. Read more about Genie in Chapter 21.

Nicaraguan sign language

Children don't just seem to learn languages; they can also create them.

In the 1980s in Nicaragua, a new centre was opened for deaf children. No sign language was available, and so the children were taught lip reading with spoken Spanish and some simple finger spelling, but with little success. However, these children did learn to communicate using a sign language they created among themselves. Linguists found it to be very rich in structure.

Pidgins and creoles

Even when learning an existing language, children are undergoing a process of guided creativity, most clearly seen in the case of pidgin and creole languages (terms used to describe two types of 'invented' language).

Seeing how children transform and improve languages

Investigating how children learn a language that's more complicated to the one they hear is a difficult task. The conditions under which pidgins were transformed into creoles are largely historical, and after a community develops a creole, it doesn't revert to the pidgin. In the modern world of global, mass communication, people are much less likely to need to develop new pidgin.

Certain situations in more recent times have been sufficiently similar to the process of creolisation, however, to enable researchers to gain insights into the process. American psychologists Jenny Singleton and Elissa Newport studied the hearing parents of deaf children who learned American Sign Language (ASL) as adults. Although highly motivated, these late-learner parents struggled to pick up the finer points of ASL grammar, though they were able to learn basic vocabulary and sentence structure. In many ways, their poor grasp of ASL resembled a pidgin version of the language. Singleton and Newport studied one deaf child, Simon, whose hearing parents were his only source of ASL. Interestingly, between the ages of 4 and 7, Simon started to add a greater fluency to his language than his parents.

One idea for how children surpass the language they hear, suggested by Singleton and Newport, is a process they call *frequency boosting* – if the parents were inconsistent in how they used a certain aspect of grammar, the child would take the most frequent pattern they used and increase her frequency. In other words, the child regularised the language. If the parents used a particular form more frequently than others, the child took the more frequent form and used it all the time.

Another process of language transformation is *grammaticalisation*, in which a form used to express a concrete meaning in a pidgin becomes used instead as a more abstract, grammatical form in the creole. Many languages, including creoles, use some form of verb of motion to express future tense. For example, in English you may say 'I'm going to Paris', in which case you're using the word 'go' to express the concrete meaning of travel. But you can also say 'I'm going to think about it', in which case you're using 'go' to express the idea that you'll be doing something in the future: no movement is necessarily involved. You can even mix the two forms of 'go' in a single sentence, as in 'I'm going to go to Paris'.

Here's a hypothetical answer to why so many languages use a form associated with travel or motion to signify the future. Many actions require people to travel to another location to perform them, and so in a natural chain of events you go somewhere and then do something. In a language that lacks future tense you may say things such as 'me go, me kill chicken' in which 'go' literally means to travel, but through a process of grammaticalisation, the child learning the language picks up a more general rule – that the word 'go' often occurs before a future event: she begins to use 'go' to signify future actions even when no travel is involved.

Numerous cases of this kind of process in language exist, but they have a similar logic – forms that are used frequently in a certain context come to express a more abstract meaning.

A *pidgin* is a language that adults create when they don't share a common language but need to communicate. Such situations occurred in the early days of international trading and also as a result of the slave trade. Usually these languages were quite rudimentary and lacked the more complex grammar of normal languages, most likely because the people creating these languages were usually late learners, and older people usually can't learn new languages to the same degree of fluency as children.

Sometimes romances developed between two people who only shared a pidgin language, and they settled down and raised children. Interestingly, the children took the pidgin language to a level beyond that of their parents, adding more grammar and increasing its richness to the point where it had most of the complexity of a full language. These enriched pidgins are known as *creoles*. A number of communities across the world speak creole today as the main language, including Tok Pisin in Papua New Guinea. The process by which children transform a pidgin into a creole is called *creolisation*.

Chapter 14

Studying the Structure of Language

• •

In This Chapter

▶ Chatting about word use

▶ Playing with sentences

▶ Telling stories

• •

Sophisticated, subtle communication is unique to people. Although many animals pass information between each other, no other species comes close to having a language system as complex as that of humans.

Language contains layers within layers of different structural levels. In this chapter, we look at these layers – from the smallest units to long stories, via words, phrases and sentences – and how people use them to build infinitely varied and complex messages to transmit information from one brain to another. We also describe some of the ingenious experimental designs that cognitive psychologists have used to investigate the ways in which people's brains process language, as well as some of these tests' intriguing findings.

Psychologists still have much to discover about how the brain processes language, but cognitive psychology reveals many surprising findings about these normally hidden mechanisms. Perhaps the most exciting discovery is just how much goes on in your brain in your everyday use of language.

Staring at the Smallest Language Units

Cognitive psychologists have been active in studying all the structural levels of language – how people piece together a sequence of processes that unfold as they listen to or read language.

Here are the two smallest parts of language:

- **Phoneme:** The smallest unit of speech sound that can change the meaning of a word. For example, 'cat' and 'bat' differ only in their first phoneme, 'bat' and 'bet' differ in their middle phoneme and 'bat' and 'bag' differ in their final phoneme. Although in these examples each word had three letters and three phonemes, you don't always get such a nice, neat correspondence between letters and phonemes: for example, 'be' and 'bee' have two phonemes.

- **Morpheme:** The smallest part of a word that has a separate or distinct meaning. For example, 'unbelievable' contains three morphemes: 'un-', 'believe' and '-able'. 'Dog' and 'elephant' are each a single morpheme, but 'elephants' is two morphemes: 'elephant' and '-s'.

The basic letters or phonemes combine to produce morphemes, which combine to make words, which combine to make phrases, which combine to make sentences, which combine to make stories. At each level, complex and specific processes take place below conscious awareness.

Working with Words

Words seem to have a life of their own – they come in and out of fashion and change their meanings over time. These changes can be historical, but other changes occur as new words enter the language and others undergo changes in their use. Sometimes a word's history can reveal something about how words interact with brains and the processes that shape language change.

In this chapter, we explore how new words are created within a language (*morphology*) and the rules that govern this process of reinventing language. People can invent new words by applying new prefixes (bits of words at the start, signified by a '-' after them, for example, 'bi-') and suffixes (bits of words at the end, signified by a '-' before them, for example, '-ing'). Whole new words can also be created but only of certain categories.

Morphing language: Fanflippingtastic!

Morphology looks at how people build new words out of old ones. But even though people can play with language, they don't do so in a random way.

Usually, people play with language in a consistent way. A basic example of morphing language comes from adding the '-s' to words in English to make a plural. Therefore, if a new concept or thing is created (say that newfangled device replacing the typewriter: the computer), you know, without being told, that adding the '-s' to the end means more than one computer. Creating new words clearly follows rules.

In 2011, US politician Sarah Palin's emails were made publicly available. Some media reports mentioned her use of the word 'unflippingbelievable', where she inserted the mild expletive 'flipping' into the word 'unbelievable' to create a new word. Interestingly, when people do this kind of thing they always tend to agree on where the word should be inserted. So if you do feel the need to insert 'flipping' into 'fantastic', you'll tend to say 'fan-flipping-tastic' and not 'fantas-flipping-tic'.

Types of morphology

While writing this chapter, a friend used the word 'Berlusconified' (based on Italian businessman and convicted criminal Silvio Berlusconi). We hoped that it would be a completely new word. But we were disappointed: the word occurred eight times on a Google search. Even so, that's still fairly rare.

People alter words using morphology in two basic ways:

- **Inflectional morphology:** The way people modify words in certain standard ways to indicate things such as tense or number. For example, 'dog', 'dog-s'; 'cat', 'cat-s'; 'jump', 'jump-ed' or 'jump-ing'; and 'fMRI', 'fMRIing' (just to try and invent a new word for using fMRI; see Chapter 1!).

- **Derivational morphology:** When people create a new type of word, such as taking a name (Berlusconi) and creating new words: 'Berlusconic', 'Berlusconified' and 'Berlusconification'.

Although certain rules guide the morphology of words, not all words follow them. Although you can say 'jump', 'jumping', 'jumped' and 'open', 'opening', 'opened', you run into problems with 'go', 'going', '*goed' or 'run', 'running', '*runned': some words (*exception words*, highlighted with the '*') don't follow the normal rules.

Creative morphology: The Wug Test

Although grammatical rules govern how new words are created, sometimes aesthetic reasons apply as well. Children use the same rules as adults in creating new words.

In 1958, Jean Berko Gleason published the results of an experiment in which she tested children's ability to use morphology correctly. She showed them a picture of a made-up creature with a made-up name and the caption 'This is a wug'. Then she showed them a picture of two of the creatures and said 'Now there is another one. There are two of them. There are two.' She waited for them to complete the sentence. Interestingly most children correctly said 'wugs', even though they'd heard only 'wug' before.

You see this kind of creative morphology at work in the mistaken use in words such as 'shopaholic' or 'chocaholic', derived from the word 'alcoholic'. The correct morphology is just 'alcohol' plus the suffix '-ic'. But people use the last two syllables '-holic' as a suffix meaning 'addicted to'. Saying 'choca-holic' rather than 'chocolatic' seems more natural, even though the latter is more like the word 'alcohol-ic'.

Inventing and accepting new words

The linguist Ferdinand de Saussure argued that words are arbitrary symbols (except for some words in languages based on glyphs, such as ancient Egyptian and Japanese): if you didn't know the English word for 'dog', you wouldn't be able to work it out by studying dogs. The English word 'dog' is no more or less appropriate than the word in French ('chien'), in German ('hund'), Turkish ('kopek'), Welsh ('ci') or in any other language.

If most words can't be guessed, no shortcut exists to learning the basic vocabulary of a language. But morphology and syntax (for more on syntax, check out the later 'Seeing What Sentences Can Do' section) allow you to combine those words to create a new meaning not heard before.

We draw a basic distinction between *open-* and *closed*-class words:

- ✔ **Open-class words:** Include nouns, verbs and adjectives. They're open classes because you can create new ones. For example, the invention of the fax machine brought the words 'fax', 'faxed' and 'faxing' with it. When people invent a new concept, language allows them to add new words to describe it.

- ✔ **Closed-class words:** A much smaller class that plays a functional role in language, including determiners (such as 'a', 'an', 'the'), prepositions (such as 'to', 'by', 'with'), pronouns (such as 'I', 'me', 'you') and possessive pronouns (such as 'his', 'hers', 'its').

Generally, you can't simply add to closed-class words at will. For example, people have made various attempts to introduce gender-neutral possessive pronouns into English to help avoid gender bias – proposing invented alternatives, such as 'Ey' 'Hu' and 'Peh', instead of 'he' and 'she'. These attempts largely failed, not necessarily for political reasons, but because of the way language works. Pronouns are function morphemes (see the next list) that people process automatically. Each language only has a small set of such words and people can't easily add to them.

Just as closed and open-classed words exist, so do the following:

- ✔ **Function or closed-class morphemes:** Tend to be small, frequently occurring words or parts of words, which carry the grammatical structure of a language. These parts of language are typically limited to a few members of each class, and you can't easily add to them.

- ✔ **Lexical or open-class morphemes:** The meaningful content-laden words of the language; you can easily add new members to these categories. For example, people can create new nouns or verbs such as 'Google' or 'Thatcherism' (shiver!), but they can't easily add new members to the closed classes, such as prepositions or determiners.

Reading the long and the short of it

George Zipf demonstrated that in many languages, more frequently used words tend to be shorter than less frequent words (perhaps unsurprisingly as people have to use them so much). If you look at a word-frequency list for English you find some interesting patterns. Some words occur an awful lot – 'the' accounts for about 7 per cent of all word occurrences in a typical English text – and the top 100 words in a language account for nearly 50 per cent of all word occurrences.

Really long words are often created, or at least used, for their own sake. *Pneumonoultramicroscopicsilicovolcanoconiosis* (apparently a type of lung disease) is often cited as the longest word in English, but this is arguable on two levels: no one uses it and people can easily create a longer word. In fact, they have: apparently a much-disputed chemical name for the protein 'titin' is more than 189,000 letters (and so not much used on Twitter!).

Creativity in language works at multiple levels. For instance, the song-writing Sherman brothers invented the word 'Supercalifragilisticexpialidocious'. But it follows the same rules as any English word and you can tell it's English rather than, say, German or Italian.

All words would probably be short if people could get away with it (you see people abbreving[!] all the time). But only enough room exists for a few distinct short words.

Seeing What Sentences Can Do

Historical change, of the sort we discuss in the preceding section on words, allows psychologists to see how language changes 'in the wild' and can help them to understand the more immediate effects that they observe in the lab. One process is *grammaticalisation*. This is where words for objects and actions (that is, nouns and verbs) become grammatical markers (affixes, prepositions and so on): for example, 'let us' meaning 'allow us' has changed to 'let's' and lost its meaning.

Some psychologists devote their whole lives to studying the inner lives of sentences – how people produce and understand them.

To investigate sentences, you need to appreciate the key distinction between syntax and semantics:

- ✔ **Syntax:** How words are combined to make phrases and sentences.
- ✔ **Semantics:** What the resulting sentences mean.

Whenever you try to communicate with people you need to understand the sentences that they use and develop your own. This complex process develops from understanding grammar. Sentence structure relates to the structure of cognition and thought (see Chapter 16), and so cognitive psychologists have to understand sentence structure. In this section, we look at how context helps resolve ambiguities in sentences and how grammatical knowledge helps people understand novel sentences.

Looking at sentence ambiguity

All sorts of ambiguities occur at the sentence level, but people rarely notice them because the context makes it clear which interpretation is correct. People rarely notice alternative interpretations unless they're pointed out – which is exactly what we do in this section!

Communicating with all sorts of methods

Language can be expressed through many media, including text, speech and sign language. Commonly, across all these media, language has the same underlying abstract structure. So although sign language may seem very different to spoken language, it nevertheless has the same basic elements as spoken language.

Babies can learn sign language just as readily and fluently as a spoken language, suggesting that the underlying brain processes aren't tied to spoken language at all, but can handle the meaning and symbols of language at a more abstract or fundamental level.

Hammering away at syntactic ambiguity

Parsing a sentence involves grouping words together according to the syntactic rules of the language. But sometimes you can apply the rules to a single sentence in multiple ways and create ambiguous interpretations.

Consider the following two short passages:

> I was attacked by two men, one of them was carrying a hammer. I hit the man with the hammer.

> I was carrying a hammer when I was attacked by two men. I hit the man with the hammer.

In the first example, the sentence 'I hit the man with the hammer' means that I hit the man who was holding the hammer, whereas in the second example it means that I used the hammer to hit the man. This distinction shows that, on its own, the sentence is ambiguous and can have two different interpretations. Figure 14-1 shows the two different ways of packaging the words in the sentence and the two different associated meanings that people can take from the sentence. These two different interpretations are called *parses* of the sentence.

The two passages show what's called *prepositional phrase attachment ambiguity*: as the brain's sentence processor builds up a phrase structure representation of the sentence, the prepositional phrase 'with the hammer' can be attached either to the verb 'hit' or to the noun phrase 'the man'. When you're reading the passages, your mental grammar allows either option, but they lead to quite different meanings. The word 'hammer' means the same in both interpretations, but how it relates to the other parts of the sentence is different – an example of *syntactic ambiguity*.

Banking on semantic understanding

In the preceding section, the two sentences in each example have different syntax, but the meaning of the word 'hammer' is the same in both cases. In the next example, the two sentences have the same syntax but the semantic interpretation of the word 'bank' is different in each case.

> I was walking near the river when I saw a man in the water who appeared to be drowning. I hurried to the bank.

> I was walking down the street when I was attacked and my credit card was stolen. I hurried to the bank.

In these two example cases, the second sentence is ambiguous, despite having the same syntax (you're hurrying to the bank). But 'bank' is ambiguous: it can mean the side of a river or a financial institution. Yet when you encounter the word in a particular context, as here, you tend to have little problem determining the intended meaning.

Figure 14-1:
Two differ-
ent parses
of the same
sentence,
showing
how words
are com-
bined
together
into differ-
ent types of
phrase. In a)
the verb 'hit'
is followed
by a single
noun phrase
'the man
with the
hammer',
whereas in
b) the verb
'hit' is fol-
lowed by
two
phrases –
the object
'the man'
and the
instrumental
'with the
hammer'.

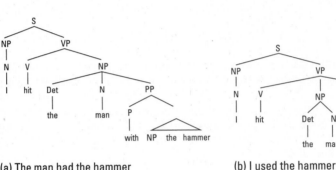

(a) The man had the hammer

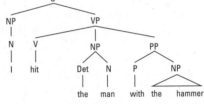

(b) I used the hammer

© John Wiley & Sons, Inc.

Occasionally, the wrong meaning is conveyed in sentence ambiguity, causing confusion or humour (such as the newspaper headline 'Man sentenced to life in Scotland') or Groucho Marx's line: 'One morning I shot an elephant in my pyjamas. How he got into my pyjamas I'll never know.' The humour arises when listeners use the interpretation in Figure 14-2(a), which means that 'the elephant was in my pyjamas'.

Figure 14-2:
The cognitive psychological explanation of Groucho Marx's joke. Interpretation a) corresponds to the funny meaning, because the phrase 'in my pyjamas' is attached to the phrase 'the elephant' and so the elephant is in my pyjamas. Interpretation b) is the intended non-humourous meaning that 'I was in my pyjamas when I shot the elephant'.

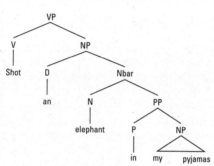

(a) The elephant was in my pyjamas

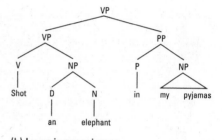

(b) I was in my pyjamas

Writing grammatical rubbish!

Sometimes a sentence can be grammatical (it has correct syntax) and yet meaningless. Even so, people can use their knowledge of syntax creatively to make 'sense' of such sentences that they've never heard before. They can do so because knowledge of language isn't simply words, phrases or sentences, but also abstract rules and categories.

A famous example is American linguist Noam Chomsky's 'Colourless green ideas sleep furiously'. Chomsky deliberately chose words that would rarely follow one another in normal language – such as 'colourless green' or 'sleep furiously'. He wanted a grammatical *and* meaningless sentence that people would probably never have heard before to argue his idea that the brain handles grammar (syntax) independently from meaning (semantics).

He also used this sentence to demonstrate the problem with behaviourist accounts of language (refer to Chapter 1). Behaviourists such as BF Skinner believed that people were able to learn language through association – for example, certain words would follow other words in chains of associations. Chomsky designed this sentence so that it has no such associations, and yet people read it with normal English intonation, pausing between the subject phrase ('Colourless green ideas') and the verb phrase ('sleep furiously').

The behaviourist account struggles to explain how people can use language creatively while still following the rules. Chomsky argued that they can handle these tasks only because they're equipped with the necessary cognitive machinery to do so.

To demonstrate, read the following two sentences and ask a friend to do the same. As you read them, ask yourself two questions: Had you heard either of the sentences before you read this book? Which one sounds more natural?

> Colourless green ideas sleep furiously.

> Furiously sleep ideas green colourless.

If, like most people, you read the second 'sentence' as a simple list of words in a flat monotone, it's because it doesn't fit the rules of grammar.

Talking nonsense

Psychologists have used nonsense poems and sentences to show how the brain processes language, as well as that humans can read such nonsense when it complies with appropriate grammatical rules. Nonsense phrases also help psychologists re-create how children may learn languages.

The author Lewis Carroll played many word games with language, creating nonsense poetry. The most famous example is 'Jabberwocky', which appears in *Through the Looking Glass*. The poem begins:

> 'Twas brillig and the slithy toves

> Did gyre and gimble in the wabe:

> All mimsy were the borogroves,

> and the mome raths outgrabe.

Carroll uses English *morpho-syntax* (written symbols represent syllables corresponding to the meaningful units). The little functional words ('the', 'and', 'in' and so on) are intact, as are the word endings (such as '-y', '-s'), but he creates new *lexical* (words in the mental dictionary) items (such as 'tove').

TIP

By making up words, Carroll re-creates the experience that children have when they encounter a word for the first time. Just as a child can work out that the plural of the made-up word 'wug' is 'wugs' (refer to the earlier section 'Creative morphology: The Wug Test'), readers of this poem can work out that 'toves' is the plural of 'tove'.

Pause for thought

Israeli psychologists Asher Koriat and colleagues Seth Greenberg and Hamural Kreiner performed studies that build on the ideas raised by nonsense language. They recorded people reading different types of sentences and analysed the intonation by measuring the length of pauses between words when speaking the sentences.

They used two types of sentence – meaningful and nonsense – and presented each type in a grammatical or a *telegraphic* form (where all the small function words and morphemes were removed). Here are four examples (including pauses):

- ✔ **Meaningful with syntax:** 'The fat cat [pause] with the grey stripes [pause] ran [pause] quickly [pause] to the little kitten [pause] that lost [pause] its way [pause] in the noisy street'.

- ✔ **Meaningful without syntax:** 'Fat cat [pause] grey stripe [pause] run [pause] quick [pause] little kitten [pause] lose [pause] way [pause] noise street'.

- ✔ **Nonsense with syntax:** 'The sad gate [pause] with the small electricity [pause] went [pause] carefully [pause] to the happy computer [pause] that sang [pause] the leaves [pause] in the front book'.

- ✔ **Nonsense without syntax:** 'Sad gate [pause] small electricity [pause] go [pause] careful [pause] happy computer [pause] sing [pause] leaf [pause] front book'.

The researchers recorded how long each person paused at each of the indicated points. What they found was intriguing.

REMEMBER

People read the syntactic sentences with normal intonation, whether they're meaningful or nonsense, whereas when the morpho-syntax was missing, their intonation became flat and unnatural. This finding suggests that fluent reading with natural intonation relies more on the syntax of what you're reading than the semantics: structure is more important than meaning.

Take notice

Count the number of times the letter 'f' occurs in the passage in Figure 14-3.

Figure 14-3:
A demonstration of how people focus on meaning rather than content.

Finished files are the result of years of scientific study combined with the experience of many years

© *John Wiley & Sons, Inc.*

If you counted 3, you agree with the majority of participants. You're also wrong. Congratulations if you said 6 – you're right. Most people miss the 'f's in the word 'of'. Before reading on, can you think why this may be the case?

We suggest two reasons why many people miss the 'f' in 'of':

✔ **It's pronounced more like a 'v' than an 'f':** So if you're relying on the sounds to decode the meaning, you may miss these non-standard pronunciations.

✔ **'Of' is a short, closed-class function word (refer to the earlier section 'Inventing and accepting new words'):** Although these functional elements are important for structuring language and for fluent reading, you don't pay much conscious attention to them.

As we describe in Chapter 15, reading involves fixations and leaps. Figure 14-4, for example, shows the eye movements recorded while a person is reading. As you see, the eyes jump over short, frequent and predictable words.

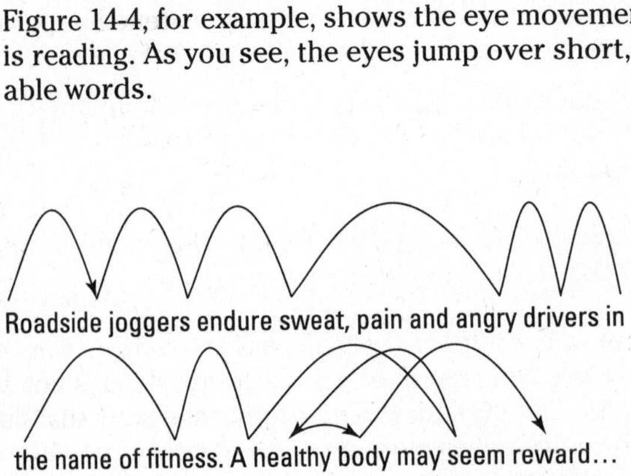

Figure 14-4:
A demonstration of how the eyes move when reading a sentence.

Roadside joggers endure sweat, pain and angry drivers in

the name of fitness. A healthy body may seem reward...

© *John Wiley & Sons, Inc.*

Interestingly, the developmental psychologist Annette Karmiloff-Smith asked young children to count the number of words in various sentences and found that they often omit these function words from their counts.

Building Stories that Mean Something

The infinite creativity we discuss in the preceding section (that allows people to produce and understand new or nonsense sentences) is central to language: people don't learn language by learning a set of sentences; they learn the rules to produce their own sentences.

Cognitive psychologists are interested in how people make sense of all this novelty – such as how they come to the right understanding of a narrative they've never heard before.

Morton Ann Gernsbacher proposed the *Structure Building Framework*, a theory of how people build a representation of the meaning of a story as it unfolds. Gernsbacher describes three sub-processes in structure building:

- ✔ **Laying a foundation:** People pay more attention to the start of a story, because it's used to 'lay a foundation' for the structure. *The advantage of first mention* refers to the fact that information mentioned at the start of a story is easier to access.

- ✔ **Mapping:** This process links new information onto the developing mental representation.

- ✔ **Shifting:** This process affects the accessibility of information. When new information can't be linked onto the existing chunk of understood text, this process shifts it into a new chunk. For example, when you cross a *constituent boundary*, such as a new phrase, sentence or paragraph, shifting involves shifting to a new chunk when new information doesn't fit the existing chunk. Information from the previous chunk becomes less accessible – you can still remember the gist but not the exact form – for example, the exact wording of a sentence.

Two mechanisms aid in these processes:

- ✔ **Enhancement:** Strengthens relevant meanings, so that accessing them is easier when you have an idea of what a story is about.

- ✔ **Suppression:** Curbs an interpretation or meaning that's not appropriate in the current context: for example, 'bug' as insect versus 'bug' as listening device in the following two sentences:

The secret agent did not like the hotel room because it was full of bugs.

The health inspector did not like the hotel room because it was full of bugs.

Recognising redundancy

One of the most important aspects about language is that it's designed to communicate. Humans have the constant need to tell each other everything, down to talking about the weather, what they watched on TV last night and who's dating whom. The most important aspect of this information transfer is that it's efficient. The brain is able to interpret incoming information in relation to the context and fill in the gaps. This allows for some redundancy in language.

Do you remember those adverts that used to appear for short-hand typing courses, such as 'Cn u Rd ths Title?' They illustrate that language contains a lot of *redundancy*: the brain can remove parts of a message without stopping the meaning of the message from being conveyed. Contrast this with using numbers on a takeaway menu – change one digit and you get a different meal.

American information theorist Claude Shannon developed a guessing game for demonstrating the redundancy of English text. You can play this with a friend.

Select a passage of text from a newspaper or book and then replace it with a series of blanks. Ask the player to guess the first letter of the text; if he gets it right, he writes it down and moves on to the next letter; if he gets it wrong, he guesses again and again until he gets it right. Keep a count of how many guesses the person needs for each letter in the text.

The following figure shows some of Shannon's results. Note that the majority of letters are guessed correctly on the first try although some take many more attempts – the R of REVERSE took 15 guesses. The players have to pick from the 26 letters of the alphabet plus the space character and so have 27 available options at each go – if they were guessing random letters, you'd expect them to take half of this number (13.5 guesses) on average per letter. But in this example, the average number of guesses was under 2 (1.84) and Shannon found that this was fairly normal for typical English text.

People need the most guesses at the beginning of new words, but within words they can often guess the correct answer first time.

```
T H E R E _ I S _ N O _ R E V E R S E _ O N _ A _ M O T O R

1 1 1 5 1 1 2 1  1 2 1 1 15 1 7 1 1 1 2 1 3 2 1 2 2 7 1 1 1


C Y C L E _

4 1 1 1 1 1
```

Cognitive psychologists found (via cross-modal priming – see Chapter 15) that when people hear an ambiguous word (such as 'bugs') it simultaneously activates both the appropriate and inappropriate interpretations of the meaning in their mental lexicon (their inner dictionary). But within a very short period of time (less than a second), the inappropriate meaning is 'shut down' or inhibited (see Chapter 8).

Chapter 15

Talking about Language Perception and Production

. . . .

In This Chapter

▶ Looking into how reading works

▶ Producing sentences correctly

▶ Understanding language problems

. . . .

People use language every day but few understand the complex structures and processes that their brains use as they produce or comprehend language. Cognitive psychologists are interested in understanding the brain processes occurring under the surface, unavailable to conscious introspection.

In this chapter, we look at the physical side of language – how people read, speak and hear language. We cover the problems that the brain has to overcome to use language, as well as some of the ways in which language production and perception can go wrong.

Cognitive neuropsychology (see Chapter 1) supports the idea that different parts of the brain handle different aspects of language. As we describe, patients with certain specific damage to the language-related areas of their brain can display surprisingly selective problems in their use of language. But although the brain may be modular in this sense, other evidence supports the idea of a complex interplay between these modules.

Decoding the Art of Reading

Learning to read is a quite different skill from learning to speak. A typically developing child learns to speak her native language without any special training, and all cultures had spoken language long before the introduction of formal education. So learning to speak seems to be a natural process.

Writing systems through history

Spoken language came first and writing systems took a long time to catch up. Over the period of recorded history, people developed various systems and different methods of recording the sounds of speech graphically.

Language is built out of units of various sizes (refer to Chapter 14) and different writing systems have tried to represent units at different levels of the language hierarchy. Languages such as English use an alphabetic system, in which visual symbols represent _phonemes_ (the smallest unit of speech sound). Some

languages, such as Hebrew, omit the vowels from the alphabet. Japanese Kana uses a syllable-based representation, hence the need for many thousands of symbols (which led to great problems in developing usable typewriters and keyboards). Other languages, such as Chinese, started with a _logographic_ system, representing words, but moved towards a _morpho-syntactic_ system, in which written symbols represent syllables corresponding to the meaningful units (called _morphemes_).

Learning to read is a different matter, however, and doesn't come as naturally as learning to speak. Historically, reading and writing developed long after humans had been speaking for many generations.

In this section, we discuss the alphabetic principle that English uses, provide insights into teaching reading, describe some fascinating experiments that show how you read in practice, and talk you through the process of the brain coming up with a word.

Reading from A to Z: Alphabetic principle

Writing systems have tended to evolve towards representing the sounds of spoken languages rather than their meanings (for some background, read[!] the nearby sidebar 'Writing systems through history').

The _alphabetic principle_ refers to the way that alphabetic writing systems map a small set of visual symbols (letters) onto a small set of sounds (_phonemes_). This system is more efficient than learning separate symbols for the much larger numbers of morphemes or syllables in a language. But alphabetic languages aren't easy to learn due to two main problems. (We talk more about phonemes and morphemes in Chapter 14.)

Abstract phonemes

The first problem is that phonemes are abstract. Although they correspond to basic speech sounds, the same phoneme can sound quite different depending on the context in which it occurs. So the child has to learn that the letter 't' corresponds to the phoneme sound /t/ (this notation is used when describing sounds), which can occur in many contexts.

Look in the mirror and watch the shape your mouth makes as you form the /t/ sound in these different words: 'tax', 'butter', 'smart', 'test'. The same /t/ phoneme corresponds to a wide range of differing mouth shapes and sounds.

In certain accents, such as those around London and Essex, UK, people often don't pronounce the /t/ sound in 'butter' at all. Instead they use what's known as a *glottal stop*: they pause and don't say anything where the /t/ sounds would occur (for example, they say something like 'buh-err').

Interestingly, the brain tends to fill in this missing sound so that it appears to be present (the *phoneme restoration effect*). This phenomenon explains how you can hear sounds even though they're missing or obscured – and so you can follow what's going on in TV's *TOWIE!* This effect is an example of *top-down processing*, where your brain uses existing knowledge to fill in gaps in your perceptual input.

Writing lags behind sounds

A second problem when learning most alphabetic languages is that fewer written vowels exist than vowel phonemes (except in Turkish). Consider how different the letter 'a' sounds in 'saw', 'cat' and 'make'. Plus, people can represent a single phoneme in several ways, using different letters or pairs of letters. For example, the /oo/ sound is a single phoneme but it appears to be quite different in the words 'moo', 'blue' and 'chew'.

English is difficult in this respect, partly because of its rich and complicated history. Written English has a *deep orthography* (that is, the spelling-sound correspondence is quite low) compared to, say, Turkish, which has a much simpler and more regular mapping between the spoken phonemes and the written letters, and thus has a *shallow orthography*. In Turkish, every letter is pronounced the same way, making it one of the shallowest orthographies.

Teaching reading

Cognitive psychologists have had a major influence on educational policy through their science-based advice in various influential reports.

Before they start learning to read, most children have already developed a reasonable level of spoken fluency and vocabulary. They acquire the basic phoneme sounds of their language in the first couple of years, but the intricacies of the system continue to develop into school. Aside from learning spoken language before written language, children also seem to find learning the spoken language much more natural. You don't need to teach children to speak in the same way that you have to teach them to read.

Reading involves two basic skills:

- **Decoding:** The ability to recognise words in their written form.
- **Comprehension:** Understanding the language and the meaning, which is the same for spoken and written language.

People should certainly be encouraged to develop their comprehension of real language, but the crucial step in learning to read is decoding.

Cognitive psychology has a lot to say about the details of learning to decode. The recommendations boil down to two main points and an interesting difference between how poor and skilled readers use context:

- **Learning to read involves learning how the written symbols represent the spoken language the child already knows.** Poor readers use the context of a story to help them decode words they may otherwise have trouble recognising.

- **The child must discover this relationship herself or be taught it explicitly.** Skilled readers can recognise words out of context and use the context for the higher-level goal of comprehending the text.

Seeing how you read

As you read this book, you may think that your eyes are moving smoothly from left to right across each line, but no: the sensation of smoothly reading a line of text is an illusion. If you watch other people's eyes as they read, you can see that they move their eyes in a series of jumps across the page: they piece together the text from a series of short instances. When you start reading, you pick a spot near the start of the first line and look at it for an instant. You then move your eyes rapidly to the right to a new spot where you pause again before jumping to a third place farther along the line.

Of course, psychologists use jargon to help describe this process!

- **Fixation:** Each instance of looking at part of the text. Fixations last for about a quarter of a second and enable you to read one or more words from a text by focusing them in your central vision, where you can perceive detail. Fixations tend to occur just to the left of the middle of words, and short words often aren't fixated at all.

✔ **Saccades:** Jumps between fixations. Saccades are much shorter (about a tenth of a second) and are fast – in a saccade you don't take in visual information. Over 10 per cent of saccades are backwards or *regressive*. Also, you need to decide where the next fixation is before you initiate the saccade, suggesting a certain amount of forward planning.

When people stare at a point in a piece of text they can see only a few letters either side of the fixation point in detail, although about 20 letters either side can be seen in a less detailed form.

We know this because of some clever experimental designs pioneered by the late cognitive psychologist, Keith Rayner.

Moving window studies

In a *moving window* study of reading, researchers alter text dynamically as a person is reading so that only letters in the immediate vicinity of the fixation point are shown normally, and letters in peripheral vision are obscured in some way (some studies blur the letters, others replace them with Xs).

For example, if a person is reading the sentence 'the quick brown fox jumped over the lazy dog' and they're fixating on the word 'fox', the sentence may be displayed as follows:

xxx xxxxx xrown fox jumpxx xxxx xxx xxxx xxx

As their eyes move, the window of visible letters moves with them. With this approach, psychologists can vary the size of the window while participants read through lots of sentences, allowing them to study how reading is affected by the changing window size. When the window is very short and only a few letters are shown, people have great difficulty reading normally; but as the window size increases, reading improves. When the window is sufficiently wide, a person's reading speed is the same as without a window.

With this approach, psychologists can estimate how many letters people take in with any one fixation while reading. The answer is about 15 letters (for adults); the average saccade jumps ahead by slightly over half that length.

Boundary studies

A *boundary study* uses eye-tracking to change what psychologists display to readers depending on where they're looking. In this case, researchers define some point in a sentence that acts as a boundary. When the reader's eye movements cross that boundary, it triggers a change in the display. For example, participants read a sentence and a key word later in the sentence changes to a different word when their eyes cross a particular boundary.

This test reveals how much information to the right of fixation affects comprehension. Results show that although readers aren't fixating on some of the words to the right, the words can influence their reading. This finding indicates some form of *parafoveal* processing: readers do process words outside the centre of vision to a certain degree. Specifically, the way words look and sound is processed before you read them, but the meaning isn't.

Looking up words in the brain

Eye-trackers and the clever experimental designs from the preceding section give cognitive psychologists a good insight into the visual processing that occurs during reading. But seeing a word is just the first step: people then have to match it against their stored memories of words, a process called *lexical access*. Psychologists can't study this process directly; instead, they infer the processes going on based on measurable quantities, such as how long a person takes to respond to a question about what she's reading.

Psychologists have found that when you hear a word that has several meanings, your brain activates all the meanings at first. But after a very short time all but the appropriate meaning are suppressed or shut down, leaving only the correct meaning active (see Chapter 14 for more).

Lexical decision task

The *lexical decision task* is used to measure a person's reaction time to different words. The participant sits at a computer and strings of letters are flashed up on the screen: the person has to press one of two buttons quickly to indicate whether the string of letters is a proper word or not. For example, if she sees 'elephant', she presses the left button to indicate 'yes'; if she sees 'ephantel', she presses the right button to indicate 'no'.

In this way, psychologists can measure differences in how long it takes to access different types of word: on average, words take longer to access if they're more unusual, and so people respond more quickly to words that tend to occur frequently in everyday language.

Usually, cognitive psychology experiments measure quite small effects that are difficult to detect, which is why psychologists don't just test something once but test it repeatedly, and measure average results.

Priming

Priming is the basic lexical decision task taken a step further. It refers to the fact that people tend to respond more quickly to a word if it's preceded by a related word. If you see the word 'doctor', you hit the 'yes' button more quickly if the preceding word is 'hospital' than if it's 'elephant'.

Priming is a well-established phenomenon, but it's hard to detect. Although people tend to respond faster to a 'primed' word, the difference is very small – maybe only 20 milliseconds. Therefore, psychologists can only reliably detect it by measuring it lots of times with lots of words and averaging the times for primed and unprimed words.

Priming is usually explained in terms of a *network model* of the brain, in which words that are related in meaning are connected: when one is activated, it sends a little wave of activation to all its relations so that they all become slightly more active (see Chapter 11).

Cross-modal priming

When you read the sentence, 'When the performance ended the audience rose to their feet and applauded', what do you think happens in your mental lexicon with the word 'rose'? In this context 'rose' is a verb meaning to stand up, but it can also mean a type of flower. So do you consider both meanings – or just the correct one for this sentence?

You can't answer this question just by thinking to yourself: the processes involved are quick and occur beneath the level of your conscious awareness.

An ingenious way of testing this issue depends on an effect called cross-modal priming. *Modal* refers to the type of presentation mode (such as whether you hear a word or see it) and so *cross-modal priming* refers to the fact that a word presented in one mode can prime a word presented in another mode. If you hear the word 'hospital', you respond more quickly to a visual presentation of the word 'doctor'.

In a cross-modal priming experiment, psychologists can study lexical access in online processing: that is, they can see how words are accessed while a person is in the middle of hearing a sentence. Here's how it works:

1. **A participant sits at a computer wearing headphones and performs a lexical decision task.** She looks at the strings of letters flashed on the screen and presses one button if the string is a word and a different button if a string is a non-word. Reaction times are measured.

2. **The psychologists play various sentences over the headphones while the person's doing this task.** She doesn't have to do anything specific with these sentences: psychologists are interested in how the words she hears affect her reaction time to the words she sees.

3. **The psychologists time the presentation of words on the screen precisely to match the words being listened to.** For example, they may present the word 'flower' on the screen 50, 100 or 200 milliseconds after the word 'rose' has been heard.

4. **The psychologists vary the time between the prime and the target.** Their aim is to see how it affects the time taken to make a lexical decision.

This cunning design makes precise measurements. Using lots of statistics, researchers have worked out what happens when people encounter an ambiguous word in a specific context. For a very short time after it's heard, the word 'rose' primes the inappropriate meaning 'flower', but the effect very quickly disappears. On the other hand, if the researchers present 'rose' in a context such as, 'For Valentine's Day I gave my sweetheart a lovely red rose', the priming of 'flower' continues for much longer.

Putting Together Coherent Sentences

People produce sentences without conscious effort, and cognitive psychologists are interested in the mechanisms involved. For example, when examining why stutterers 'get stuck' at the starts of words, most cognitive psychological models of speech production look at the mechanics rather than the emotions (even though, undoubtedly, stress and anxiety can make matters worse by imposing a greater load on the brain, which makes it harder for the speaker to attend to the task of speaking).

The Lord is a shoving leopard

A *spoonerism* is a speech error in which the speaker swaps parts of two words and produces different words that change the intended meaning, often to humorous effect. The Reverend Charles Spooner of Oxford University was notorious for making such slips of the tongue: 'The lord is a loving shepherd' became 'The lord is a shoving leopard' and 'You've wasted a whole term' became 'You've tasted a whole worm'.

Spoonerisms and related 'slips of the tongue' have played an interesting role in the cognitive psychology of speech production. Although perhaps 'slips of the brain' may be more appropriate, because the brain is the source of these mistakes.

In this section, we discuss the difficulties of researching this area and some models that have, to an extent, overcome them.

Producing a sentence

When psychologists study language perception, they typically set people tasks in which they have to identify words or sentences under various different conditions. But studying the process of language production is hard under laboratory conditions. For example, some of the most compelling evidence about the processes involved in speech production comes from the study of speech errors and these tend to occur in normal conversation when people mix up their words. Eliciting such naturalistic errors under laboratory conditions is difficult. Instead, most studies use a less-controlled diary method, where researchers simply keep a note of every speech error they encounter in their everyday life.

This kind of approach is perhaps less reliable than a lab-based study and may be prone to selective bias on the part of researchers (in what they notice or choose to record). Despite these limitations, some interesting patterns have emerged that reveal a lot about the complex sequence of processes that takes place when people produce a sentence.

Looking at models of sentence production

Merrill Garrett used a diary approach to gather speech errors. He used the patterns of observed speech errors in designing a model of speech production that attempts to account for the series of separate processes involved when people speak.

In Garrett's model, a sentence passes through the following three levels of representation before you speak:

- **Message level:** A representation of the meaning that you want to convey. If you're a bilingual speaker, this level may be the same whichever language you want to express yourself in. Bilingual speakers often switch language mid-sentence without altering the meaning of the original message.

- **Sentence level:** You take the message to express and choose the particular words and grammatical forms you want to use to express it. Two separate processes exist here: the functional and the positional levels.

- **Articulatory level:** You take your constructed sentence and work out the precise sequence of articulatory processes needed to say it. A complex mix of muscles movements is required to produce the sounds.

Slipping into a Freudian error

Sigmund Freud's writings on speech errors gave rise to the modern term *Freudian slip*. This isn't a silky undergarment he wore to feel comfortable, but the idea that the error reveals something about the hidden meanings that a person is trying to repress.

Gerald Ford once referred to his US presidency as 'a single four-year sentence' (rather than 'term'), implying that he viewed it like a prison sentence. Whereas a Freudian interpretation would focus on hidden, repressed meanings, cognitive psychologists may note that 'term' and 'sentence' are interchangeable when following the word 'prison', and so they may have already been associated in Ford's mental 'dictionary'. When he looked for the word to describe the length of a presidency, 'sentence' may have become activated by its related meaning.

When a friend informed the psycholinguist Gary Dell of another Ford slip, he said 'I heard Freud made a Fordian slip'. Interestingly, the speaker switched 'Freud' and 'Ford', units of speech with several overlapping properties: they're both proper names, they both begin with 'F' and end with 'd', and they both contain one syllable. This mistake is an example of a morpheme exchange error, because the morphemes rather than words are exchanged. A person saying 'I heard Freudian made a Ford slip' is unlikely. Instead the ending 'ian' of 'Freudian' remains in place and is attached to the misplaced 'Ford'.

Garrett's model proposed that the sentence level involves the construction of a functional frame containing the *function morphemes* (small words or parts of words that carry the grammatical structure of the sentence). This frame contains slots into which are inserted the lexical morphemes that carry the semantic payload of the sentence. For example, Garrett reports this error: 'How many pies does it take to make an apple?' Here, 'pie' has slotted into the frame 'How many ___-s' and 'apple' has slotted into the frame 'a ___'.

The late American linguist Victoria Fromkin was a pioneer in the study of speech errors. You can access her speech error database online at the following address: http://www.mpi.nl/dbmpi/sedb/sperco_form4.pl.

Recognising Speech as Speech

After you've planned what you're going to say, you need to put it into practice by manipulating the muscles of your vocal system in just the right way to give rise to the spoken words.

Distinguishing different meanings from the same sound

If spoken in normal fluent speech, the two sentences 'It's not easy to recognise speech' and 'It's not easy to wreck a nice beach' sound practically identical. This is down to two factors: the phonemes that make up the phrases 'recognise speech' and 'wreck a nice beach' are almost identical, and people tend not to pause between words. The same bit of speech can be interpreted as a two-word or a four-word phrase.

We use *The CMU Pronouncing Dictionary* to produce the following phonetic transcriptions of the two phrases:

Words	*Phonemes*
RECOGNISE SPEECH	R EH K AH G N AY Z S P IY CH
WRECK A NICE BEACH	R EH K AH N AY S B IY CH

Segmenting speech

The problem of how the human brain splits language up into words is the problem of *speech segmentation*. You may think that the preceding section's example is unusual and that normally the spaces between words are clear. But, in fact, normal speech rarely contains clear pauses between words.

Psychologist Jenny Saffran and colleagues played a recording of a nonsense language to infants and found that, apparently, they learn statistical associations between the syllables of the language. To create the nonsense language, they combined nonsense syllables to produce words like 'pabiku' and 'golatu', and then strung them together without any pauses or spaces to produce a few minutes of monotone computerised nonsense speech.

The infants just listened to the speech. They received no feedback or reward, and at the end they were tested on pairs of nonsense words. As infants, they couldn't be asked to choose a word and so instead they were played the pairs of words; researchers recorded how long the babies attended to each word. For example, the infant may hear a sequence beginning as follows:

'tupirogolabubidakupadotitupirobidakugolabupadotibidakutupiropadotigo labutupiro . . .'

The researchers strung together nonsense words: 'Tupiro golabu bidaku padoti tupiro bidaku golabu padoti bidaku tupiro padoti golabu tupiro'.

Then the child was played two stimuli – one a word from the language such as 'bidaku' and another a 'part-word' consisting of the end of one word followed by the beginning of another such as 'pirogo'. Saffran and her colleagues found that infants spent longer attending to the part-words than the whole words, indicating that they're more familiar with the words – the part-words seem more novel to them and so they're more interesting. In turn, this suggests that children use the statistical patterns between words to help them work out where one word ends and another begins.

Without spaces between words, how did the children learn to distinguish the words from the part-words? The researchers argue that the infants must be keeping track of how often one syllable is followed by another – within a word, each syllable is always followed by the same syllable but at the end of a word the choice of the next syllable is more variable. The infants keep track of these transitional probabilities and use them to carve the speech up into its constituent words.

Delving into Language Problems

Much of this chapter concerns how cognitive psychology can help people to understand language problems, but language problems can also help people develop cognitive psychology. Various types of language problems exist that may be due to a variety of factors, including brain damage, genetic mutations and learning. Here we look at just four such problems.

Being lost for words: Aphasias

Aphasia refers to language impairments. Two well-known types have been known since the 19th century and they're named after their discoverers:

- **Broca's aphasia:** Identified by Paul Broca, it's caused by damage to an area in the frontal lobes (now called *Broca's area*) that's responsible for motor control of speech. Broca's aphasia is typified by disfluency in speech and a tendency to leave out grammatical morphemes: the patient's speech uses a very simple sentence structure and lacks in normal intonation. People with Broca's aphasia would find the sentence 'Peter gave Mike beer' easy to understand but 'The beer was given to Mike by Peter' more difficult.

- **Wernicke's aphasia:** Identified by Carl Wernicke, it's caused by damage to an area in the parietal and temporal lobes (now called *Wernicke's area*) that seems to be responsible for understanding meaning. Patients are usually quite fluent but tend to produce the wrong words and even create their own words (*neologisms*). A person may say 'I will sook you dinner' instead of 'I will cook you dinner'.

These problems seem to affect different aspects of language, which is sometimes used as an example of a *double dissociation*: two separate parts of the brain handle different aspects of a task independently. Broadly speaking, Broca's aphasia is characterised by intact semantics but damaged syntax and fluency, and Wernicke's aphasia is associated with almost the opposite pattern – fluent speech, with correct syntax but impaired semantics.

These two types of aphasia are typically produced by damage to the left side of the brain. Damage to the corresponding right areas produces different language issues, such as complementary problems with production (damage to Broca's area) and comprehension (damage to Wernicke's area) of the emotionality of speech.

Sequencing the genes: Specific language impairment

Specific language impairment (SLI) is a rare condition that appears to run in families. Sufferers tend to have specific problems with grammar, leading some people to see this as evidence for a kind of 'language gene'.

More recent research, however, suggests that SLI may not be specific to language, but that the genetic difference underlying this condition may be responsible for a more general mechanism for handling sequences. For example, the same gene occurs in a very similar form in other mammals, including mice. When this gene is mutated, the mice have problems with organising a sequence of actions.

Speaking in foreign tongues

Brain damage can also affect the pronunciation of speech: some people who suffer a brain injury start speaking in a foreign accent. This problem indicates that brain regions exist that process particular ways of pronouncing and speaking. These brain regions may control the motor system of speech and if damaged cause people to speak in an odd way. To a listener it may be that this new speaking pattern sounds foreign.

Having trouble reading: Dyslexia

People are usually classified as *dyslexic* when their reading ability trails behind their other cognitive abilities. But this definition is complicated by the fact that dyslexia isn't a single condition. It can include people with a specific neurological impairment that affects their reading and people who, for one reason or another, haven't learned the specific decoding skills necessary for reading.

In practice, little evidence exists of a specific neurological or genetic problem underlying most cases of dyslexia. In her book *Why Children Can't Read* (Penguin), the cognitive psychologist Diane McGuinness outlines the results of many studies suggesting that people diagnosed as dyslexic may often simply not have acquired the necessary decoding skills. This situation can be fixed with the right kind of remedial programme, and these people can then be taught to read correctly.

This research suggests that, in many cases, a diagnosis of dyslexia doesn't imply a permanent inability to read. Instead, the problem may reflect the fact that the person learned to read in a way that didn't emphasise the correct mappings between the letters and sounds required to become a skilled reader. By training people in the necessary phonological decoding skills, these adults can be brought up to a reading level more compatible with their general level of intelligence.

Chapter 16

Discovering the Links between Language and Thought

In This Chapter

▶ Exploring whether language affects thought

▶ Asking whether thought can exist without language

▶ Contrasting the two different views

*T*ake a moment and think about your breakfast this morning (we hope you've eaten; otherwise, this introduction may give you the munchies). Although you probably conjure up some mental imagery when asked to think about a particular concept in this way – for example, melted butter running off a slice of toast and onto your clean jacket – predominately you employ words and language to articulate your thoughts.

Does this vital use of words mean that the entire thought processes of humans are based on language? If you think yes, that would mean that people who speak different languages think differently to each other and those without language can't think (which seems highly unlikely).

The breakfast thought experiment hints at a long-lasting, fiercely contested debate in psychology: does language affect or indeed guide thought? Does thought direct language? Clearly the two aspects are related (and in this chapter we often describe language and thought together), but what's the nature of this link?

Two rival schools of thought exist, as follows:

✔ **Realists:** Believe that language and thought are unrelated.

✔ **Constructionists:** Believe that language influences thought. Many traditional thinkers thought, seemingly logically, that thought comes before language, but this opinion has been challenged.

In this chapter, we discuss the links between language and thought, including the most famous theory in this field (the Sapir–Whorf hypothesis) and the extensive evidence that supports it. We also look at the equally extensive evidence contrary to this theory. Throughout, we try and form a coherent response to the question: does thought require language?

Investigating the Idea that You Need Language to Think

Much evidence suggests that language affects thinking in profound ways. In this section, we back up this assertion of an intimate and essential link between language and thought. We look at language differences, colour perception and how children think, among other aspects.

Connecting language to thought

Russian psychologist Lev Vygotsky believed that language and thought are intertwined and that during childhood development this relationship changes. Early on, thought and language are unrelated, but as children get older, language and thought become loosely related, with a behaviour preceding a verbal description. Subsequently, speaking out becomes internal speech, which allows people to create complex thoughts.

The main proponent of the idea that people require language in order to think and that language dictates how they think was American linguist Benjamin Whorf (don't confuse with Mr Worf, the *Star Trek* character!).

His hypothesis is usually known as the *Sapir–Whorf hypothesis* (or *linguistic relativity*). The idea is that the structure of someone's language dictates how that person sees the world – how he devises concepts and categories, and memorises and thinks about his surroundings.

Psychologists talk in terms of strong and weak views of the Sapir–Whorf hypothesis:

> ✔ **Strong view:** Language must affect thought in all cases. In fact, you can't have any kind of thought without language. Certain concepts that are expressible in one language can never be described in another language and a large number of untranslatable sentences are bound to exist: presenting the issue of *translatability*. Little evidence has been produced for the strong view.

✔ **Weak view:** Language influences thought. Plenty of evidence supports this form of linguistic relativity (that is, language causes differences in mental processes). The form of people's language affects how they think (called *linguistic determinism*). This view is similar to Vygotsky's perspective that some thought requires language.

Considering cross-cultural language differences

Here we present the evidence for the weak view of the Sapir–Whorf hypothesis, which we introduce in the preceding section. The first line of evidence is the difficulty of translating between languages. However, this aspect is hard to assess because literal translations don't necessarily translate to conceptual translations. Thus, researchers have devised more precise studies.

Many of these studies involve how people describe colours in different languages and reveal that language affects perception and, by extrapolation, thought.

Colour-recognition experiments show that lacking the word for a particular colour causes difficulty for people trying to remember that colour. For example, members of a Native American tribe who use only one word to describe yellow and orange *(luptsinna)* made more errors when spotting yellows and oranges than English speakers. Similarly, a New Guinean tribe with only two colour words demonstrated a worse recognition memory for colours than that of English speakers. (You can read more on this research in the later section 'Seeing the same: Universal perception'.)

I can think it but not say it

Alfred Bloom, an American psychologist, suggests that, because of the grammatical structure of Chinese Mandarin, native speakers are unable to process counter-factual statements and to reason counter-factually. An example is when a statement involving an 'if' statement is followed by something other than a clearly related fact, such as 'would have' – as in,

'If I had revised, I would've passed the exam'. This sentence is counter-factual, because sometimes even people who revise fail exams. But Bloom's data have been criticised, because only the grammatical structure is unusual: employing an alternative grammatical structure can allow for such thoughts in Mandarin speakers.

In another experiment that tested English participants only, participants were asked to either give names to colour chips or not. Their memory was subsequently tested. Naming the colour chips caused them to be recognised less accurately than not naming them, again highlighting how language interferes with perception.

Telling this from that: Categorical perception

Categorical perception is where people find that discriminating between two similar stimuli is easier when they're from different categories (*between-category*) than if they're from the same category (*within-category*). This tendency is found in the perception of colour, phonemes (spoken sounds; see Chapter 13) and emotional expressions.

Categorical perception is a prime candidate for showing the effects of language affecting perception. One example is that in Japanese the sound 'r' and the sound 'l' aren't distinguished (which in the past led to countless, deeply unfunny racist 'jokes' centred on mixing up 'rice' and 'lice'). No categorical boundary exists between these two sounds, because the language doesn't feature a difference.

Similar effects exist in the cross-cultural categorical perception of colour. Tarahumaran speakers don't have different names for blue and green, whereas English does. English speakers show a categorical boundary between green and blue, whereas Tarahumaran speakers don't.

Presenting the evidence from child development

Further evidence that language is necessary for perception comes from studies with children. For example, they seem to require the language skills to express differences between two related items in order to solve problems associated with such relationships (check out the nearby sidebar 'Articulating relationships between things' for more details).

One useful method for assessing how language affects thought is to test people who don't have language. New-born infants haven't developed language yet and so are ideal participants.

Articulating relationships between things

If you're familiar with developmental psychology, you may well have heard of Jean Piaget, a French developmental psychologist. Piaget created a theory to explain how children develop through a series of stages.

One of those stages is based on children's understanding of relationships and concepts (the *pre-operational* stage). At this level children who're able to verbalise relationships between two things (such as 'bigger than') can solve problems that involve such relationships.

In contrast, children who can't verbalise the relationship can't solve the problem. Thus, the necessary cognitive ability requires the language.

General cognitive development and language ability are developing at the same time, however, and so separating the two is difficult. Saying this, Piaget believed that language develops because of cognitive development, suggesting a cyclical relationship between language and cognition.

Research on children has tended to explore colour perception and categorical perception (refer to the two preceding sections). Many studies show that children find it harder to discriminate between colours for which they don't have verbal labels. In addition, categorical perception boundaries aren't so readily identifiable in children.

Although some developmental changes in the perception of colour may exist, the *focal colours* (the 11 basic colour terms of English, including red and blue; see Chapter 5) do appear to be learnt earlier without words.

Covering other cognitive abilities

Here we provide more evidence of how language affects thought.

The way people label objects affects the accuracy with which they're recognised. In one experiment, participants were presented with a series of fairly ambiguous objects that had been labelled or not. Labelling aided memory for the ambiguous objects, suggesting that language helps memory.

When presented with a series of shapes to remember, if participants verbally label based on distinctive labels (for example, crescent), they're more likely to remember them than if participants verbally label based on common shared labels (for example, square). This is consistent with the weak form of the Sapir–Whorf hypothesis, because the language used has affected memory (refer to the earlier section 'Connecting language to thought').

A similar example of how language affects memory is the *verbal overshadowing effect*. This is where using language to describe objects actually makes them harder to remember subsequently. It's found quite consistently with faces: after seeing a face, participants in a study were asked to describe it. Subsequently they had to identify the face from a line-up. Participants were very inaccurate at this task – worse than if they hadn't described the face. This result provides evidence that language can alter the way people remember faces, which is consistent with the Sapir–Whorf hypothesis.

Another similar example is that of some false memory research. Elizabeth Loftus, an American psychologist, found that memory for events can be substantially altered after people are presented with leading questions. The results suggest that language can affect people's memories, and thus their thoughts.

Some psychologists indicate that *functional fixedness* (that is, being unable to disengage the proper use of a particular object to solve an insight problem; see Chapter 17) is a consequence of language. In other words, if people didn't have words for the objects, they'd be able to use the objects for something else.

One method to show how language affects cognition is to explore cultural stereotypes in bilinguals. For example, English contains a stereotype of an artistic type (moody, bohemian and a bit weird). But this stereotype doesn't exist in Chinese Mandarin speakers. When asked to provide free interpretations, people are able to provide more detail if they meet up with a stereotype used in the language in which the participant was speaking. That is, people draw inferences based on the language they're speaking. When bilinguals speak in one language, they're thinking in a different manner than when speaking in their other language.

Evidence suggests that performance in a spatial-reasoning task (such as map reading) is affected by the language of the speaker. Participants whose language employs a *relative spatial coding* (that is, an object is described as being next to or left of, and so on, of another object) perform in a completely different manner to those whose language employs an *absolute spatial coding* system (when an object is described according to absolute positions such as north and south). So think carefully next time you're giving directions to someone, if you want to arrive on time!

Thinking without Language: Possible or not?

The thinkers we discuss in the earlier section 'Connecting language to thought' believe that cognition drives language development. But others think the opposite – that language and cognition are independent faculties.

In this section, we introduce the research that indicates that thinking without language is possible. We look at evidence from consciousness, universal perception, expertise and work on children.

Bringing consciousness into the debate

Cognitive psychologists study how different processes work in the brain to enable human behaviour (see Chapter 1). For example, when you produce a sentence, a complex chain of events needs to occur – involving many different brain areas and different stages of information retrieval, planning and complex motor control – before you can utter a word. Yet, you aren't consciously aware of all these underlying processes.

Sometimes psychologists use the term *zombie brain* to distinguish these many separate processes from conscious thoughts.

The human conscious mind is like the swan floating elegantly on the surface of the water while underneath its legs paddle furiously to cause the movement. This situation raises the following question: if conscious thoughts are in language but language is the result of lots of processes occurring in areas of the brain of which humans aren't conscious, are humans really coming up with these thoughts themselves – or is the zombie brain doing it and letting the conscious brain know the result?

We look at consciousness here to explore whether unconscious thought, which typically isn't based on language, exists and what its nature may be.

How do you know you exist?

French philosopher René Descartes famously wrote 'Cogito ergo sum' ('I think therefore I am').

This was long before the concept of virtual reality or the kind of illusory experience portrayed in films such as *The Matrix,* but Descartes was pondering the question of what people can know is real. He imagined a situation in which people's senses were being fooled by demons so that what seemed liked reality was in fact an illusion. He asked what they could be certain of in these circumstances and came to the conclusion that although all their senses could be fooled, the one thing that people could be sure was real is their own consciousness. Yes, even your own body may be an illusion – you may be a brain in a vat being fed illusory sensory information from a computer (or demon). (Ah, 'illusory sensory information', as Homer Simpson would say, drooling.)

People can be sure that the thoughts they're thinking are real – that is who they are and, so, they think therefore they are. The flip side of this idea is that people can only ever know their own consciousness – they can never know whether someone else is conscious or whether that person's experience is like theirs.

Halt! Who goes there? I or iPad?

In the 1950s, computing pioneer and wartime code-breaker Alan Turing posed a related question – how would people know whether a computer was intelligent? The problem is similar to knowing whether another person is conscious – you can never really know, and instead you have to infer what's going on inside based on their external behaviour. So Turing proposed a behavioural measure of intelligence, which is now known as the Turing test in his honour.

In the Turing test, a human judge communicates with two or more entities, which may be real people or computers pretending to be people, via a text-only medium – nowadays, with mobile phone text messages or chat software. Then the person judges the entities on the basis of what they say and how they interact with him rather than on how they look or sound. The test involves having conversations with the entities about whatever subjects the judge chooses and, based on their interactions, he has to decide which is human and which is the computer.

An annual competition (the Loebner Prize) implements a restricted form of the Turing test – researchers enter programs known as chatbots that have to compete with humans to convince human judges that they're people. Judges are only allowed to converse on very narrow topics but, despite this, no computer program has yet claimed the prize for being a sufficiently convincing human, indicating that thought can go beyond language.

Seeing the same: Universal perception

Earlier in this chapter, we describe how language affects the perception of colour (in the section 'Considering cross-cultural language differences'). However, cross-cultural language differences in colour perception aren't always found. Eleanor Rosch Heider believes in something called the *universals of perception*, which is where people perceive the same thing regardless of their language.

Rosch Heider tested colour perception of a stone-age tribe from the rain-forests of New Guinea called the Dani. The Dani had vastly different words for colours to English speakers. In fact, they had only two (*mola* for bright, warm hues and *mili* for dark, cold hues). But they were able to discriminate between two colours presented to them as accurately as English speakers. Given the existence of memory differences for colour stimuli between the Dani and English speakers, this suggests that language may affect memory but not perception.

The studies also found that the recognition memory for colour words was better for *focal colours* (the 11 basic colour terms used in English) compared with non-focal colours in English and Dani speakers. Thus, Dani speakers were better at remembering particular colours over other colours even though they don't have the words to do so, but they weren't as good as the English speakers.

Similar results have been obtained with memory for focal shapes. Dani speakers don't have the same words for basic shapes as English speakers, and yet they can still discriminate between them.

Brent Berlin and Paul Kay also believe in the universals of perception and suggest a hierarchy of colour terms (black and white at the top, red next, as shown in Table 16-1), with those higher up the hierarchy existing in all languages and those lower down becoming less and less focal. Nevertheless, all peoples can discriminate the 11 focal colours. (Check out the later section 'Comparing the Opposing Arguments' to discover some compromises involved in this research.)

Table 16-1	Hierarchy of Basic Colours		
Black	White		
Red			
Yellow	Blue	Green	
Brown			
Purple	Pink	Orange	Grey

Based on the results of Rosch Heider and Berlin and Kay indicating that every human perceives the same colours (except those who are colour-deficient, obviously!), researchers concluded that perception is biologically derived; because people have a particular physiology (they have only three colour receptors; see Chapter 5), they perceive in a particular way. For example, you can distinguish the shade of a green basil leaf from a green spinach leaf (we've been gardening today, as you may be able to tell!), because the receptors in your eyes allow you to detect this difference. People whose language doesn't have the word 'green' can still tell them apart, because the biology of their visual system allows them to see green.

Thus, perception is biologically determined rather than language determined. By extrapolation, other mental processes, including thought, aren't language determined.

'Well, I just dunnit really': Expertise

If you ask expert footballers to describe the steps behind how they play, they often have difficulty. Being an expert at something often changes the mental processes involved so that describing how you do that activity is very difficult.

The fact that experts find it hard to verbalise their activity is evidence for thought processes that exist beyond language. However, this can be extended further: when expert sports people have to describe how they play their sport, they often become worse at it. This difficulty arises because they have to use language to describe an activity that they think about without language. In other words, behaviour can exist without language.

Automaticity is another form of thought without language. Tasks that people perform automatically are done without the need for language and thus highlight how language isn't a requirement for thought.

Similarly, people may very easily describe a face, but research shows that their descriptions of faces don't always match up to how they remember them; that is, people can't actually describe the mental processes involved in recognising faces. The right words aren't always available to represent the thought process accurately.

It started with a thought: Mentalese

The term *mentalese* refers to a special language of the brain. The idea is that when people produce a thought it starts out in some language of the brain, which is then converted into spoken language to enable them to communicate the thought to others. Similarly, when people speak to you, their language is converted into mentalese before you understand it.

Here are several of the arguments in favour of the theory that people think in mentalese rather than their normal spoken language:

- ✔ People often have trouble putting ideas into words – if ideas already were in words, this wouldn't be an issue.
- ✔ People can coin new words or phrases for novel concepts, suggesting that ideas can precede the language needed to express them.
- ✔ Pre-linguistic children and animals seem to be capable of some degree of thought prior to language. Helen Keller, who was blind and deaf from an early age, describes having thoughts without language.

✔ The meaning of a sentence can be ambiguous when the intended meaning isn't, which suggests that thoughts are less prone to ambiguity than the language used to express them. For example, the newspaper headline 'Prostitutes Appeal to Pope' is intended to mean one thing, but you could easily (and embarrassingly) interpret it in a very different way.

'*I don't remember doing that – honestly!*'

If people need language to think, a natural conclusion is that before they have language, they can't think. But children have cognition and thoughts, and their language develops out of that, which is consistent with the view that cognition precedes language development.

The evidence comes from studies on cognitive abilities in children. As soon as children develop the concept of *object permanence* (that is, when an object is obscured by something, it still exists), they're then able to use language to describe the object.

Thinking back to when you were a young child, before being able to talk, I'm sure that you believed you could think. The concept that you didn't think at some point in your life is difficult to grasp. However, people don't seem to have any memory before they develop language (called *infantile amnesia*; see Chapter 10). Thus, perhaps humans need language to form memories.

Comparing the Opposing Arguments

The preceding sections discuss two rival views: that thought *is* dependent on language and that thought *isn't* dependent on language.

If you're looking for a definitive answer in the published scholarly scientific articles, you may be disappointed. Researchers are providing more and more evidence for language affecting thought *and* for the exact opposite. In fact, the debates can get quite heated, with researchers for one perspective often criticising the methods employed by the opposing researchers!

Here we compare the arguments in a balanced view (to be honest, we don't have a strong opinion either way – though maybe by the end of this section we will!).

We present the overall arguments in Table 16-2.

Table 16-2 Arguments For and Against the Sapir–Whorf Hypothesis

Thought and Language Are Connected	*Thought Doesn't Require Language*
Poorer recognition memory for colours not in the language (see the earlier 'Considering cross-cultural language differences' section)	Better recognition memory for focal colours even without the words
Discrimination of colours equally good without words (see the earlier 'Seeing the same: Universal perception' section)	
Verbal overshadowing effect (see the earlier 'Covering other cognitive abilities') section	Mentalese (flip to the earlier 'It started with a thought: Mentalese' section for more)
Infantile amnesia (see 'I don't remember doing that – honestly!' earlier in this chapter)	Consciousness (the earlier section 'Bringing consciousness into the debate') has the details
Functional fixedness (which we also discuss in the 'Covering other cognitive abilities') section	

Two differences between the results concerning perception differences due to different language are worth noting:

- ✔ **Language does seem to affect recognition memory.** But when two colours are presented simultaneously or close in time, discrimination of colours is unaffected by language. Thus, language may not affect perception because of the basic physiological system, but may affect memory because memory is based on culture and experience.

  Another problem with research conducted in this field is the often-found lack of control in these studies. For example, some research into the universals of colour perception failed consistently to apply the criteria used to define a focal colour. Such problems suggest that the universals of perception findings (such as the ones we discuss in the earlier section 'Seeing the same: Universal perception') are likely to be the result of poor methods.

- ✔ **Environment influences the exposure to certain colours and physiology dictates what colours are likely to be best recognised.** Related to this finding is that although a linguist may suggest that a language doesn't have a word for a particular colour, often those who speak a particular language do have a word to describe such things. For example, speakers of languages that use the same word for blue and green (linguists have said this about Welsh, but Welsh speakers say that they do have a word for green) may use another word to discriminate (for example, attaching the word 'sky' or 'grass' to differentiate the two colours). Check out the nearby sidebar 'More than just Uncle Ben's!' for another example.

The environment may cause people to devise different words: that is, language and thought may be partially environmentally determined. Separating out the effects of the environment and culture from language is virtually impossible.

In part to resolve this debate, researchers have put forward a *cognitive computational approach*, which highlights that different languages can be used to transmit different information more easily than others. The idea is that when flexibility is involved in a particular task, language is likely to affect performance, but with no flexibility, physiology, biology and environment takeover. When people have one word to represent a particular concept, no load is placed upon their cognitive resources. But if they require more words to represent the same concept (because their language doesn't have that word), a greater load is placed upon working memory.

This load can have knock-on effects on thought processes. For example, Chinese Mandarin has single words for the numbers 0–10, 100, 1,000 and 10,000 but, unlike English, not for 11, 12 or the teens. So when an English person says 11, a Mandarin speaker requires two words, 10 and 1 combined, which involves more cognitive effort (though only slightly!).

So, sometimes thought is dependent on language and sometimes it's not (isn't that always the case in psychology!). This is pretty much what Lev Vygotsky said in the 1930s (that some thoughts don't require language because they're biologically predetermined, but more complex thoughts do require language): check out the earlier section 'Connecting language to thought' to find out more.

Whatever the truth, the relationship between language and thought is a complex one.

More than just Uncle Ben's!

The evidence for many words for a particular set of concepts in one language but not in another suggests that the subject needs more thought. For example, the Hanuxoo language of the Philippines has 92 names for rice, which seems to suggest that they can tell more types of rice apart than English speakers. Then again, this usage may simply be a result of the environment: people eat more types of rice in the Philippines than in English-speaking countries.

Part V

Thinking Your Way around Thought

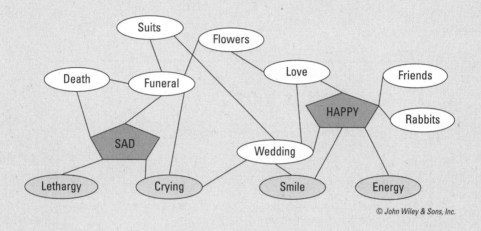

© John Wiley & Sons, Inc.

web extras

Take your cognitive psychology journey further, with a free online article that contains the truth about lying at www.dummies.com/extras/cognitivepsychology.

In this part . . .

✔ Look at how people solve problems rationally, logically, or with insight and creativity.

✔ Get to grips with the cognitive processes involved in making decisions.

✔ Discover the rules of logic and rationality, and just how irrational humans really are.

✔ Find yourself in the mood to examine how your emotions affect your cognitive abilities – it's not as simple as you may think!

Chapter 17

Uncovering How People Solve Problems

. . . .

In This Chapter

▶ Revealing mental processes with the Gestalt school

▶ Solving problems with computers and experts

▶ Considering cognitive research in learning

. . . .

The film *Apollo 13* depicts the true story of how disaster struck this lunar mission. An explosion forced the crew to retire to the spacecraft's small command module and use it as a 'life boat' to return to Earth. But the module needed a better air filter for them to survive the journey and they didn't have one that fit its life support system.

A famous scene in the film dramatically depicts the NASA engineers on Earth re-creating the available materials on the stricken spacecraft and frantically trying to use them to construct an air filter. They succeed and instruct the astronauts how to make a filter out of (among other things) a pair of socks, some duct tape and hoses from the space suits they no longer needed.

This event is a particularly compelling example of problem-solving, but innovative thinking isn't limited to NASA engineers (it's not rocket science . . .): you see or use this skill on a regular basis. People solve problems all the time, although they may take the ability for granted and not notice when they're doing it. When someone asks you how you solve problems, you can struggle to put the processes into words. Try it now: think about the mental processes you go through when solving a problem.

For example, our current problem is to write this paragraph and yours is to understand the psychology of problem-solving. The fact that you're reading this text suggests that you're actively engaged in solving that problem. The means at our disposal are words, which we're free to arrange in any order – though only certain orders will do the job. The problem is *ill-defined*, because no single correct paragraph or simple process exists to solve the problem. For this reason, psychologists often focus on *well-defined* problems – ones with definite goals and clearly specified rules.

The ability to solve problems is important for coping with the demands of everyday life. This chapter covers the main perspectives on how people develop ways of solving simple and complex problems. We look at the methods psychologists use to study problem-solving and some of the theories that have emerged to explain how people go about it.

Experimenting to Reveal Thought Processes: Gestalt Psychology

Before cognitive psychology emerged in the mid-20th century, two prominent schools of thought existed on how people solve problems:

- ✔ **Behaviourists:** Liked to limit their studies to observable behaviour; their explanations of problem-solving focused on the concepts of trial and error and reinforcement.

- ✔ **Gestaltists:** Disagreed with the behaviourists on the issue of studying mental processes and mental representations. They sought to explain the psychological activities behind problem-solving. In this sense, they're like the forerunners of cognitive psychologists, and so they're the focus of this section.

Trial and error versus thought

American behaviourist Edward Thorndike studied how cats learnt to open the doors on specially designed puzzle boxes through what appeared to be a process of trial and error. The cats tried out various apparently random actions and repeated any that resulted in a positive outcome. Actions that never led to a positive outcome became less frequent. As a result, Thorndike proposed his *Law of Effect* – the idea that people try out ideas, and those that work get reinforced and are used more often. Later,

American psychologist BF Skinner's theory of *operant conditioning* built on this idea, using schedules of rewards or punishments to shape behaviour.

In contrast, the Gestalt school designed clever experiments that revealed details of the underlying mental processes involved in problem-solving, which enabled them to study the role of insight and fixed thinking patterns in humans' and animals' problem-solving abilities.

Defining the problem

Karl Duncker, a German Gestalt psychologist, stated that 'a problem arises when a living creature has a goal, but does not know how this goal is to be reached. Whenever one cannot go from a given situation to the desired situation simply by action, then there has to be recourse to thinking'.

When talking about a problem, the desired situation is called the *goal state* and your starting position is the *initial state*. You have at your disposal a range of actions (or *operators*) that you can apply. A problem can require you to overcome some specific obstacles or come up with an efficient solution, such as achieving the goal with the fewest actions.

Well-defined problems are ones in which the goal state, the initial state and the operators you can apply are all well-defined. Many puzzles, such as the Rubik's cube, fall into this category, but lots of real-world problems vary in the extent to which they're well-defined.

Monkeying around with insight

Wolfgang Köhler, another German Gestalt psychologist, believed that animals and people are capable of more complex learning, involving insight and thought, than the trial and error approach that behaviourists put forward. He studied problem-solving by chimpanzees at a primate research station on the island of Tenerife, and published this research in a famous book entitled *The Mentality of Apes* in 1917.

Köhler argued that Thorndike's puzzle boxes (see the nearby sidebar 'Trial and error versus thought') were unnatural and went so far outside an animal's experience that the cats couldn't apply their normal thought processes. He wanted to test animals with puzzles more suited to their natural intellect to see them demonstrate their mental abilities.

Köhler devised various puzzles in which chimps had to use objects to retrieve out-of-reach bananas. In one example, a chimp who'd already learned to use a stick to reach a banana was given two sticks, neither of which was long enough. At first the chimp tried both sticks and gave up when neither worked. But after some time sulking, the chimp stuck one stick into the end of the other to make a stick long enough to retrieve the cherished banana. A delicious result!

Behaviourists would object to us using words such as 'sulking' and 'cherished'. They'd see them as too *mentalistic*, because they refer to concepts that can't be observed and shouldn't be assumed; yet they'd have trouble explaining this apparent moment of 'insight' by the chimpanzee. No trial and error learning existed before the chimp combined the two sticks, and it's unlikely that the animal had previous experience of this type of problem. Therefore, it seems to have arrived at the solution purely by thinking.

The behaviourist and Gestalt schools' disagreement reached beyond non-human animals. The former didn't just object to *anthropomorphising* (attributing human-like qualities to animals); they also objected to explanations of human thinking that referred to mental states or processes. Sidney Morgenbesser, an American philosopher famous for his witticisms, asked BF Skinner: 'Let me see if I understand your thesis: you think we shouldn't anthropomorphise people?'

Getting stuck in a rut: Functional fixedness

Karl Duncker identified a particular limitation that often restricts people from spotting novel uses for familiar objects. He called this *functional fixedness*, because humans' idea of how an object can function is fixed by their past experience. For example, perhaps you've been at a party or picnic when everyone has brought beer bottles but no one has a bottle opener. Resourceful individuals look for something else to open the bottles while others panic or sulk, their ability to see alternative uses for objects limited by functional fixedness.

To illustrate his idea, Duncker provides this problem. You're given a box of drawing pins (thumb tacks), a candle and a book of matches. Your task is to fix the candle to the wall. Try to solve it before reading on.

The solution is to empty the drawing pins out of the box, use them to attach the box to the wall and use the box as a candle holder. People often have difficulty solving this problem, because they can't see beyond the box's use for holding the pins to its more general possibilities.

We may have primed you to get the right solution by talking about seeing alternative functions for objects, but Duncker's participants didn't have this prompt. In general, a good tip for solving these kinds of problems is to question your natural tendency to make assumptions about how things can be used or how your actions are limited.

Watching the Rise of the Computers: Information Processing Approaches

Although the Gestalt psychologists' experiments (refer to the preceding section) showed that cognitive processes and representations, such as insight and functional fixedness, occur in problem-solving, they didn't address the question of how. That issue was left until the cognitive revolution (see Chapter 1) prompted a return to the study of problem-solving and the attempt to pin down precisely what processes happen in the brain when a person, or an animal, solves a problem.

Yet how to study thought is a problem for cognitive psychology; despite what popular culture may have you believe, you can't observe thoughts.

What psychologists can do is use technology, such as functional Magnetic Resonance Imaging (fMRI), to observe the physical activity in the brain that's associated with thoughts. They can detect differences between distinctly different kinds of thought so that, for example, by asking a person to think of one situation or another, they can see relatively distinct patterns of activity. (Such techniques have been used to test patients in a persistent vegetative state.) Psychologists can also see the effect that damage to different areas of the brain has on a person's problem-solving ability. For example, patients with damage to the frontal lobes of the brain often show problems with planning and problem-solving.

Welcoming computers to the struggle

Computers provided a new way of thinking about thinking and were soon being applied to the study of psychology. In this new *information processing approach*, problem-solving was broken down into its basic constituent processes, which psychologists then simulated on a computer.

Nobel-prize winners Alan Newell and Herb Simon set about developing computer programs to simulate the processes a person goes through when solving a problem. On the one hand, they were developing ways to program computers to solve problems and thus contributing to computer science. On the other hand, they were trying to replicate the processes that occur when a person solves a problem; in trying to understand this, they contributed to the study of psychology as well. In other words, they were using computers to demonstrate how humans may solve problems.

Newell and Simon worked on a general approach to solving well-defined problems (with clear goals and specified rules), such as the following one. Try it out but also think about what makes it so tricky to solve.

A farmer has to cross a river with a wolf, a goat and a cabbage. (Don't consider why or we'll never get to the problem. Just say that he's a bit batty and leave it at that!) He has a rowing boat that can carry himself and one of his three items of cargo at a time. He has to get all three items across the river, but he can't leave the wolf alone with the goat or wolfie will eat it, and he can't leave the goat alone with the cabbage for the same reason. How does the farmer get the three items across the river?

Here's the solution:

1. **Take the goat from side 1 to side 2.**

2. **Return to side 1.**

3. **Take the cabbage to side 2.**

4. **Return to side 1, taking the goat with you.**

5. **Take the wolf to side 2.**

6. **Return to side 1.**

7. **Take the goat to side 2.**

How did you get on? The difficulty in this problem lies in the need to make moves that appear to be moving away from the solution. When the farmer takes the goat back from side 2 to side 1, you appear to be undoing your actions. But you aren't returning to the initial state, because the cabbage is no longer on side 1. Therefore, you can now leave the goat on side 1 while bringing the wolf across.

Seeing the state space approach

To tackle well-defined problems, Newell and Simon proposed a *problem space*. Starting with the goal state, you consider what would happen if you were to carry out each of the possible moves. The result is a state space diagram showing all the possible moves, which allows you to find the shortest path from the start state to the goal state (see Figure 17-1).

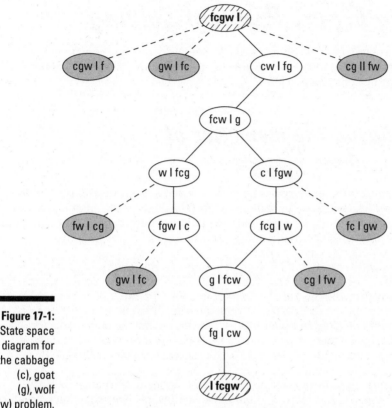

Figure 17-1:
State space
diagram for
the cabbage
(c), goat
(g), wolf
(w) problem.

Note: Grey states are invalid states due to violations of the game rules.

© John Wiley & Sons, Inc.

Perusing protocol analysis

Newell and Simon also used a technique called *protocol analysis*, in which they asked participants to talk through their thinking process as they solved well-defined problems. Protocol analysis established that people often use *means-ends analysis*: they start with the goal they want to achieve (the ends) and work backwards, identifying which methods (the means) at their disposal they can use to achieve the ends.

Examining Expert Problem-Solving

As well as studying how people solve individual problems, cognitive psychologists are also interested in how people develop expertise in solving problems of a particular type.

Analysing the memories of expert chess players

Human short-term memory has a limited capacity for storing units of information, which George Miller called *chunks* (see Chapter 8). Miller estimated that people can remember about seven chunks of information, although more recent studies suggest that people's capacity is even lower than that.

Research with expert chess players has revealed this ability. One clue to what changes in the brain and in processing as a person becomes an expert at chess is provided by a study on their memory for chess board positions. Expert chess players are better at remembering different arrangements of chess pieces on a board than novices. But this advantage only works for genuine arrangements of pieces from real chess games. When tested using random arrangements of pieces, the experts fare little better than novices.

Expert chess players can remember more positions not because their memory capacity has increased but because they've amassed a much greater 'library' of chess positions, which they can recognise and store as a single chunk. Whereas a novice may have to remember each of three pieces as three separate chunks, an expert can recognise the configuration of pieces as a single chunk. As when learning a language, the novices are treating each piece like a separate letter, whereas the experts know larger 'words' involving common arrangements of pieces.

Learning to become an expert

Newell and Simon's ground-breaking work on human problem-solving (refer to the earlier 'Welcoming computers to the struggle' section) established certain general principles, such as means-ends analysis, by which experts solve problems. John Anderson developed the *ACT* theory,* which incorporates not only a mechanism for general problem-solving but also addresses the question of skill acquisition – how do people build the knowledge that enables them to become better at a skill?

At its heart, Anderson's model has a *production rule*, which is a basic unit of a procedural skill composed of two parts: a condition that gives the context in which the rule applies and an action that specifies what to do in that situation. For example, if someone knocks on your door (the *condition*) then the action is that you get up and open the door (unless your favourite programme is on the TV!).

Anderson's model allowed him to construct computer models of how students develop skills in areas such as mathematics and computer programming. This model simulated the learning of a skill as the gradual development and strengthening of specific production rules and was able to identify errors due to the misapplication of specific rules. So, in the preceding example, you hear a knock on the door and the action is to open it. But learning applies such that you may need to specify the condition (for example, at night opening the door may not be safe, and so you don't, or during the day the caller may be a door-to-door salesperson and so you pretend not to hear it). With experience, the production rule becomes refined.

Emulating the experts to improve your problem-solving

Even if you don't want to become a chess grand master, you can still become an expert problem-solver by following these helpful hints:

- ✔ **Practice:** Learning develops slowly, piece by piece. To be an expert you need to amass a vast number of chunks of relevant experience. Some research shows that around 10,000 hours' practice is typical (though this is a bit of a myth with caveats regarding how often the skill is practised and the type of skill), though you can become proficient with less practice at lots of smaller skills.

- ✔ **Vary your experiences:** If you deal with too many problems of the same kind you can become mired in repeated patterns of thinking (see 'Getting stuck in a rut: Functional fixedness' earlier in this chapter). Instead, try to build up a rich memory of different patterns (read the research in the later section 'Improving problem-solving comes with experience').

- ✔ **Group problems sensibly:** Doing so allows you to tackle ones with similar underlying structures together and promotes the development of helpful analogies and more abstract patterns (see the later 'Using analogies in problem-solving' section for more).

✔ **Keep an open mind:** Don't assume that limitations apply, but instead consider how a new problem may resemble a familiar one. Analogies may exist with situations that seem different on the surface.

✔ **Relax:** After you've done the hard work, take some time off. Many people report that novel and useful solutions to problems come to them after they stop working, relax, go for a walk or even to sleep. An unconscious process seems to sift through your memory looking for something that matches the structure of your current problem.

One example is the dreams of Friedrich August Kekulé, a German chemist. After struggling to discover the chemical makeup of a particular molecule, he slept. In a dream, he saw atoms dance around and then form themselves into strings, moving in a snake-like fashion. The snake of atoms formed a circle and it looked like a snake eating its own tail. Allowing his mind to relax and wander, Kekulé was able to discover the cyclic structure of benzene.

Modelling How Learners Learn with Intelligent Tutoring Systems

Intelligent tutoring systems aim to model students' and learners' thought processes as they develop a skill and attempt to identify gaps or misunderstandings in their knowledge. For example, computer models such as ACT-R have been applied to everyday areas.

British psychologists Richard Burton and John Seeley Brown studied how children solved basic mathematical problems such as addition, subtraction, multiplication and division. Getting computers to calculate sums correctly is easy, but Brown and Burton wanted to reproduce the faulty thought processes that lead to wrong answers. For example, a child may forget to carry the tens when adding two numbers.

Brown and Burton took children's answers to a series of simple calculations and used a computer model to simulate the pattern of correct and incorrect answers that they produced. The psychologists simulated the children's thought processes using a set of production rules, each of which addressed different stages in a calculation (such as carrying tens). They then systematically replaced these rules with 'buggy' versions, which simulated a particular misunderstanding that a child may have. By trying out different combinations of correct and buggy rules they found the combination that re-created the child's answers. This enabled the model to diagnose what particular mistakes each child was making.

Brown and Burton's work was pioneering in the 1980s, but such cognitive modelling of the learner is at the heart of much recent research in online education. The ability to test automatically students' understanding and diagnose the reasons for their mistakes can greatly enhance online assessment. It can enable a computer program to be more responsive to students' needs by identifying their misunderstandings.

Improving problem-solving comes with experience

Psychologists can produce a model of a human learner that identifies the areas where the person lacks knowledge or has particular misconceptions. Harriet Shaklee and Michael Mims studied the way in which people form associations between events. In this fascinating area of study, you encounter all sorts of interesting questions about everyday experience. For example, people often form *illusory correlations* between events (see Chapter 10), which are when the human brain links two rarely occurring events together.

Shaklee and Mims hypothesised that people use increasingly better strategies as they develop. They created a set of problems that were carefully designed so that they could distinguish between several different cognitive strategies for forming associations. They then gave these problems to different age-groups and recorded the errors made by each group. They found evidence of increasing use of more advanced cognitive strategies with age. All groups could tackle the simplest versions, but only older, better educated individuals correctly answered the most difficult problems.

Using analogies in problem-solving

If you've already experienced and solved a problem, you're more likely to be able to solve a dilemma with the same underlying structure, even if it appears different on the surface. By applying Newell and Simon's state space analysis (refer to the earlier section 'Seeing the state space approach'), you can identify that underlying structure. Psychologists call two problems with an identical underlying structure *isomorphic*.

For example, the problem of getting a goat, cabbage and wolf across a river has the same structure as a number of other popular puzzles, including the fox, goose and bag of beans one (where you can't leave the fox and goose or the goose and bag of beans alone together). If you draw the state space graph for the two different versions of the puzzle, you find that they have identical structures and the optimal path from the start state to the goal state is the same.

Therefore, when you know how to solve the wolf, goat and cabbage problem you can apply the same skill to the fox, goose and bag of beans one. You just need to recognise how the new problem maps onto the one you've experienced. This is a form of what's called *analogical problem solving,* which is solving a new problem by recognising how it resembles a problem you've experienced before. You thus have a solution, or at least a method, for solving the problem without having to go through the much longer learning process of tackling such a problem for the first time.

In the real world, however, problems have so many variations that a new problem rarely matches one that you've previously experienced in every detail, and so you have to look for similarities rather than exact fits.

Psychologists Mary Gick and Keith Holyoak used a range of related problems to study how people use the knowledge gained from solving one problem to solve another similar problem. In particular, they were interested in how people find analogies between two problems as part of creativity, and how they come up with new ideas or new solutions based on existing knowledge.

Consider these two connected scenarios. The first one has a surgeon trying to remove a tumour from a patient using powerful rays without damaging the surrounding healthy tissue. The solution involves targeting the tumour with multiple weaker beams that converge to a point focused on the tumour. The second problem involves an army marching to attack a fortress, but it has to avoid triggering mines on the road that explode if too large a force crosses. The solution requires splitting the army up into many small groups who'd then converge on the fortress.

Neither of these problems is well-defined, but you can see an underlying similarity – both problems involve splitting a stronger force into weaker ones that converge at a target.

Gick and Holyoak wanted to know whether, and how, their participants would use analogical problem-solving. To do so, the participants needed to notice the relationship and then map the corresponding elements between the original and the new problem (for example, fortress = tumour, rays = army and so on). They then needed to apply the existing solution to the new situation.

Gick and Holyoak found that people generally aren't very good at noticing analogies unless they're fairly obvious in the surface form of the story. Giving participants a hint that a relationship is present between the problems helps considerably. The task of mapping between problems is also quite demanding, because it can involve people holding several items in their working memory simultaneously. After the analogy is found, people have to implement it, which can also impose a big cognitive load.

Chapter 18

Thinking Logically about Reasoning

. . . .

In This Chapter

▶ Revealing flaws in human logic

▶ Thinking logically and illogically

▶ Modelling how people reason

. . . .

*R*easoning is the human ability to think logically and rationally. In this chapter, we look at questions such as, 'How do you know whether someone is thinking logically?' To address this issue, we explore formal and computational logic models and the cognitive models used to explain rationality. We also discuss whether purely rational logic is appropriate to apply in humans when dealing with real-world problems.

To show what psychologists mean by logical thinking and the rules of logic, we use examples of problems that have been widely used in cognitive psychology experiments.

Testing Human Logic

Cognitive psychologists have adopted a long history of theories of formal logic (from philosophy, mathematics and, more recently, computer science) to act as a benchmark against which to compare human thinking.

In this section, we look at just how logical humans really are.

Introducing humans: The logical animal?

In the past, a lot of people liked to think that humans were the rational animal – the one able to think things through logically. But cognitive psychologists burst that bubble by demonstrating that people don't think logically. Research shows that human reasoning is often illogical and that most people are quite poor at reasoning in an abstract way. Later studies then rallied in defence of humans, suggesting that although humans may not think logically, they do think in a way that's well-suited to important real-world problems.

The fact is that people perform much better when problems are presented in a way that makes them familiar. Much human reasoning seems tied to the specific experiences people have encountered, and their ability to deal with new problems is determined to a large extent by their ability to recognise similarities to previous problems (check out Chapter 17 for more on problem-solving).

Confirming confirmation bias with two problems

In this section, we describe an error of logic that people make in experiments, called *confirmation bias*. This is the tendency to seek *confirmatory* evidence – examples that fit the rule – rather than *falsifying* evidence – examples that break the rule.

We present two problems that we'd like you to try for yourself before reading the explanations. Make a note of your answers, because we use them to help explain the proposed theories on how and why humans think the way they do.

Four-card trick

The four-card trick is based on a famous cognitive psychology problem – Wason's Selection Task. British psychologist Peter Wason used the task to test whether people do make the logical error of confirmation bias.

Imagine that you have four cards in front of you (as in Figure 18-1). Each card has a letter on one side and a number on the other side. Your task is to test the rule that 'if a card has a vowel on one side of the card, it has an even number on the other side'. What's the minimum number of cards you need to turn over to test this rule, and which card or cards should you turn over?

When you've written down your answer, consider this question: do you think most people would get the same answer as you? If not, write down the answer that you think most people would give to the problem.

© John Wiley & Sons, Inc.

Before we consider the answers, try the next problem.

Logical drinking problem

You're charged with checking age restrictions on drinking alcohol in a bar. You have to enforce the local rule that nobody under the age of 18 can drink alcohol there. You have four cards representing the four drinkers in the bar (as in Figure 18-2). Each card has the age of the drinker on one side and what the person's drinking on the other side.

© John Wiley & Sons, Inc.

You need to test the rule that 'if a person is drinking alcohol, he must be over 18'. What's the minimum number of cards you need to turn over in order to test this rule, and which card or cards should you turn over? Again ask yourself whether you think most people would give the same answer as you, and if not, make a note of what answer other people would be most likely to give.

Two problems, same structure

Despite appearing different on the surface, the four-card trick and the logical drinking problem have the same underlying structure (we discuss this situation in more detail in Chapter 17). Experiments reveal that people are very poor at choosing the right cards in the first (abstract) problem but perform better with the second (real-world) problem on beer and age. See whether you find that as well. Both problems have a rule of the same form: if something is true then something else is true. You can write this formally as 'If P then Q', using the 'code' in this table:

Symbol	Wason Selection Task	Beer Task
P	Vowel	Beer
Q	Even number	Over 18
~P	Consonant	Cola
~Q	Odd number	Under 18

For example, in the beer problem, P = drinking alcohol and Q = being over 18. The opposite cases are written with a squiggle (~P and ~Q), which correspond to not being over 18 and not drinking alcohol, respectively. You need to check that the person who's not over 18 (~Q) isn't drinking alcohol and that the person who's drinking beer (P) isn't under 18 (~Q).

To explain the four-card trick, we work backwards from the correct answer. You're asked which cards to turn over to test the rule that if a card has a vowel on one side of the card then it has an even number on the other side. The answer is that you need to turn over two cards: the A and the number 7. But when Wason gave this problem to his participants, they were more likely to choose the A and the number 4. This pattern is an example of confirmatory bias: participants turn cards over in order to confirm the rule.

The point is that the rule tells you only that Q must be true if P is true, and not vice versa. If you turn over the even number 4 and it doesn't have a vowel on the other side, it doesn't tell you anything about the rule. For the age and alcohol problem, the equivalent of turning over the number 4 would be turning over the cola.

A large number of experiments using variations of the Wason Selection Task confirm these interesting findings:

- ✔ The majority of people get the wrong answer when faced with the abstract, logical version of the problem.
- ✔ People are much better at choosing the logically correct cards when the task is framed in a particular social context.

'It's Only (Formally) Logical, Captain'

Philosophers and mathematicians have tried to develop formal systems of thinking for centuries. The aim is to come up with systems of logic that are guaranteed to produce the right answer to a question (if one exists).

Logical thinking tends to be quite mechanical in that each step follows another in a predictable way with no uncertainties – the rules of logic tell people what to do at each step. The simple mechanical nature of logic made it ideal as the basis for building computer programs. For example, when you tap the 'home' icon on a mobile phone, the software follows some rule of the form, 'if the user taps the home icon then navigate to the home screen'.

Formal logic was inspired by human thinking, and so for many years people thought that human thought was, in most cases, rational, and follows the rules dictated by logic. But a range of results from cognitive psychology experiments in the 1960s and 1970s highlighted that this wasn't always the case: in some situations, the vast majority of people behave illogically.

Identifying four reasoning rules

Logicians define four specific types of conclusion that people can reach. Two are logically valid and two are logically invalid:

- **Modus ponens (affirms by affirming):** A type of valid logical argument where you know that two things *always* co-occur and one is present, therefore the other must be present.

- **Modus tollens (denies by denying):** A type of valid argument where you know that two things *always* co-occur and one isn't present, therefore the other must not be present.

- **Affirmation of the consequent:** An invalid argument where an outcome is observed that can co-occur with something but can also occur without the second thing.

- **Denial of the antecedent:** An invalid argument where the premise of the argument implies an outcome and when the premise isn't present, the outcome may still be present because the outcome may have other causes.

Table 18-1 illustrates these rules with examples for the statement, 'if a person is a pirate then he has a beard'. People are best at reasoning with modus ponens but have more trouble with modus tollens. They often make invalid inferences, such as the last two examples of incorrect reasoning in the table.

Table 18-1	Four Types of Formal Logical Arguments with an Example and Their Validity		
Rule	*Form*	*Example*	*Valid*
Modus ponens	If P then Q; P therefore Q	If a person is a pirate then he has a beard.	
		John is a pirate; therefore John has a beard.	Correct!
Modus tollens	If P then Q; not Q, therefore not P	If a person is a pirate then he has a beard.	
		John doesn't have a beard; therefore John isn't a pirate.	Correct!
Affirmation of the consequent	If P then Q; Q therefore P	If a person is a pirate then he has a beard.	
		John has a beard; therefore John is a pirate.	Wrong!
Denial of the antecedent	If P then Q; not P, therefore not Q	If a person is a pirate then he has a beard.	
		John isn't a pirate; therefore John doesn't have a beard.	Wrong!

Understanding the importance of context

As we describe in the earlier 'Confirming confirmation bias with two problems' section, people are far better at solving problems with logic when they're presented in social (real-world) contexts as opposed to being purely abstract. People appear to have special logical skills that only kick into action when they're presented with a realistic setting. But quite a lot of debate exists about why this may be the case:

- **Evolutionary theories:** American psychologist Leda Cosmides and American anthropologist John Tooby's view is that people have evolved reasoning mechanisms for the specific task of understanding social relationships. Humans live in social groups and these groups maintain cohesion through various social contracts that make sure that everyone contributes their fair share of work and benefits equally.

- **Experience-based views:** An alternative view is that people gradually learn to apply logic in particular contexts. With American psycholinguist

Diana Shapiro, Wason compared performance on the abstract form of the Wason Selection Task with one phrased in terms of transport, where each card had a destination on one side and a mode of transport on the other. Participants had to check the rule, 'every time I go to Manchester I travel by car':

Manchester   Leeds   Car   Train

In this form, people were able correctly to turn over the cards for Manchester (to check that it has Car on the other side) and Train (to check that it doesn't have Manchester on its other side). This led some psychologists to conclude that humans' logical thinking emerges from their experience with specific situations. Yet people can also reason about fictional situations with which they have no specific experience.

✔ **Pragmatic reasoning schemas:** Psychologists Patricia Cheng and Keith Holyoak proposed this theory (a *schema* is a mental representation of the gist of a type of situation or object). The idea is that with repeated experiences of a particular type people can develop a schema for that situation. Cheng and Holyoak proposed that a schema-based theory may account for the pattern of results observed in experiments on the Wason Selection Task (see the earlier 'Confirming confirmation bias with two problems' section).

For example, you've experienced various situations where you've encountered age limits on drinking, driving, voting and the like. From these experiences you extract a general principle of the logic of age restrictions that you can apply to novel situations (such as unfamiliar age restrictions in other cultures) without requiring direct experience of each specific situation.

A variety of cunningly designed experiments demonstrated that the common factor between versions of the task that people can solve easily is the concept of *permission*. This is where participants have to establish whether something is permitted or allowed in a real-world sense. When participants consider permission, they're better able to solve logical problems.

People's ability to deal with abstract logic is affected because the examples used to research it often don't hold true in the real world. The trouble with logic is that it's all or nothing, whereas in the real world things are rarely so clear-cut. For example, a rule of driving, such as 'if you're turning left at the next junction then you should indicate left', describes what *should* be the case, not what necessarily *is* the case. A driver can turn without indicating, and so you shouldn't assume that because a car isn't indicating it's not turning. The real world contains more uncertainties than logic allows for, and thus it struggles with the all-or-nothing implications in logical rules that don't come naturally to people.

Reasoning with Uncertainty: Heuristics and Biases

Formal logic (refer to the preceding section) is great for simple situations where everything is known and certain. But its definite, all-or-nothing rules make it less good at handling uncertainty. When outcomes are unsure, psychologists turn to alternative theories of reasoning that take into account uncertainties by attaching probabilities to events.

Israeli-American psychologists Daniel Kahneman and Amos Tversky extended the idea that human reasoning is flawed to judgements involving probabilities or uncertainties. They ran a series of experiments in which they set their participants a variety of problems involving making judgements about the relative probabilities of different events.

Kahneman and Tversky found a consistency to participants' errors, with different people giving the same wrong answers to questions. They put the reason down to humans using mental shortcuts called *heuristics*. These heuristics can be useful, because they often enable you to come up with answers quickly and easily, but in certain situations they mislead you into making the wrong judgement.

Taking a shortcut – to the wrong answer!

Heuristics cause people to prioritise excessively things that are more familiar or recent to them. Consequently, they may act illogically. Try the following exercise, which demonstrates heuristic thinking in action.

Do more words begin with the letter K or have the letter K in the third position?

Most people estimate that more words begin with K, whereas a lot more English words have K in the third position than in the first. What's interesting here isn't the question's answer, but *how* people answer it. Kahneman and Tversky proposed that when people get asked this sort of question they try to think of examples of each category.

Now, because the way that people's brains represent words emphasises the first and last letters, and maybe also because people have experience of using first letters when searching alphabetical lists, coming up with a set of words that begin with a certain letter is much easier than those containing that letter in the third position. People can also read sentences that have words with the letters in a random order, provided the first and last letters are in the correct places. People can easily access such words, which makes them more available and thus biases people's answers – they assume that because they can think of more words beginning with K, more words must begin with K, but this isn't true.

A similar process seems to affect people's perception of risk. After the movie *Jaws* (killer shark attacks bathers) came out, researchers recorded a noticeable drop in the numbers of people swimming off the California coast. Releasing the movie hadn't increased the risk of shark attack, but the vivid imagery made it readily available to people's minds, making them overestimate the risk and the likely severity of a real shark attack. (Incidentally, one estimate put the risk of an American being killed by a shark at approximately half that of being killed by a vending machine!)

Weighing down people's thinking: Anchoring

Anchoring, where people's opinions and actions are fixed by a preceding statement or event, is another effect of using heuristics.

In one Kahneman and Tversky experiment, a researcher spun a wheel with percentages printed around its rim. The wheel stopped at a certain value and participants were asked a question about some probability, such as, 'what proportion of African nations are members of the UN?'

Kahneman and Tversky found that participants' answers were strongly influenced by whatever number the wheel stopped at. If it stopped at 10 per cent, people made much lower judgements than when it stopped at 90 per cent. People seemed to be 'anchored' by the 'starting' number even though they'd seen that spinning a wheel had produced it randomly.

Anchoring effects can come into play when two people barter over a price: the buyer and seller can to some extent be 'anchored' by the starting price. Similarly in food labelling, manufacturers often emphasise a low value such as '0 per cent fat' while not mentioning a very high sugar content, in the hope that people's judgement of sugar content is 'anchored' by the low fat content.

Ignoring the base rate

Another heuristic-based error involves the *base rate* – the basic statistical information about the likelihood of events. People all too readily ignore the base rate. In an experiment, Kahneman and Tversky set people the following problem related to the reliability of courtroom evidence.

A taxi was involved in a hit-and-run accident at night. Two cab companies, the Green and the Blue, operate in the city. Eighty-five per cent of the cabs in the city are Green and 15 per cent are Blue. A witness identifies the cab as Blue. The court tests the reliability of the witness under the same circumstances that existed on the night of the accident and concludes that the witness correctly identified each one of the two colours 80 per cent of the time and failed 20 per cent of the time.

What's the probability that the cab involved in the accident was Blue rather than Green, knowing that this witness identified it as Blue?

The most common answer is 80 per cent, which seems logical because the witness says it was Blue and in the tests he'd been shown to be correct 80 per cent of the time. But wait a minute. To get the correct answer you have to take into account not only the witness's accuracy but also the relative likelihood of the cab being a particular colour. This is the base rate and Kahneman and Tversky found that people tend to ignore it.

The actual odds that the cab was Blue are considerably lower than 80 per cent, because you need to take into account the accuracy of the witness and the likelihood that the cab was Blue to begin with. Green cabs are much more common, and so a good chance exists that a Green cab was misidentified as Blue.

Explaining Reasoning with Models

Psychologists and other thinkers have created a number of theories and models to investigate human reasoning. We describe a few that represent two basic approaches: one that confirms that humans are sometimes surprisingly poor at reasoning but stops there; and a second that aims to address these deficiencies and so improve people's reasoning skills.

Using probabilities and Bayesian reasoning

Recent years have seen a resurgence of interest in the mathematical work of an English church minister and mathematician born in 1701, Thomas Bayes. *Bayes's theorem* is a statistical approach used to work out the probability of an event occurring or of something being true given that another event occurred or something else is true. Some evidence exists for people using their own intuition to estimate probabilities of events occurring; therefore, cognitive psychologists need to understand how it applies to human reasoning.

Bayes's theorem enables people to answer questions such as the taxi problem (hitch a ride to the earlier 'Ignoring the base rate' section) and has much relevance in fields such as medical diagnosis. His work is even the basis for spam filters – software that automatically detects and removes marketing email spam from your inbox.

Unfortunately, Bayes's theorem is complicated and difficult for most people to understand. This complexity doesn't matter if the problems are abstract mathematical ones with no real-world relevance, but it does when the theorem is applied to reasoning and making real life-and-death medical decisions.

A branch of cognitive research studies human reasoning in professionals making medical diagnoses. Doctors and nurses are often required to explain test results to patients, and doing so correctly involves Bayesian reasoning, because Bayesian reasoning doesn't ignore base-rate information and allows for accurate judgements to be made (without Bayesian reasoning, diagnoses would be far less accurate). People do quite badly at this kind of reasoning, and worryingly lots of studies show that medical professionals make the same errors as the general population.

In one study, researchers gave doctors a question based on the diagnosis of breast cancer from mammograms scans: 'if a patient has a positive mammogram, what's the probability that she has breast cancer based on the following facts':

- ✔ The probability that a patient has breast cancer is 1 per cent.

- ✔ The probability of obtaining a positive mammogram if the patient has breast cancer is 80 per cent.

- ✔ The probability of obtaining a positive mammogram if the patient doesn't have breast cancer is 10 per cent.

Only 1 in 20 of the doctors got close to the right answer, which is around 7.5 per cent: the majority came up with figures closer to 75 per cent! (We describe the working-out process in the next section.) Just like the participants in the taxi problem, many doctors tended to ignore the base rate, which in this case is 1 in 100. Even though the false-positive rate is quite low, it gets many more opportunities to occur, and so false-positives can drown out the true positives, which are relatively rare.

If the story ended here, you'd be left with the gloomy conclusion that doctors aren't very good at interpreting the results of medical tests. But cognitive psychology research is increasingly emphasising more positive aspects, such as using psychologists' knowledge of human reasoning to improve it – as we discuss in the following section.

Solving problems with similar structures

German psychologist Gerd Gigerenzer studied how psychologists can teach people to improve their reasoning and so solve base-rate related problems, such as the taxi driver one (in the earlier section 'Ignoring the base rate') and the diagnosis problem in the preceding section.

These problems are examples of *homomorphic* ones, which means that they share the same basic structure and so can be solved using the same method. (Chapter 17 covers *isomorphic* problems – ones with an *identical* underlying structure.) You can solve homomorphic problems in two ways – the hard way uses Bayes's theorem, and Gigerenzer's method is the easy way. We consider the latter, which still takes a bit of explaining.

Gigerenzer's approach is based on the idea that people have evolved the ability to think about real things rather than abstract concepts, and so to make solving these problems easier people should convert them into a frequency-based format. The key to the *frequency format* is to get rid of abstract measures such as probabilities and percentages and instead use real numbers. So when you're given a problem like the medical diagnosis one in the preceding section, you follow these steps:

1. **Convert the base-rate probabilities to real numbers.** In this case, imagine a real sample of 1,000 women being tested with a mammogram. Use the base rate to determine how many would be expected to have the disease. In the diagnosis example, that's 1 per cent and so 10 women would have the disease and the remaining 990 women wouldn't.

2. **Work out the correct hit and false negative rates.** In this case, doctors know that 80 per cent of women with the disease get a positive mammogram (8 of 10 women with the disease get an accurate positive result and 2 get a false-negative).

3. **Work out the false hit and correct diagnosis rates.** Take the remaining number of women who don't have the disease and determine what number of them will receive a correct negative or false-positive test. Of the 990 women, you'd expect 10 per cent (99 women) to obtain a false-positive.

4. **Compare the number you obtain in Step 2 with the sum of those obtained in Steps 2 and 3.** In this case, the result determines how many people with a positive test actually have the disease.

Restricting screening to high-risk groups

The fact that medical test results are sometimes unreliable when the base rate is relatively small is one reason why medical screening for conditions such as breast cancer is rarely extended to the whole population. Instead it's reserved for high-risk groups (the expected base rate is higher). If hospitals (and the NHS in the UK) screened the whole population, the number of false-positives would create such anxiety and require so much re-testing that it's not considered feasible unless a test is very accurate.

We put the results in a table to make the numbers clearer:

	Has Disease	Doesn't Have Disease	Total
Positive	8	99	107
Negative	2	891	893

The sample of 1,000 women would have 107 positive tests, of which only 8 are accurate. In this case, you divide the number of true positives by the total number of positive tests to get 8/107, or just under 7.5 per cent.

Gigerenzer and his colleagues produced tutorial materials to teach this method of solving Bayesian problems to novices in a couple of hours. Given the importance of this kind of problem in understanding medical test results, and the fact that people aren't naturally good at solving them, at least people can be taught to do them correctly.

Using heuristics successfully in the real world

Gigerenzer and his colleagues looked at how people use heuristics in reality and came to different conclusions from previous research. Whereas Kahneman and Tversky illustrated how heuristics can lead people to make consistent errors (biases; refer to the section 'Taking a shortcut – to the wrong answer!' earlier in this chapter), Gigerenzer's research emphasised the benefits of using heuristics in many real-world problems.

In one experiment he asked groups of financial experts and non-experts in the United States and Germany to pick stocks to buy in a range of US and German firms. He found that the best-performing stocks were those companies chosen by non-experts in a different country.

Gigerenzer and colleagues explained this result in terms of the *recognition heuristic* – people choose what's most familiar. Being recognised by a member of the public is a good predictor of a company's rising profile and likely success; a person who only recognises a few companies can pick those ones and they're likely to be among the more successful. A financial expert is familiar with all the companies and therefore can't use recognition as a useful heuristic.

Gigerenzer and colleagues demonstrated many other cases where simple heuristics can produce better results than more complicated decision-making methods. One of these heuristics is called *take the best*, which means making choices based on a single best distinguishing property. (For lots more on decision-making, move decisively to Chapter 19.)

Making mental models

According to the Scottish psychologist Kenneth Craik, to make sense of reality the human brain constructs 'small-scale models of reality'. These *mental models* allow people to make predictions about the likely outcomes of a situation and adapt this to novel situations. But because reality is so complex and the models are considerably simpler, inevitably they're incomplete and don't fully reflect real-world situations. Therefore, mental models are most successful in situations that can be simplified without losing important details.

Mental models are an important concept in the design of user interfaces for computer software. For a user to be able to use an app, he needs to have a mental model of the app that matches that of the designer in order for a maximised 'fit' between the user's mental model and how the system works. One method is to use metaphors for real-world objects, such as pictures of documents and folders and rubbish bins as metaphors for their real-world counterparts. Another method is to use established conventions, such as copying whatever the most popular software does.

Chapter 19

Making Up Your Mind: Decision-Making

A possibly apocryphal story concerns a leading researcher in decision-making trying to decide whether to take a new job or not. Advised simply to use the techniques from decision-making theory, the expert said, 'Don't be silly, this is important!'

This story is all too believable: a lot of people working on cognitive psychology don't necessarily apply their knowledge in everyday life. Yet making decisions is socially and cognitively important.

In Chapters 17 and 18, we look at how people solve problems and approach reasoning tasks. But when talking about decision-making, we also have to consider other factors, such as risk-perception, emotions and how people judge the value of different potential outcomes. Also, when making important real-world decisions (outside of formal experiments), people don't know what the future holds or what other options may become available in the future.

The research we present in this chapter focuses on the cognitive processes involved in making decisions. Cognitive psychologists have identified many of the processes involved in decision-making and some of the problems that people can experience. Being aware of these issues can affect your decisions, helping you to discover how to make better decisions and avoid being led into bad ones.

Researching Real-World Decision-Making

The various theories and experiments that we discuss in Chapters 17 and 18 often focus on abstract problems with little relevance to the real world. Such controlled studies can tell you a lot about the mechanisms underlying your thought processes but, as with much experimental research, they lack *ecological validity*: that is, they don't closely represent the real world (see Chapter 1).

One thing missing from decisions made in the artificial setting of the laboratory is the importance of the outcome. Experimenters sometimes offer small awards to participants for making successful choices, but the stakes are never as high as for some real-world decisions. In the lab, people don't have much to win or lose and so they may not approach problems as they would when the consequences really matter.

As a result, when people 'have skin in the game', psychologists can't consider their decisions purely in terms of logic or mechanical processes. Instead, they have to take into account the effects of emotion and the complexity of the real-world environment.

For example, one big decision concerns how people choose a partner – 'the one' for them – when they rarely have perfect knowledge about the people they meet and don't know whom they're going to meet in the future. How do people decide when they can't make an optimal decision? As you may expect, scientists tend to take rather an unromantic view of such matters.

How do you know when to stop your search for love? The answer lies in the odd word *satisficing* (a combination of 'satisfy' and 'suffice'), which describes how people look for something that satisfies their basic requirements but stops short of waiting for their best possible outcome. A person waiting for all the necessary information to choose the perfect partner would die of old age before committing.

Thinking speedily

The result of one type of test helped psychologists discover more about why people make wrong decisions – fortunately in the safety of the lab! This test has more ecological validity, because it isn't based on weird and abstract logic problems and because the wording is more familiar.

This exercise is called the *cognitive reflection test,* because it tests something about your style of thinking. Take a look at these three questions that vary in difficulty. Answer them as quickly as you can:

- ✔ A bat and a ball cost £1.10 in total. The bat costs £1.00 more than the ball. How much does the ball cost? _____ pence

- ✔ If five machines take five minutes to make five widgets, how long does it take 100 machines to make 100 widgets? _____ minutes

- ✔ A lake contains a patch of lily pads. Every day, the patch doubles in size. If it takes 48 days for the patch to cover the entire lake, how long would it take for the patch to cover half of the lake? _____ days

How did you do? Check the answers at the end of this paragraph. If you got all three correct – well done! If you got the obvious but wrong answers, don't worry; you aren't alone. The idea is that to get the correct answer in each case you need to inhibit the impulsive part of your brain that wants to blurt out the obvious answer and instead 'reflect' on your answer. The answers are 5 pence, 5 minutes and 47 days (not 10 pence, 100 minutes and 24 days).

In his book *Thinking Fast and Slow* (Penguin), Nobel Prize–winner Daniel Kahneman splits the brain into two systems:

- ✔ **System 1 does the 'fast thinking':** It operates automatically and quickly with little conscious effort or control. In some ways it reflects the ingrained knowledge of 'crystallised' intelligence.

- ✔ **System 2 handles 'slow thinking':** This more deliberate system uses conscious, effortful processes and allocates resources in your working memory to solve problems.

If you answered two or three questions correctly, it suggests that you tend to engage System 2 more; if you got mainly the obvious but wrong answers, you're relying on System 1 to get you through.

This exercise isn't a test of intelligence. American economist Shane Frederick tested various university students and the majority went for the obvious but wrong answers. Even at the Massachusetts Institute of Technology (renowned lair of geeky scientists) less than half of the sample got all three questions right. The average score across all university students that were studied was just slightly above 1 out of 3.

One of the reasons why people jump to the wrong answers so readily in these questions is that they seem obvious. Interestingly, you can improve people's performance on the test by printing the questions in a hard-to-read font. Doing so seems to cause the brain to slow down and be careful, thus engaging a more analytical thinking style.

Studying how people make decisions: Normative theories

To study decision-making scientifically, psychologists need a way of evaluating decisions objectively. They require a *normative* theory that offers a 'norm' against which to assess people's decision-making skills, and so allows them to evaluate whether a decision is good or bad. One such normative tool is *utility theory*, which provides a rational method for making decisions that weighs up the likelihood of success as well as the relative benefits of success and costs of failure. According to this theory, the best choice is the one that maximises the expected benefits.

But this approach has problems. Perhaps the most serious one is that people rarely know all the relevant information when making a decision; coming up with accurate values for the likelihood of success or the value of an outcome isn't always possible.

In Chapter 18, we describe Kahneman and Tversky's influential research that emphasised how human thinking is riddled with errors due to people using mental shortcuts (heuristics) that often lead to wrong answers. We also explain Gigerenzer's contrasting view that heuristics are in fact a 'toolbox' – exquisitely adapted to the needs of the real world – and the power of the *recognition heuristic*: that is, given a choice between two things, people tend to go with the most familiar.

Gigerenzer gives a good example of a real-world, decision-making heuristic. People used to think that a fielder running to catch a ball (in cricket, rounders or baseball) was making complex mathematical calculations about her speed and angle relative to the ball, implemented by part of the brain inaccessible to conscious introspection. But Gigerenzer shows that in fact people use a much simpler heuristic method:

1. **Run towards the ball, fixing your gaze on it.**

2. **Try to keep your head at a constant angle while running.**

3. **Speed up if you have to *lower* your head to keep the ball centred, but slow down if you have to *raise* it to keep the ball centred.**

This surprisingly effective strategy requires no mathematical calculations or knowledge of the laws of physics (in contrast with the view presented in Chapter 4!).

Understanding why heuristics work when normative theories fail

A surprising, apparently counter-intuitive finding from Gigerenzer's research is not only that heuristics can match the performance of normative theories, but also that sometimes they outperform them.

How can that be? Surely a normative theory that takes account of all available information should outperform a heuristic that only uses one or two salient points on which to base the decision? But in fact, if models are based on all the available information from past occurrences, they can become too specific to those events and not sufficiently applicable to the current decision.

A second problem is that normative methods often require you to have perfect knowledge of the state of the world, which is rarely the case. In experiments that pit experts against amateurs (such as when choosing stock options; refer to Chapter 18), experts certainly take into account many more factors but often without adding a lot of potential information: their model is never complete, just more complicated.

If you develop too complicated a model of the world based on past experience, you can end up with a world view that's too specific to your own personal set of experiences. The more factors that you take into account, the more your view becomes associated with the specific events that you've experienced.

Framing the problem

Another factor affecting decision-making is the *framing effect*, which is when people alter their decisions depending on how they are presented, for example, as a loss or as a gain. Typically people avoid risky decisions when the choice is presented positively but take more risks when the choice is presented negatively.

Kahneman and Tversky asked two group of participants this question:

> *Imagine that the United States is preparing for the outbreak of an unusual Asian disease, which is expected to kill 600 people. Two alternative programmes to combat the disease have been proposed. Assume that the exact scientific estimates of the consequences of the programmes are as follows.*

One group was given these figures:

- ✔ If Programme A is adopted, 200 people will be saved.
- ✔ If Programme B is adopted, a one-third probability exists that 600 people will be saved and a two-thirds probability says that no one will be saved.

A second group was given these different figures:

- ✔ If Programme A is adopted, 400 people will die.
- ✔ If Programme B is adopted, a one-third probability exists that nobody will die and a two-thirds probability says that 600 people will die.

In fact, the options have identical consequences: the numbers of expected deaths are the same for Programmes A and B in both versions. But the first is framed in terms of lives saved and the second in terms of lives lost. People shown the first version were more likely to take Programme A, which guaranteed saving 200 people, whereas those who saw the second option were more likely to take a chance on Programme B.

Deciding to Look into Your Brain

In this section, we ask you to get inside your brain and look at the parts involved in decision-making. For example, the pre-frontal cortex (PFC) is a region associated with *executive functioning,* which includes the kinds of problem-solving ability that we cover in Chapters 17 and 18. We also discuss brain development and studies of patients with neurological damage. These helped psychologists understand how different regions of the brain are involved in weighing up the consequences of decisions.

Handling annoying issues: The multiple demand system

Much research associates many areas of the human brain with a *modular architecture*, in which specific areas perform specific functions. For example, certain areas are devoted to different aspects of visual perception, such as motion, colour and form, and other areas deal with specific auditory aspects, such as sounds with a particular musical pitch.

But the *multiple demand system* (a set of areas in the brain) is different: it's designed to handle whatever problem is currently vexing you. John Duncan identified this system, which consists of parts of the PFC and the parietal system of the brain. Its neurons can't be devoted to specialist functions but must instead be able to handle novel situations dynamically. The neurons in this area can be recruited for multiple purposes depending on the demands of the current situation.

The one thing that's common about the situations in which the multiple demand system is particularly active (as shown by functional magnetic resonance imaging – fMRI – scans) is that they involve the use of *fluid intelligence*: that is, the problem-solving ability associated with novel situations is more associated with long-term memory (the wisdom of experience). This evidence shows psychologists that decision-making, thinking and reasoning are complex processes that require multiple brain areas. It also shows that one core characteristic of intelligence is the ability to make logical decisions.

Seeing how brain damage affects decision-making

If you think of thought as a singular thing, you may expect a patient suffering with PFC damage (which has impaired her ability to solve problems or make decisions) to seem obviously impaired. You may not expect the person to be able to act normally or hold a conversation.

But patients with localised damage can come across as quite normal in their behaviour, with their impairments only becoming noticeable with the kind of problems that tap into fluid intelligence: they can hold conversations, watch television and follow instructions. But the apparent normality of the person's behaviour is coupled with them making bizarre choices in problem-solving situations or real-world decisions.

Experiments of decision-making that employ gambling-type tasks are relevant here. Participants' choices are monitored under different conditions, in which the odds of various outcomes can be manipulated and the effect on their subsequent choices is measured. Real prizes of small amounts of money or other rewards can be used to motivate the participants.

 Patients with PFC damage produce a pattern of results on such tasks that's consistent with anecdotal evidence of their problems in making real-life decisions. They show a poor ability to think through the likely negative consequences of many choices and display a greater tendency to base decisions on short-term reward and positive associations.

Forensic psychologists using such tests show that many career criminals display similar patterns of performance on problem-solving tasks as those with PFC damage. This highlights how the PFC is important for making appropriate decisions.

Tracing the development of decision-making

Traditionally, people thought that most interesting changes in the brain occur in early childhood, and that differences in thinking or decision-making by teenagers is attributable to the hormonal effects of sexual maturity and the social world in which they live, with effects such as peer-group pressure. But an emerging view suggests that the differences in the thinking of teenagers may be down to fundamental physical differences in the structure of their brains.

Analysing the teenage brain

Cognitive neuroscientist Sarah Jayne Blakemore researches the major changes that occur in the brain throughout life. The PFC goes through considerable development during adolescence, and Blakemore studied how this fact should influence the way teenagers are educated.

In this view, people have two competing systems:

- **Limbic:** Gives people a rush of excitement when they engage in risky behaviour.
- **Pre-frontal cortex (PFC):** Involved in making executive decisions; it inhibits behaviour that's too risky.

According to Blakemore, the teenage brain has physical differences from the adult brain. These differences are caused by the fact that the limbic system reaches a fully mature state earlier than the PFC. In this two-horse race between the impulse-driven limbic system and the more considered and sensible PFC, the limbic system wins; until the PFC catches up, the teenage brain is more prone to impulsive decisions and risky behaviour. Indeed, the PFC doesn't seem to reach maturity until the mid-20s, which may explain the average age for criminality (from dangerous driving to participating in terrorism) is late teens and early 20s.

Getting through to the teenage brain

If you're a teenager, please don't take offence – you obviously have a more mature PFC because you made the great decision to read this book! If you're still offended, you're paying too much attention to your limbic system – instead, allow your PFC to take more control.

One way that public health and safety campaigns have targeted the teenage mind is through emotive and visceral advertising. For example, one advert conveyed the dangers of texting on a mobile phone while driving with a vivid reconstruction of a resulting car crash, including a long and harrowing focus on the physical injuries and long-term emotional damage caused by the accident.

By associating the behaviour with strong visual and emotional content, this advert is well-designed to target teenagers. The strong negative emotional association with the behaviour of texting while driving taps into the more primitive, associative mechanisms used by the limbic system – your basic 'gut feeling' about a situation.

Emotional advertising may be less appealing to people with a well-developed PFC. They may find the message too emotive and prefer evidence that texting while driving impairs a driver's attention and reaction times, such as an advert showing a driver's stopping distance when using a mobile phone compared to normal. Both styles are effective, depending on the target audience.

Remembering the role of experiences

Psychologists have to be careful about how they interpret developmental changes to the brain. Thinking of changes in the brain as following some biological programme, which triggers certain changes at certain stages in life, may be natural, but an alternative view is that experiences determine changes to the brain.

People take more risks when they're younger, because building up a catalogue of experiences that end badly takes time. Only with more experience and knowledge of the potential risks do they begin to inhibit these risky decisions. The limbic reward system gets positively reinforced quickly by short-term thrills, and it takes longer to accumulate enough of the rarer (but necessary) negative outcomes from making risky decisions to engage the executive inhibitory processes of the PFC.

Altering People's Decisions

Cognitive psychology's discoveries of how people make decisions can be used to influence those decisions so that people make better ones – or to help them resist negative or inappropriate manipulation.

Assisting public-health information

Sometimes people's logical reasoning is fine but their premise is wrong. Logic only works to help people make the right decision when they have the right mental model of the situation. If their understanding is wrong, they may well make the wrong decision while being perfectly rational. When that's the case, the solution is to frame the problem better with appropriate language and examples.

A growing medical problem is the emergence of antibiotic resistance in germs. This emerges partly because people are taking antibiotics more than they should for conditions that don't improve as they take them, such as viral infections. In addition, people stop taking the antibiotic before finishing the full course, usually because the symptoms go and they assume that they're better; unfortunately, the antibiotic may not yet have killed lingering germs. Therefore, the infectious organism has time to regroup. Repeated across many different patients, this process gives those organisms more time to evolve antibiotic-resistant strains.

The medical charity, The Wellcome Trust, researched people's attitudes and beliefs about antibiotics to try to determine why they often stop taking the course of treatment early and how medical professionals can overcome this behaviour. They found that many people believe that antibiotic resistance occurs in their body rather than in the bacteria (in which resistance actually evolves). If you think that your body is becoming resistant to germs, stopping a course of antibiotics makes sense, but in fact it contributes to the ability of bugs to gain resistance.

One effective strategy is to show patients with infections a picture of the organism that causes their infection and say, 'this bug is going to gain resistance to the antibiotic you're taking, not you . . . unless you take the full course of treatment'. Another suggestion is to modify the language, using terminology that promotes the correct understanding of the relationships. For example, instead of talking about 'antibiotic resistance', doctors should say 'antibiotic resistant germs', because this anchors the concept to the bug rather than the patient.

Tackling supermarket manipulation

As well as the big decisions you make, your life can also be affected dramatically by the cumulative effects of all the little decisions you make every day.

People in developed countries tend to have the luxury of choice, but their choices often leave a lot to be desired. Many of these countries have problems with poor diet, leading to growing levels of obesity and resulting health problems. Decisions on what to eat are affected in different ways by different cognitive processes:

> ✔ **Recognition:** Advertisers target people's more simple heuristics and associative learning. By ensuring that their logo is visible as often as possible to as many people as possible, big brands exploit the *mere exposure effect* – the sense of familiarity in the absence of negative effect that leads to a positive feeling towards the brand (and brand recognition is a good predictor of success).

- ✔ **Positive association:** Advertisers also actively promote positive associations with the brand: for example, they show healthy young people having fun while using the brand. These kinds of associations target the limbic system's associative response rather than the more reasoned, logical processing of the PFC (refer to the earlier 'Tracing the development of decision-making' section for more).

- ✔ **Availability:** Big brands have more money to spend on advertising than public health campaigns, and so getting their message across is easier. Consumers bring to mind the messages from the advertising more easily compared to warnings.

- ✔ **Halo effect:** A single positive attribute can have an effect on how people judge other information in the situation. For example, one positive health claim can cause people to overlook more negative aspects. Sometimes this halo effect can lead to strange outcomes: people's estimates of the calories contained in a meal were lower when a healthy salad was added to a picture of a plate of junk food. Even though the amount of junk food was the same on both plates, calorie estimates for the overall meals were lower for the junk food plus salad than for the junk food alone, as if people estimate that the salad is adding negative calories!

- ✔ **Unit perception:** People seem to estimate portion size based on container size. For example, people tend to eat less in a buffet when portions, scoops, plates or bowls are smaller, even when they can visit the buffet to refill as often as they like.

Cognitive psychology can help public health policy by designing systems for nutritional labelling that take into account how people make decisions.

Deliberating about jury decision-making

In an example of the halo effect from the preceding section, mock jury decision-making studies found that people are positively swayed in their judgements by the physical attractiveness of the defendant.

In addition, one theory from American psychologists Nancy Pennington and Reid Hastie suggests that jurors build a kind of simple mental model of the sequence of events being described in a case. Jurors are more likely to believe a statement if they can incorporate it into a plausible story model of what happened and more likely to believe evidence for the prosecution or defence when it's presented in story order rather than witness order.

This theory fits with the more general discovery that people find some representations easier to work with than others: specifically, they find representations consistent with their internal schemas easier to use (see Chapter 12). What's important isn't simply what information you're presented with, but *how* it's presented.

Chapter 20

Thinking Clearly about the Role of Emotions

*E*xperiments show that people remember emotional events more vividly and accurately than unemotional ones. If, say, you try to remember an event from your own life from three years ago, most likely the memory is emotional – perhaps your first kiss, a tricky exam or the death of a beloved pet. This finding that mood can improve memory is one of the ways in which emotions impact cognition, but the story is more complicated than that.

Emotions can also affect other cognitive processes. For example, when you're in a bad mood (say you've been told off by a teacher or had to take a pet to the vet), you don't work as efficiently. Research suggests that when people are in an emotional state, they seem to concentrate on emotionally relevant things. In particular, when you're sad you don't concentrate as well as when you're happy.

Understanding the vital role that emotions play in cognitive processing is important when considering the clinical conditions that affect your emotions, such as depression and anxiety disorders. In fact, awareness of these issues shows more widely how 'hot' your cognitive abilities can be. They aren't stable ('cold'), slowly changing only as you learn new things. Instead, the effect that emotional states have on cognition shows that constantly changing environmental changes affect your abilities. Put simply, emotions have a bearing on *what* you think and *how* you think.

In this chapter, we show how emotions and moods affect the ways in which people behave, learn, remember and make decisions. We look at how emotion influences how things are detected (*encoded*) and perceived, and how people attend differently to emotional stimuli (objects, words, people and sounds) than to unemotional stimuli. We also describe how people tend to remember things because of their emotional state – either because that state is the same as it was when they learnt the information or because the information matches the emotion. We also cover two examples of clinically relevant cases of emotion affecting cognition.

In other words, this chapter shows how emotion affects everything we discuss in this book!

How Do You Feel? Introducing Emotions

You may think that you know exactly what emotion is, but as a scientist you need to take a step back and question any easy assumptions.

Consider this example: in *Star Trek IV*, the computer asks Mr Spock, 'How do you feel?' This question stumps the friendly Vulcan because he has no emotions and is always confused by his 'flawed feeling human' friends. If, suddenly, he felt an emotion, how would Spock know what it was? That's a tricky question! You know when you feel happy, but what is happiness? The answer to that question goes well beyond the scope of cognitive psychology, or even psychology (try philosophy!).

In this section, we describe what cognitive psychologists mean when they refer to *emotion*, show how people learn emotions and explore the thought processes surrounding emotions.

Emotions, moods and affective states are similar but distinct concepts:

- ✔ **Emotions:** Brief, but intense, experiences
- ✔ **Mood:** Prolonged, low-intensity experiences
- ✔ **Affect:** The whole lot of experiences, including emotions, mood, preferences and *arousal* (the bodily reactions to stimuli such as sweaty palms or increased heart rate)
- ✔ **Valence:** The subjective quality of a particular event, such as thinking something is good or not good

Looking at ways of defining emotion

Broadly speaking, psychologists describe *emotions* as a combination of the following:

- ✔ **Physiological changes and arousal:** How your body changes due to a stimulus. For example, when you're afraid, your heart rate increases and your pupils dilate.

✔ **Facial expressions:** When you feel a particular emotion, your face contorts into a specific pattern. For example, when you're happy, the corners of your mouth tilt up, and if you're very happy, you open your mouth to reveal your teeth – in other words, you smile!

✔ **Cognitive appraisals:** When you feel an emotion, you evaluate the event cognitively and decide whether it's positive or negative. For example, if you've just been asked out by the guy you've fancied for months, you're probably able to work out that you should be happy.

At this point, you may be thinking that people display emotions and appraise their feelings in different ways. Indeed, a number of experts believe that cross-cultural differences exist in facial expressions – if you meet someone from a tribal village in Papua New Guinea and he reveals his teeth, you may not know for certain whether he's happy or hungry.

American psychologist Paul Ekman claims that six basic emotions and their associated expressions are *universal*. They're the same across all peoples of the world, because they're genetic: happiness, surprise, anger, sadness, fear and disgust. You can classify these six emotions by relating them to the fight-or-flight response as follows:

✔ **Approach emotions:** Happiness, surprise and anger make you feel as though you want to draw nearer to the thing causing the emotion.

✔ **Withdrawal emotions:** Sadness, fear and disgust make you feel as though you want to move away from the thing causing the emotion.

You can also use the response of the *sympathetic nervous system* (part of the nervous system that controls the basic physiological responses to stimuli) to classify these emotions. For example, happiness, anger, surprise and fear result in an increase in activity, whereas sadness causes a depletion of the emotional resources.

Ouch! Developing emotional responses

Emotions are externally mysterious. Why does something become emotional for you? Why do some people develop phobias? Places, items, songs and people all have emotional value – some more than others, depending on the person and his experience.

One of your authors has a phobia of elastic bands – we don't want to stretch the point (groan!) but he gets anxious when he sees one. On the other hand, driving down the street where his first love lived always makes him feel happy. How do such connections – between, say, a street and an emotion – develop?

One theory to explain how people discover that particular things have emotional value is through *classical conditioning*. Simply put, emotional value can be paired with an object. People learn to associate a particular place or thing with a particular feeling or emotion.

Ivan Pavlov was one of the first scientists to test this phenomenon systematically, having noticed that the dogs in his lab salivated at the sound of a trolley bringing the food, instead of just the sight of the food. The dogs seemed to have paired the sound with the food they'd receive.

Similarly, classical conditioning has been used to explain how some phobias may develop. *Fear conditioning* is when a particular neural stimulus (such as a word) is paired with an electric shock. The unpleasant electric shock causes arousal and fear, as shown by elevated skin *galvanic response* (slightly sweatier hands). Eventually participants associate the stimulus with the shock and the stimulus alone produces arousal.

Liz Phelps, an American neuroscientist, identified that the amygdala (part of the brain about 5 centimetres behind each eye) is critically important in fear conditioning. She tested a patient, SP, who had damage to the amygdala. SP was able to remember an experiment and report receiving electrical shocks in it. However, she never showed the elevated skin response associated with fear of the stimulus. Thus, Phelps concluded that the amygdala was critical for processing fear.

Although fear conditioning is readily demonstrable – you can pair almost any previously neutral stimulus with a fear response – some stimuli can be fear-conditioned much more easily. Snakes, spiders and other normal phobia objects (unlike a fear of elastic bands) can be fear-conditioned more quickly and more easily than less terrifying stimuli (such as a cute guinea pig). So humans may have some kind of genetic predisposition to fear certain animals, and only minimal learning is required to develop this fear (although check out the nearby sidebar 'Watch and be afraid . . . very afraid'). Alternatively, these fears may be more socially and culturally expected so that people expect to fear them more.

Advertisers use a similar form of emotional classical conditioning (evaluative rather than fear-based) when they pair a product with something desirable. The old-fashioned, sexist example is pairing scantily clad women with fast cars. Advertisers also use endorsements from (supposedly) popular celebrities so that you pair the feeling of liking the celebrity with the product. Advertisers can also make their adverts funny so that you connect the amusement and liking of the advert with the product.

People can also learn fear, and by extrapolation all forms of conditioning, through observation. You don't need to receive the shock to be afraid of a particular object; simply witnessing someone else getting the shock is sufficient for you to pair the stimulus with the shock.

Watch and be afraid . . . very afraid

A study demonstrating observational fear learning used two groups of monkeys: one raised in the wild and the other in captivity. The former group had a natural fear of snakes, whereas the group raised in captivity had never seen a snake. The two groups were put in a cage and had to reach past a snake to get some food. The wild group refused but the captivity-raised monkeys reached for the food, indicating that phobias aren't genetic.

But when the monkeys raised in captivity could see the wild monkeys demonstrating fear of the snake, they subsequently showed fear of the snake and refused to reach past it for food. The conclusion is that monkeys can learn fear through observing other monkeys.

Thinking about emotion

Here's an interesting question that fascinates cognitive psychologists. When you have the physiological responses that are generally associated with an emotion, do you need to know why they're happening in order to feel the emotion? Put another way, can you have an emotion without any cognitive awareness?

On one side of the debate, the American-Polish social psychologist Robert Zajonc claims that you can experience emotions without any conscious awareness as to why you have them: this is called the *affective primacy hypothesis*. He suggests that affect (the collection of all your emotional experiences) and cognition are based on two separate systems.

As evidence, Zajonc demonstrated the *mere exposure effect*, where people rate things more favourably if they've seen them before, irrespective of whether they remember seeing the object.

In a contrasting view, Richard Lazarus, an American psychologist, proposes that *cognitive appraisal* plays an important role: you can't have an emotion without thinking about the object or event. Individuals carry out a primary appraisal of a situation, regarding the situation as positive, negative or irrelevant. They then perform secondary appraisals, to assess their coping ability by implicating someone as responsible and to establish the expectancy of the event occurring in the future. They then re-appraise and monitor these conclusions.

To back up cognitive appraisal, Lazarus presented emotionally stirring films, after which participants were given instructions to intellectualise or deny the events of the films. These instructions reduced the physiological response to the films relative to a control condition, indicating the importance of thinking about events and the emotional response.

So, which view is more accurate? Do you need to think before you have emotion or not? Well, neuroscience provides some answers: noted American neuroscientist Joseph LeDoux identified two emotion-related neural circuits:

- ✔ **A slow-acting circuit:** A slow-acting circuit that involves conscious detailed cognitive processing of an emotion, supporting Lazarus.

- ✔ **A faster circuit:** A faster circuit that bypasses the conscious processing and the cortex, supporting Zajonc.

Therefore, both are correct! Fast emotional responses don't require thought whereas slower ones do – which is why you should count to ten when you get angry!

Recognising the Reach of Emotion

Most experimental studies show that sad moods are detrimental when people are performing cognitive tasks. Sad moods impair performance on reasoning, thinking, memory and face recognition, whereas happy moods tend to be beneficial in many of these tasks. But things aren't quite that simple (they never are in psychology!). These mood differences tend to occur only during difficult or complex tasks. Fewer differences exist between happy and sad people with simpler tasks.

Emotions affect cognition on many levels. In this section, we explain how they impact all the basic processes that we describe in this book, from perception and attention to memory, language and thought.

Attending to emotions and perception

Mood affects how you perceive the world and attend to things in it. Here we describe how this happens.

Emotional perception

On some occasions, emotion can affect what you perceive. When provided with ambiguous stimuli, sad people tend to interpret them negatively, whereas happy people interpret them positively. For example, when participants are shown a neutral face and asked to rate its emotion, sad people perceive it as sad and happy people as happy.

Differences also exist as to where sad and happy people look when viewing visual scenes. During face-perception tasks, sad people tend to look at features other than the eyes, whereas happy people tend to look at the eyes more. Further experiments show that sad people look around a room more than at the person with whom they're talking.

Emotion and attention

Generally, emotional material grabs your attention more than non-emotional material. This tendency makes sense, because emotions are likely to portray important information for your survival or well-being.

In Chapter 7, we introduce the Stroop effect (where naming the colour of ink in which a colour word is written takes longer when the word's meaning fails to match the ink's colour: say, 'red' written in green ink).

The similar emotional Stroop task uses emotional or phobia-related words in different colours (for example, 'snake' for those with snake phobias). Emotional words interfere with colour ink naming more so than neutral words, showing that emotion interferes with attention.

Researchers have also used the *Posner cueing paradigm* – where a cue precedes the location of a target on valid trials and doesn't precede the location of a target on invalid trials (refer to Chapter 7) – to examine how emotion affects attention. When the cue is a threatening stimulus (such as an angry face), the effect of an invalid cue is greater than when the cue is neutral. In other words, participants fixate on an angry stimulus and can't disengage from it. Emotional cues hold the attention.

But instead of showing simply that emotion affects attention, research also reveals that specific emotions affect attention in different ways. In visual search tasks, people find angry faces easier to detect, even in a crowd of other faces. But the same effect doesn't occur for happy faces, highlighting how valence (refer to the earlier section 'How Do You Feel? Introducing Emotions' for a definition) influences cognition.

Experiments have unearthed another effect in sad and depressed people: *defocused attention* is where fixing attention on one thing is difficult. Instead of being a spotlight, attention is more spread out. Scientists have long known that depression is associated with many intrusive thoughts. If depressed people can focus their attention on a particular task and block out these intrusive thoughts, they're better able to perform the task.

In one experiment, sad participants were presented with words surrounded by a coloured frame in the left- or right-hand side of a computer screen. When given a word-recognition task, happy and sad participants performed equally well. For each word they recognised, they were then asked about the coloured frame and the position. Happy participants were unable to remember either bit of extra information, but sad participants did. Sad moods seem to cause people to attend to lots of extra, unwanted, irrelevant information.

Both the emotion of the stimuli and the emotion of the observer affect how something is likely to be attended to. We cover further attentional biases that emotions cause in the later section 'Worrying about Anxiety'.

Remembering to cover memory and mood!

Mood affects how participants remember information, what information is remembered and what's recalled. Here we describe these effects.

Mood dependency

Many people remember things more effectively when they're in the same emotional state as when they learnt them (the *encoding specificity principle* from Chapter 9). A version of this effect has been discovered using emotions: if people learn items in a particular mood they're better able to recall that information when in the same mood (known as *mood-dependent memory*). So, if you revise for an exam when you're happy, you perform best during it when you're also feeling happy.

In one study of mood-dependent memory, participants were made to feel a particular mood: in this case, happy or sad (called *mood induction*). They then learnt a list of words. Half the participants recalled the words in the same mood, whereas the other recalled the words in the contrasting mood. Participants whose mood matched from learning to test recalled more words than those participants whose mood didn't match.

Research also shows the effects of mood-dependent memory on recalling childhood memories: when happy, people recall about four times more happy childhood memories than sad ones. Clinically depressed patients tend to rate their own parents as having been more rejecting and distant when the patient was a child. But when not depressed, the same patients rate their parents as being warmer and kinder.

Although the logic of mood-dependent memory is simple and compelling, it isn't found consistently. A number of researchers have failed to find it, leading some people to consider it an unreliable effect. In fact, three principles exist in order to obtain mood-dependent memory effects:

✔ **The emotion must be seen to be causally belonging to the material.**
   That is, the information must somehow relate to the emotion.

> ✔ **Mood-dependent memory is more likely for less meaningful stimuli or ambiguous stimuli.** That is, mood affects memories that are not very important.
>
> ✔ **Without any other cues to memory, mood may be useful.** Thus, mood-dependent memory effects are more likely in free recall experiments than recognition or cued-recall tests.

Despite not being consistently found, mood-dependent memory effects are more likely if the mood is strong and stable and is used when learning about the information. Just being in a particular mood doesn't mean that you remember things learnt previously in that mood – you remember them only if they relate to the mood. For example, depressed patients often report intrusive negative thoughts: that is, the negative mood causes negative memories to resurface.

Mood congruency

Mood-congruent memory is similar to mood-dependency and is where your present mood aids the recall of information that's congruent with the mood, regardless of your mood at the time the information was learnt. Therefore, currently happy people tend to remember happy events more than sad events and currently sad people tend to remember sad things better than happy things.

Mood-congruent memory effects have been found in clinically depressed patients. Depressed people given word lists to memorise tend to recall more negative items than positive. Furthermore, mood-congruency is present in the *amount* of cognitive effort paid to particular stimuli. Participants in a sad mood are likely to pay more attention and spend more time viewing sad stimuli than participants in a happy mood.

These effects of mood-congruency may be down to mood congruency during learning of the information, mood congruency during the encoding or storage processes, or better mood-congruent recall. Researchers tested this effect by getting participants to learn emotional material after or before a mood induction. Typically, mood-congruency effects are much stronger at learning than at retrieval.

Encoding when emotional

In Chapter 9, we present the levels of processing framework, which identifies when you're more likely to process things more deeply and so remember them better. The more elaborate and semantic the learning, the more likely you are to remember something. Some research explores how elaboration is affected when you feel emotional.

Using mood induction, experimenters found that sad participants don't benefit from deeper encoding (at least when limited time is available to process information). The conclusions are that sad mood impairs memory for elaborative encoding and only under higher cognitive load. Other researchers found that people in sad moods tend to find using deeper encoding more challenging than people in happy moods: that is, they don't show the same levels of cognitive processing effects. Participants in a sad mood, or depressed patients, recall words that they should've deeply encoded at the same level as shallowly encoded words. The conclusion is that sad mood disrupts effortful coding.

Organising thoughts when you're emotional

Sad participants seem unable to organise material to be remembered. For example, when word lists are given to sad, happy and emotionally neutral people, typically the sad people recall fewer words. However, if the lists of words are organised in a meaningful manner (that is, words relating to similar concepts are put together), all participants perform equally in this recall task. When the list of words is highly disorganised, sad participants show an even larger recall deficit.

Although sad people can better recall organised information, they're more likely to remember associated words falsely when using the DRM paradigm (refer to Chapter 12). Here participants are presented with a series of words related to a particular concept (say, 'doctor', 'nurse' and 'medicine'). Sad people are also more likely to make false recognitions when researchers present lure words in a recognition test (words related to the concept, for example, 'hospital'). The lure word isn't presented first, and so shouldn't be recognised, but sad people tend to recall seeing more lure words than neutral people.

Another method for showing organisation in memory is looking at the order in which words are recalled. Typically people recall words in a clustered manner – they tend to recall words related to a similar concept at the same time. Sad participants don't show this effect. Depressed mood thus affects people's ability to organise material.

Speaking about language and emotion

Mood also affects how people comprehend information. In one study, participants read a passage that was hard to comprehend without a title providing context. The ambiguous passage describes, say, washing clothes without using the word 'washing' or 'cleaning' (try it in Chapter 12). Sad participants comprehended and recalled much less than neutral participants and were less confident in judging what they'd remember.

In lexical-decision tasks (where participants have to identify whether a word is a word or not) happy participants are faster when the words are happiness-related than when they're sadness-related, highlighting how mood affects the very early stages of coding. Some degree of precision applies with these effects, too. Sadness doesn't speed up decisions on general negative words, though, only specifically sadness-related words.

Another assessment of how mood affects reading comes from word-naming tasks, where participants simply have to read words. Again, research finds mood-congruency in the speed of naming words: happy people read happiness-related words faster than sadness-related words.

Thinking that you may be in a mood

Mood has pervasive effects on how people think. Consider someone who's feeling sad or depressed. If you say something innocuous, the person often immediately associates it with something bad. This reaction isn't simply a depressed person moping but a consequence of the semantic and emotional network.

Mood and how you think

Research shows that if you ask depressed people to name a type of weather beginning with the letter 's', they often describe less pleasant weather such as a 'storm'. If you ask happy people the same thing, they say something like 'sunny'. Mood thus affects what springs to mind. Try it on your friends to identify the Down Dereks from the Happy Harrys!

Mood also influences preferences and likes. When you're happy, you tend to prefer to be outside and active; when you're sad, you prefer to be inside and sedentary. Happy moods also cause you to integrate your knowledge into larger, more inclusive units. People include more things in positive categories when they're happy.

Emotional decision-making

Mood also affects the way you encode messages, with sad people processing the world very differently to happy ones.

When presenting persuasive messages to happy and sad people, the latter appear less likely to be swayed by a weak argument than happy people. Sad people are more likely to process the information deeply using more elaborative cognitive processing (which may seem contradictory to what we say at the start of this section, but it isn't, honest!), a case in which sad mood seems to *benefit* cognitive processing.

Happy people tend to employ faster and simpler cognitive processing, characterised by more *heuristic* use (mental shortcuts based on schemas and stereotypes; see Chapter 12) and more superficial encoding. They look more at the gist of situations, without focusing on the detail, and tend to use more open, flexible and creative processing.

Sad people's processing tends to be slower, more systematic and analytical. They focus more on the details of scenes and are more vigilant in their processing and less flexible in their problem-solving. Perhaps they're deliberately more accurate at these tasks to improve their mood by being more successful.

Looking Behind the Reality: How Mood Interacts with Cognition

A number of theories explain how mood interacts with cognition. In this section, we review briefly four of these models. Most were devised with the intention of explaining cognitive deficits in people with depression.

Activating feelings: Emotional network

In 1981, Gordon H Bower, an American cognitive psychologist, used a *neural network model* to explain how emotions can affect memory and other cognitive structures. Simply put, knowledge is represented in memory through a series of nodes (refer to Chapter 12). Each node represents an idea or a construct and is connected to other nodes that represent related constructs. Emotional nodes are also connected to the physiological systems. Whenever an emotion is activated, it activates all the nodes connected to it (called *spreading activation*). When the activation reaches a certain threshold, the ideas become conscious. Critically, a node can be activated by external or internal causes.

We summarise this theory in Figure 20-1. The ovals represent nodes of semantic information, autobiographical memories, physiological responses and behaviours. The pentagons represent the emotion.

So, if the emotional node 'happy' is activated, it causes the face to smile and the physiological system to release endorphins. It activates the connected memory nodes of a happy time (say, a particular holiday or a successful date) and also any items learnt during a happy state. Activating these nodes causes them to be easier to bring to the conscious mind: that is, the affect (flip to the earlier section 'How Do You Feel? Introducing Emotions' for a definition) primes all connected nodes.

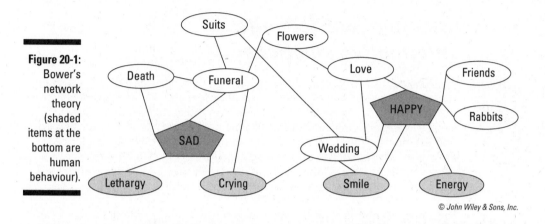

Figure 20-1: Bower's network theory (shaded items at the bottom are human behaviour).

This simple model accounts for mood-dependency and mood-congruency effects (which we describe earlier in the section 'Remembering to cover memory and mood!'). For mood-dependent memory, the idea is that word lists are learnt while attached to the emotional node. If this link is strong, the connection between the word list and the emotion is stronger. Thus, when the emotion is reinstated, the words are as well. Mood-congruency is accounted for because when an emotion is activated, so are all the attached nodes, making them easier to access.

Maintaining focus: Resource allocation model

American psychologists Henry C Ellis and Patricia Ashbrook identified that, based on the network theory (refer to the earlier section, 'Activating feelings: The emotional network'), participants experiencing a particular emotion are likely to have related thoughts activated. This effect is particularly noticeable in depressed patients with intrusive thoughts. The extra emotional thoughts entering the mind mean that the attentional system (refer to Chapter 7) must work overtime to block out distracting thoughts, which isn't easy. So, unwanted emotional material takes up too much of the working memory.

This *resource allocation model* (RAM) is based on the principle of limited attentional and/or working memory resources being available. Emotional states moderate the amount of resources available for other tasks, but take up some of those resources with irrelevant information.

This model suggests that mood-congruent memory effects occur because the emotion causes the attentional system to allocate more resources to mood-congruent stimuli. It explains why mood causes deficits in cognitive processing information but fails fully to describe mood-dependent memory effects.

Trusting your feelings: Informative emotions

The *affect-as-information model* suggests that when presented with a particular stimulus, people simply decide how they feel about it and this decision guides their cognitions. (We define 'affect' in the earlier section 'How Do You Feel? Introducing Emotions'.) In a memory experiment they see a word and decide whether it 'feels' good or not (a very subjective feeling indeed). Subconscious knowledge of the mere exposure effect (which we describe earlier in the section 'Thinking about emotion') means that if the word feels good they're likely to think that they've seen it before.

This model requires establishing how you feel at that particular moment and linking it with the stimulus presented. People consult their emotions to make quick and not fully thought judgements about something, suggesting that judgements aren't based on detailed elaborative coding.

One piece of evidence for this model comes from a telephone survey. Experimenters telephoned a random selection of the public and during the conversation asked for quick judgements about their mood and general life satisfaction. On sunny days, participants tended to report being happier and more satisfied with their lives. On rainy days, they were less happy and less satisfied. But when researchers made the participants aware of the probable source of their mood, by asking them about the weather, these effects disappeared. Thus, people tend to base a judgement about their mood on the weather, unless they know that it's the cause.

The affect-as-information model accounts for mood-congruent memory effects by suggesting that mood guides the search process used by cognition. Mood guides how people look through their memory system, but only affects cognition in the absence of an identifiable reason for the emotion. If the emotion stems from an unrelated stimulus, it's ignored.

Although this theory is simple and general, a number of studies find that its basic premise (that only emotions without an obvious cause are used to guide cognitions) is false. The theory also predicts that mood only affects judgements (whether evaluative or recognition-based), and yet plenty of data show that mood impacts learning and encoding. Thus, affect seems only to be used as information under a limited set of conditions when quick and schema-based processing is all that's required.

Choosing an appropriate processing type: The affect-infusion model

Incorporating the preceding models, Australian psychologist Joseph Forgas developed the *affect-infusion model* (AIM). This model brings in evidence suggesting that emotions affect cognition in varying ways and that this effect is highly context-dependent. The model is based on the idea that humans put the minimum amount of cognitive effort into performing any task, employing the easiest strategy to succeed at a task. However, different tasks require different strategies and levels of effect. Several types of cognitive processing exist and emotion is infused into the processing for only some of them.

The different types of processing are based on the following:

- **Features of the information:** For example, familiarity, complexity

- **Features of the person:** For example, motivation level, cognitive capacity

- **Features of the situation:** For example, expectations, time pressure

These factors combine and allow for four possible processing types:

- **Direct access:** This simplest type is *crystallised* (it can't be altered): you have set-in-stone opinions or facts. You use this form of processing for highly familiar tasks, such as stating your name or where you grew up. These facts are so readily available that you need no elaborate processing, and the processing is so robust that it resists the influence of emotions.

- **Motivated:** When you have a strong desire to search for a particular piece of information. This processing is goal-directed, meaning that you use it to seek out particular information. It involves quite a lot of cognitive resources.

- **Heuristic:** Relies on minimal information and is used when no personal relevance or motivation is present to process more deeply. In other words, it's a shortcut. For this reason, processing may be based on irrelevant social factors or, indeed, irrelevant internal factors, such as emotion. When using heuristics, people may say, 'I feel happy; therefore, that thing must be good'.

- **Substantive:** The most elaborate and extensive processing type is used only when easier strategies can't be. It's the most susceptible to the influence of emotion, and is employed whenever a task is complex or personally relevant, or when you need accuracy. Mood can affect many different sub-processes within this type, which is why it's the most likely to be affected by emotions.

Motivational and substantive processing are those employed when more elaborate encoding is required. However, affect is likely to have a bearing on heuristic and substantive processing more than the others.

Many factors can affect which processing a person employs. Table 20-1 summarises a few of these influences and how they may work.

Table 20-1	Factors Affecting the Type of Cognitive Processing Employed within the Affect-Infusion Model	
Processing Type	**Features**	**Degree of Affect Infusion**
Direct access	Familiar	No affect infusion
	Not relevant	
	Not important	
Motivated	Relevant	Low affect infusion
	Important	
	Specific motivation	
Heuristic	Typical target	High affect infusion
	Simple processing	
	Low cognitive capacity	
	Positive emotional state	
	Accuracy not required	
Substantive	Atypical and unusual target	Highest affect infusion
	Complex processing	
	High cognitive capacity	
	Negative emotional state	
	High motivation for accuracy	

Encountering Emotions Going Wrong

Sometimes severe emotions affect cognition. We describe two of these cases here: arousal (which for this context we define in the earlier section 'Looking at ways of defining emotion') and anxiety.

Stimulating arousal for memory

One of your authors remembers clearly a small event: he was trying to get his teacher's attention in class by shouting her name, but for some reason he yelled 'Mum!' Everybody turned and laughed. He wanted to run away and cry and is still embarrassed thinking about the event. The question is: why can such embarrassing memories remain so vivid for so long?

The reason seems to be that the emotional sequence causes arousal and activation of the amygdala, which helps the hippocampus (necessary to store memories; refer to Chapter 9) consolidate memories. Thus, arousal helps build stronger memories by making the memory centres work better.

Arousal also helps to prevent memories from being forgotten. Whereas people tend to forget low-arousing stimuli relatively quickly after learning, they recall highly arousing stimuli efficiently for 24 hours and even longer after learning.

A limit exists to the effects that arousal has on memory. When things are moderately arousing, memory is more efficient. But for intensely arousing events, memory is often worse. As Freud's ideas of repression say – highly emotional events are too painful to be kept in memory and so are prevented from being recovered. Similarly, Tim Valentine, a British cognitive psychologist, has shown that highly scared participants at the London Dungeon (a horror museum) recalled less information accurately than lowly scared participants. Therefore, memory is better for moderately arousing stimuli than neutral or highly arousing stimuli.

Worrying about anxiety

Socially anxious people demonstrate a convergence between mood and stimulus valence (refer to the earlier section 'How Do You Feel? Introducing Emotions'). They detect threatening stimuli (for example, an angry face) faster than people without social anxiety. When detected, socially anxious people avoid looking at the threat further.

Together, these two performance patterns form an attention bias known as *hyper-vigilance avoidance*.

Socially phobic patients recognise critical faces more accurately than non-critical faces. They're also more likely to think that they've seen a critical face before and to believe that they experience more criticism than they do. Whereas control participants show enhanced memory for happy expressions relative to sad expressions, social phobic participants don't.

Part VI
The Part of Tens

To discover that you have many more senses than you think (and whether a 'spidey' sense is one of them), head to www.dummies.com/extras/cognitive psychology.

In this part . . .

- ✔ Get to know ten famous case studies of individuals whose particular disorders taught the world a lot about cognitive psychology.

- ✔ Avoid the common errors that students make when writing research reports.

- ✔ Dispel the myths that the media perpetuates about cognitive psychology.

Chapter 21

Studying Patients with Brain Damage

• •

In This Chapter

▶ Using case studies to understand cognitive psychology

▶ Caring about the clinical cases

• •

*I*n Chapter 1, we mention that some of what cognitive psychology knows about cognition comes from *neuropsychology*: the study of patients with different forms of brain damage. Here we present ten famous case studies and what they reveal about some complex cognitive psychology problems.

In case studies, neuropsychologists collect and analyse the notes from loads of different sources: doctors' medical histories, neurosurgeons' and neuroscientists' information about brain structure, family history and any significant events. Neuropsychologists use this information and lots of cognitive psychology tests and neuropsychological assessments to establish the cause of the brain damage, diagnose and in some cases treat the patient.

Smelling More than Normal

Robert Henkin, an American doctor, reported the case of a woman with *hyperosmia* (heightened sense of smell). She was exposed to highly toxic gases and incurred damage to her nasal passageway, which caused her nose to receive more signals than was typical. She was able to smell much more vividly than previously and more than other people. Her sense of smell was so accurate that she could distinguish between all the perfumes in a pharmacy!

Her threshold for detecting smells was reduced: that is, she needed less smell particles in order to smell something. Typically, hyperosmia fades with time, because the brain isn't used to processing so much smell.

This study tells you that people's noses are capable of smelling much more than they normally do. In fact, your brain must prevent your conscious mind from detecting so many smells. One reason why is that smell is considered a 'basic' sense. Humans are supposed to be civilised: they don't need to smell. Instead they prefer to use more 'advanced' senses such as hearing and seeing, or indeed language, to communicate.

Losing Track of Movement

German neuropsychologist Joseph Zihl described patient LH in 1983. She suffered from headaches and felt shaky and sick at heights (*vertigo*). The problem was caused by an uncommon damage to blood vessels in the brain that can lead to strokes (called *superior sagittal sinus thrombosis*) towards the back of her head in an area of the brain called V5 (just above the ear).

Zihl and his colleagues tested LH extensively and found that her vision was perfectly normal – except that she couldn't see depth or movement. These deficits were only in her central vision, but she was unable to cross roads, pour cups of tea or watch TV; she understood that things were moving by listening to moving sounds. LH described her experience as seeing the world in snapshots. It was like those flip-drawings where one image leads to the next, but with a big gap in the position of objects.

Using video-production software on a computer, watch a film at only 2 frames per second (rather than the more common 24 frames per second) and you experience what life may be like for LH.

This case study and many others show that part of the brain specifically processes motion. If damaged, people can't see fast motion of objects. It also shows that the periphery (the edges of vision) sends its visual signals to different parts of the brain to detect more global motion (movement that isn't part of objects).

Unfortunately, no treatment exists for *akinetopsia* (the inability to see motion). Psychologists did give LH strategies to help her adapt: using sound more readily to detect motion (the pitch of liquid filling a cup gets higher as it reaches the top) and using her peripheral vision to see whether things are moving.

Failing to Recognise Faces

British-American neurologist Oliver Sacks reports on Dr P, a noted musician and teacher, in his book *The Man Who Mistook His Wife for a Hat* (Touchstone). The first signs of problems were when Dr P couldn't recognise his students from their faces. As his symptoms grew worse he couldn't tell the face of a person from the face of a grandfather clock. He started to interact with fire hydrants and door knobs, thinking that they were faces. One time he tried to grab his wife's head thinking it was a hat.

Dr P had no sign of dementia or mental problems. His visual acuity was perfectly fine, though he did have slightly odd eye-movements: his eyes seemed to dart over lots of little features instead of processing things as a whole. When he concentrated, he was able to figure out what he was looking at, but not faces. He recognised certain people if they had very distinctive features: Winston Churchill by his cigar and Einstein by the crazy hair.

Dr P demonstrated a classic pattern of severe *prosopagnosia* (an inability to recognise faces). More specifically, he seemed unable to link all the features of a face together, providing evidence that faces are one particular stimulus that requires *configural processing* (the ability to code the whole face in one lump; refer to Chapter 6).

Unfortunately, prosopagnosia is untreatable.

(Almost) Neglecting the World

In Chapter 7, we introduce the neuropsychological condition *spatial neglect*. Of the many reported cases of this debilitating disorder, we look at British neuropsychologists John Marshall and Peter Halligan's study of patient PS.

Patient PS's right parietal cortex was damaged due to a brain injury. She displayed two deficits:

- ✔ **Hemianopia:** Loss of vision to one half of the visual world (refer to Chapter 4). PS's hemianopia was to the left side.

- ✔ **Neglect:** Patient PS displayed neglect to the left side, meaning that she couldn't see the left side of objects even if she turned her head to look at them. She displayed the classical patterns of neglect. If you asked her to cross out objects, she crossed out only those on the right. She ate only food on the right side of her plate. When copying objects, she drew only the right side.

Patient PS had an interesting pattern of neglect. She demonstrated conscious unawareness of the left side of objects, but did have covert (unconscious) awareness of it. When presented with images of two houses, one on the left with fire coming out of the left window and one on the right with no fire, she said that the two images were identical. However, when asked which house she preferred, she chose the one on the right, suggesting an unconscious awareness of the fire.

The way in which the human brain codes left and right isn't simple. People code left and right according to the space relative to themselves. They also code the left and right of objects. These two types of left and right are processed differently in the brain.

No treatment is available for hemispatial neglect. Psychologists can only offer ways to adapt to not seeing the left side of objects, such as ensuring that objects are turned periodically to see both sides.

Forgetting What You Learn

Patient HM is the single most researched person in the history of psychology. In 1953, to treat very severe epilepsy, he had brain surgery that involved removing the hippocampus. Although his epilepsy was cured, he suffered devastating side effects: he was unable to transfer information from short-term to long-term memory. He never learnt the names of anyone new, never learnt current affairs and couldn't store the knowledge of his father dying. For him, every day was like the day before he had his operation.

HM's working memory and language skills were perfectly normal. His memory for people he knew before his operation was perfectly fine and he was able to learn new skills – but he had no knowledge of being able to do so. He was always surprised that he could do something he thought he'd never done before.

The hippocampus is crucial to the formation of long-term memories and a difference exists between knowing things and knowing how to do things: one ability can be damaged while the other remains intact.

Like many other brain injuries, this kind of *anterograde amnesia* isn't treatable. Patients can just be reassured that they haven't lost any skills and experiences from prior to the injury, to help them avoid suffering with depression (which is quite common).

Knowing that Knowledge Is Slipping Away

Karalyn Patterson, a British neuropsychologist, and her colleagues reported several cases of patients with left temporal lobe damage. One was PP. For two years, PP's memory of names of people, places and things had been getting worse. She was asked about whether she had been to America and her reply was 'what's America?' She didn't even know what food was.

Even with these severe memory problems, she was perfectly able to remember events and appointments. She cooked, cleaned and cared for herself and her visual abilities were perfectly normal. Unfortunately, her awareness of the problems led her to suffer depression.

Although her grammar and understanding of personal events seemed perfectly fine, PP had problems finding the right words when speaking (*anomia*) and showed signs of surface dyslexia. Her condition got steadily worse; she became unable to shop or cook because she didn't know what items to choose.

This condition, called *semantic dementia*, is untreatable. It demonstrates that semantic knowledge and words are stored in the brain somewhere different to language. Grammar and syntax are located in different areas to the words.

Developing without Language

Susan Curtiss, an American linguist, was one of the principle scientists who investigated the tragic case of Genie. Genie was a severely abused child who was locked in a room with no human contact from the age of 20 months until she was discovered by the authorities at the age of 13 years. Evidence suggested that Genie was quite a normal child until the age of 20 months.

Genie was found to be quite feral. She performed poorly on virtually all cognitive and social tasks. She didn't speak at all.

After a few months of interaction with psychologists and doctors, Genie began to make progress. She was able to develop some cognitive skills and to communicate her needs and wants; she even started to utter a few single words. But she was never able to understand grammatical structure.

The work with Genie reveals a lot about how language develops. It suggests a critical period between early childhood and puberty when language learning must take place. Fully learning a language outside this period isn't possible.

Reading but Not Understanding Words

Myrna Schwartz and her colleagues at Johns Hopkins University studied patient WLP in the late 1970s. WLP came to the hospital with symptoms of dementia that gradually worsened over the next 30 months. She had particularly unusual problems with understanding the meaning of words, which provided some of the first direct evidence of a purely *lexical route* in reading (where readers recognise words by sight alone without needing to sound the word out). WLP was able to read words relatively fluently and showed little evidence of surface dyslexia, but she had problems understanding them. For example, she could read out a list of animal names and pronounce them correctly, but she had trouble matching the words to pictures of the animals.

WLP's case provides evidence to support the existence of a pathway in the brain that relates the visual form of written words to the knowledge of how those words sound, and which bypasses the knowledge of what those words mean. She also provides some support for a *modular view* of language, with distinct processes for handling the meaning and the sounds of words.

Her case was an early documented case of what's now called semantic dementia. It raises the important point that not all patients suffering from this condition show the same pattern of problems. This terrible condition can selectively damage certain mental capacities while leaving others relatively spared.

Struggling to Speak Grammatically

In her book *Fractured Minds* (Oxford University Press), the neuroscientist Jenni Ogden describes the case of a patient called Luke. Luke had suffered a brain hemorrhage that damaged a small area in the frontal lobe of the brain called *Broca's area* (after Paul Broca, who first identified the region in the 19th century).

Luke displayed a pattern of cognitive symptoms that are characteristic of damage to this area. He could understand the meaning of words and simple sentences, but he struggled with grammar. In a standard comprehension test, he was shown several pictures and asked which one matched a particular sentence. When given the sentence 'The cat is under the chair' he was as likely to choose a picture of a cat on a chair as a cat under a chair.

When speaking, Luke was able to produce the meaningful, lexical words but struggled with the grammatical function words, so he said things like 'Phone Mum. Clothes, umm, coat, black, umm'. Such speech is often described as *agrammatic* (because it lacks grammar) and is typical of *Broca's aphasia* (as the condition is known).

This case study and the one in the preceding section support the idea that separate processes in the brain handle the meaning and grammar of language. Luke also suffered from a degree of *apraxia* (an inability to perform purposeful actions), which isn't unusual: Broca's area is located in the part of the brain that handles the planning of complex sequences of physical movements, as well as spoken language.

Changing Personality

One of the earliest neuropsychological case studies was that of Phineas Gage, a 19th-century railway worker from America. In 1848, while using explosives to clear the way for a new railway track, a metal rod was driven through Gage's skull, damaging the frontal lobe of his brain.

The resulting symptoms were typical of what's now recognised as a common form of brain damage. Such patients often seem quite unimpaired and able to behave in ways that seem normal, except for the changes in their behaviour and personality. People who knew Phineas Gage before his accident said that he was no longer the same person.

The frontal lobes house the executive areas of the brain, which make high-level decisions and decide what you're going to do next, and which things to focus on. They're also important in inhibiting the more impulsive parts of the brain. People with frontal lobe damage often start to behave in unusual, and sometimes socially inappropriate, ways. They have trouble regulating their behaviour and resisting spur-of-the-moment decisions. They can develop gambling problems, lose their jobs or have trouble maintaining relationships.

Chapter 22

Ten Tips for Writing Successful Research Reports

*A*s a cognitive psychology student, you'll almost certainly be expected to write a research report. These reports are designed to present your own experimental findings: that is, you need to design, carry out and run your own experiment. After all, cognitive psychology is a science.

You have to follow certain rules when writing these reports, as set out in the *Publication Manual of the American Psychological Association* (APA). The APA developed these rules over many years to ensure that all scientists produce work that's similar and that everyone can easily understand. Some of these rules may seem pedantic or even downright silly, but you must follow them.

Even if you don't have to write a research report, knowing how they're constructed is definitely useful. Given the ever-increasing number of online free-to-access scientific journals, more people are being exposed to cognitive psychology research than previously. Journalists read scientific reports and then write stories about them. Often, however, they make mistakes or interpret these reports incorrectly. Thus, being able to read scientific reports accurately is vitally important.

In this chapter, we present eight dos and two don'ts of writing cognitive psychology research reports. We give you the tools to write, and read, scientific reports appropriately. The tips are based on what professional researchers (like us) do. Therefore, check with your tutors that the advice is the same for your specific course.

We know that you expect good value from *For Dummies* books and so here's a bonus tip. Take a look at these free online journals to get a feel for what published cognitive psychology papers look like: *Advances in Cognitive Psychology* (www.ac-psych.org), *Frontiers in Cognition* (http://www.frontiersin.org/cognition) and *Journal of Vision* (www.journalofvision.org).

Using the Correct Format

The APA's rules for writing reports tell you what font to use, how to set the margins, what subsections to include and how to write scientifically.

Your chosen font needs to be easy to read in terms of design and size. Fonts such as Arial and Times New Roman are known to be easier to read than, say, Comic Sans or Brush Script. The size has to be big enough to read, but not too large to waste paper. So use size 12 Times New Roman. Also, always double-line (or 1.5-line) space your text. Reading is easier when you use extra line spacing and it gives room for your tutor to write comments on your work!

Research reports need to contain these seven sections in this order:

- ✔ **Title:** Tells readers what the study is about.
- ✔ **Abstract:** Brief summary of the report (no more than 120 words).
- ✔ **Introduction:** Tells readers why you're doing this study.
- ✔ **Method:** Describes *exactly* what you did . . . in detail . . . no really, more detail than you're thinking, and then add more detail!
- ✔ **Results:** What you found (the important bit).
- ✔ **Discussion:** What your findings mean.
- ✔ **References:** List of all the other research reports you read to help you write yours.

Place only the title, abstract and references on their own pages. Everything else can follow on to save paper.

Tables and figures are great for showing off results, but do label them correctly and clearly and don't put them in colour. For figures, label all axes and place a caption underneath (readers have to be able to understand a figure without reading the text). Don't use vertical lines in tables, because it clutters the space and makes them hard to read.

Within the correct format, use the appropriate concise scientific language. Scientists like bland, plain and simple sentences. They hate long sentences, with lots of clauses and lots of commas. Just give the information in simple terms. Use short sentences. Make sure that you use scientific words and phrases correctly (often this means that you don't need to define them). Only ever write the amount that's necessary to get your point across – no need to write more.

Including Background Research

In the report's introduction, justify everything to do with your study, including why you're doing it: that is, explain the purpose from a scientific point of view. Simply being interested in a topic isn't sufficient (though it helps!); your research needs practical application.

The opening of an introduction usually sets the scene for the research. Explain why the research is useful for society and any practical reasons for doing the work. Memory research is often useful for understanding and improving eye-witness testimony, for example.

The rest of the introduction describes the kinds of work that have been published previously. These descriptions need only to include relevant and important studies – not everything you've read. In fact, include only the absolute minimum to get your point across.

Aim for a logical progression in the background research you describe. Present all sides of a debate, if there is one. Also explain what your work adds to the debate, what's different about it and why it's the best piece of work done on the topic.

Criticising Existing Research

Part of the fun of writing research reports and generally being a cognitive psychologist is getting to criticise existing work. No published papers are perfect (except ours, obviously!) so always look for ways of criticising them. Criticisms form the basis for pushing science forward and establishing new, better ways of testing things.

Some good things to criticise are the appropriateness of the methods and procedures. Often researchers conduct a study and have a *confounding variable* (a second variable may explain their findings but isn't the one they describe). Recently, for example, we read a paper stating that mood affected the recognition of facial expressions but not their identity. But the researchers told the participants to remember the face identity and didn't mention the expressions. So a *confound* existed between expression/identity recognition and the learning instructions.

You can also criticise the appropriateness of the tools used to measure a certain effect. Does a particular experimental variable really measure what it's supposed to? In other words, try to explain someone else's results in another way. Develop your own explanation of their results.

Also up for criticism is the statistical approach used in a particular study – though this probably requires you to understand statistics (perhaps *Psychology Statistics For Dummies* by Donncha Hanna and Martin Dempster [Wiley] can help!).

Developing Testable Hypotheses

Ensure that your experimental hypothesis fulfils these four requirements:

- ✓ **Simple:** It needs to describe how one thing affects another (possibly only under certain circumstances). Don't produce a convoluted set of propositions before coming to a suggestion (it's not philosophy). As we state in Chapter 18, the logic of a simple hypothesis is that if one thing happens then something else should happen as a result.

- ✓ **Clear:** It needs to make obvious what you're talking about: that is, clearly identify what variables you're investigating. This aspect is perhaps the hardest thing for students to get right first time. You have to turn a complex hypothetical construct (say, personality) into something simple and easy to measure (such as extraversion scored on Eysenck's Personality Inventory). You need to state clearly how that variable affects something else. Your hypothesis must also stem from the background literature you summarise.

- ✓ **Controlled:** Many professional researchers fall foul of this requirement. A controlled experiment has no room for confounds (refer to the preceding section) or error. A hypothesis has to be specific to the set circumstances under investigation. From your experiment, you're able to draw the intended inferences about the concept, because you can compare to the relevant control conditions. A *control condition* is like a neutral condition or a baseline to which everything else is relative.

- ✓ **Testable:** No point devising a hypothesis about something that you can't test (such as humans evolved from monkeys – how would you experimentally test that?). A hypothesis must take clearly defined concepts that you can measure or manipulate easily. You can easily measure memory performance by administering a recall test, for example, but you can't easily measure brain power. With a testable hypothesis, you're stating exactly how you're going to measure and manipulate everything in your experiment and you're describing, broadly, the paradigms and procedures you intend to use.

Providing Detailed Methods

In the method section you describe exactly what you did: state every single thing that happened – and then add more information. Too often writers' method sections miss things out. You want to ensure that you give readers your method so that they can repeat your *exact* experiment.

Method sections are usually divided into four subsections:

- ✔ **Participants:** Describe your participants, how you recruited them and why they took part, because evidence suggests that different people perform differently. For example, men and women give different results in the DRM paradigm of false memory (check out Chapter 11), and paid participants give different results on personality questionnaires than those who volunteer.

- ✔ **Materials:** Describe everything you used in *lots* of detail. If you did a memory experiment with words, describe what type of words. Evidence shows that shorter words are remembered better than longer words, as are distinctive words, high-frequency words and so on. You can also justify why you chose these particular materials.

You can't put too much information into this section about the materials used (though don't include pedantic detail such as the type of pencil used to fill in a questionnaire!).

- ✔ **Design:** Tells readers the type of experiment you've chosen and identify the variables. Basically, did all participants do all conditions (*within-subjects*) or did different groups of participants do different things (*between-subjects*).

- ✔ **Procedure:** Detail exactly what happened to the participants during the experiment. Often procedures describe trials and phases:

  - **Trial:** Sequence of events leading to a single participant response.

  - **Phase (or block):** Where a group of similar trials are put together in a sequence. Recognition experiments, for example, feature a phase of learning trials (where stimuli are first presented) and then a test phase involving recognition trials (where the learning stimuli and new stimuli are presented and participants say whether they've seen them before or not).

We can't overstress the critical importance of detail in the method section. Papers often contradict other papers due to subtle differences in the methods, including the mean length of the words used or whether the participants sat 60 or 100 centimetres from the computer!

Presenting Your Results Clearly

The whole point of reports is to collect data and show them off. Thus, the results section of a practical report is one of the most important – clarity and understanding are vital. Make sure that anyone would understand your results and that they relate to your hypothesis.

Always describe what your numbers are and what they mean. Basically, what can the scores range between? Also describe the trends and patterns in the data (that is, which condition produces a higher mean than another?). Then comes the pretty bit, the table or figure (it's a graph, but the APA guides always refer to 'figures', and so don't use the word 'graph' in your research reports).

The table or figure presents the *means* of your results, which summarise all the participants' data nicely and succinctly. Throughout this book, we refer to experimental effects where something was 'bigger than' something else. These come from results of research reports. The beauty of figures is that they show visually differences between numbers clearly – but they aren't as precise as numbers in tables.

Make sure that your results reflect your hypothesis (refer to the earlier section 'Developing Testable Hypotheses'). The variables in an analysis must be the ones you describe in the introduction (many people do the statistics without thinking about what they represent).

Interpreting Results within Theories

You need to interpret your results within a theoretical framework. Refer again to the theories and background research you present in your introduction: are these theories supported? If they're not, why not?

When you interpret inconsistent results, make sure that you refer to theoretical reasons as to why this may be the case. Perhaps the reason is down to differences between your study and those conducted by other people. Make sure that any reason you suggest as to why you obtained different results is based on some form of scientific theory.

Ensure that your interpretation of results considers any arising potential bias or validity issue, including imprecision of measures. You want to explain the psychological mechanisms that account for the effect you're investigating. These mechanisms need to be *causal* where possible – that is, try to explain why something happened the way it did.

Attempt to interpret your results within other theoretical perspectives than the one you necessarily believe in – to show off your true genius!

Suggesting Future Research

With your results interpreted within various theoretical frameworks (refer to the preceding section), you can really shine by describing how readers can practically test between these theories. In this way, you can suggest new and important investigations based upon theory and extra background reading. Don't simply suggest something because you think it would be interesting: only make suggestions for work because of some important theoretical use.

You can also propose future work that may make your results more generalisable to other samples of people, or even to the real world. In other words, you can say why your results are really important and what can be done to make them revolutionise the whole world and the way people look at psychology. Don't be afraid to be a bit pompous!

Often professional researchers use the suggestion of future research as a way of hinting that psychologists should be paid more money to do more research! Think of it as being like a job request!

Avoiding Criticising the Sample

Often students make general and vague criticisms of their own and published studies, such as 'the sample size is too small', 'the sample involved only psychology students' or 'a random sample would have been better'. All these criticisms are wrong. Here's why.

When psychologists conduct and experiment and find a statistically significant result, the sample size is the right size. End of. This practice is a rule within statistics, because every time you test a new participant, it costs a lot of money. Testing the fewest number of participants is better to find a significant result. If you don't find a significant result, however, your experiment may lack *power* (the necessary statistical quality to find a significant result) and require more participants – but better ways exist of increasing power than simply testing more people.

Don't criticise the fact that you tested only psychology students. Would they perform differently from other people on your cognitive tests? The answer is almost always no. If you have evidence from published papers that says different you can use it, but you must have a theory. If you think that psychology students may know what an experiment is about, and the participants can influence the results, you have a bad experiment and need to design it better before running it.

Also don't criticise the lack of random samples. Although they're technically better than opportunity samples, achieving them is nearly impossible, as well as far too expensive and difficult to organise. Given that you describe the participants that you tested, the readers need to determine whether your results would generalise to other populations.

Don't Knock Ecological Validity

Students tend to make the mistake of criticising published and their own papers for lacking *ecological validity*, which is where the results obtained in the experiment are unlikely to replicate in the real world.

Although many experiments are conducted in the laboratory, this is the only way to create controlled environments to explore specific processes. This isn't a problem, but is actually a good thing.

You can say that although the results may only generalise across a limited range of conditions, further work can use the experimental findings and try to replicate them in the real world. For example, if researchers investigating language find an effect in the laboratory, they can then devise a new way of helping people with dyslexia, and test this in the real world. Without the original lab work, the helpful new technique wouldn't have been devised.

Chapter 23

Busting Ten Cognitive Psychology Myths

*M*any people think that they know a thing or two about cognitive psychology – and some of it is common sense. But most of it, as you discover throughout this book, is a bit more technical and (we hope you agree) more interesting.

Here we expose ten commonly held myths related to cognitive psychology. Most of them connect to the brain (as if people don't really understand it!). Sometimes we give an example of the myth's use (usually by Hollywood or television) and provide the science behind why it's wrong.

Using Your Whole Brain

In the film *Lucy*, the main character takes a drug that allows her to use her whole brain and develop frankly ridiculous powers. The notion is that people use only 10 per cent of their brains.

This myth is plain wrong. Certainly learning increases the amount of brain connections and brain matter – and people may only use part of their brains at one time. For example, you're reading right now and so the reading parts of your brain are doing something. But the part of your brain that recognises faces or controls playing football isn't needed and isn't as active.

Brain scanning, such as fMRI, shows that most of the brain is active all the time (even during sleep), even if some parts are more active than others. Furthermore, damaging any part of the brain causes some form of cognitive deficit – clearly every part is used for something. Some parts of the brain are used more for some tasks and behaviours than others (called *localisation of brain function*).

The basis of the film *Limitless* is that if humans used their whole brains they'd have superhuman powers. Ridiculous! If your whole brain was equally active at once, you'd be doing and thinking everything at the same time and your brain would go into some form of sensory overload. In fact, autism is thought to be down to too much sensation. Overstimulation in the sensory parts of the brain causes people with autism to retreat into themselves and avoid any extra sensation (such as social stimulation).

Seeing Depth with Two Eyes

In Chapter 5, we describe the various sources of information needed to see three dimensions. Only one source, *stereopsis*, requires comparing the images across the two eyes, which means that you can obtain many sources of depth perception from one eye. Therefore, you don't lose depth perception if you have only one eye (that means you, Leela from *Futurama*).

Undoubtedly, seeing depth with only one eye is more difficult, particularly if you haven't seen the object before or you're looking at something in an empty space (such as a wide open field, far from any trees). Clearly, these situations are rare.

If you lose one eye, therefore, you lose only stereopsis. For the vast majority of situations you don't notice any difference.

Failing to See Colour, in Men

Various types of colour-blindness exist (as we describe in Chapter 5) and one myth says that only men can be colour-blind. Putting aside the fact that most people with colour-blindness aren't blind to colour at all (they just confuse certain colours), colour-blindness can affect men and women.

The main reason for colour-blindness lies in a particular gene on the X chromosome. Men have only one X chromosome, whereas women have two. Therefore, to be colour-blind women need to inherit the problem on both chromosomes, whereas men just need it once. Colour-blindness can also be the result of diabetes and brain injury (*achromatopsia*).

Therefore, men are roughly ten times more likely to be colour-blind than women, though this depends on the type of colour-blindness. Women are more likely to be *deuteranopic* (a colour deficiency in which yellows and reds are confused) than *protaneropic* (colour deficiency in which greens to reds are confused), whereas for men the percentages are the same. Overall, approximately 8 per cent of men and 0.5 per cent of women are colour-blind.

Also, to dispel two more myths, colour-blindness isn't passed on from fathers to sons (though if a mother is colour-blind, all her sons will be) and dogs aren't colour-blind.

Falling for a Symmetrical Face

Symmetry is attractive to the human eye. This 'fact', and some scientific research, led to the theory that symmetrical faces are attractive. The research responsible involved a series of faces that were seemingly rated as symmetrical and as more attractive. But good scientists look behind such basic findings to explore the *confounding variables* – things that occur at the same time within an experiment but weren't measured.

If symmetrical faces were attractive, when you take a picture of your face and make it fully symmetrical (mirror one side) it should look more attractive than your normal face. But it doesn't: people typically don't rate artificially symmetrical faces as attractive.

In fact, the confounding variable of symmetry is average faces. Attractive faces are average. Average faces typically have no blemishes, marks or weird features. They show good health. Typically, average faces are symmetrical, but not always. Average faces are more attractive than symmetrical faces.

Memorising like a Tape Recorder

In *The Big Bang Theory*, the character Sheldon Cooper claims to have an *eidetic memory*: he remembers things with an amazing degree of accuracy. He only needs to see or hear something once and can recall it perfectly. The ability is similar, but not identical to, a *photographic* memory (where someone can look at a page of text and instantly remember it all).

Some cases of eidetic memory are found in children who can recall, for a short time, something they've been told almost exactly. Their understanding of it, however, may not be entirely accurate and so it's unrelated to someone's intelligence.

But no cases of people with eidetic memories have been found. The outcome of every single case of someone who claims to have it has been disproved. What they are very good at is remembering the gist of all situations and often creating false memories. They may be able to recall more detail than most (people with *hyperthymestic syndrome*), but their memory is certainly not eidetic (if anyone reading this believes they have an eidetic memory, please get in contact with us!).

Listening to Mozart Makes You Smarter

A commonly held myth is that listening to Mozart makes you smarter: known as the *Mozart effect*. A company in America sells material based on this myth, and leading politicians recommend listening to Mozart in schools and even giving CDs to new-born infants.

This myth is based on a study conducted in America in which mostly white middle-class participants listened to Mozart while performing a series of spatial tasks. Although their performance improved on spatial tasks (only), no effect lasted more than 15 minutes. Further studies show that spatial abilities improve with playing Mozart on the piano compared with no training (obviously), singing (again, obviously) and playing on the computer.

The key problem is what listening to Mozart is compared to – typically, paper folding or another boring task. If you give people the chance to read or watch something they enjoy before doing these tasks, they usually do better than if you give something they don't enjoy. The participants in the original study probably enjoyed Mozart. When the BBC replicated this study on people from the UK (not just white middle-class), their IQ was found to improve listening to pop music but not Mozart. Indeed, the original study's results haven't been replicated even when it was closely replicated.

In fact, the original researchers clarified that they never said listening to Mozart made you smarter. People misread and misreported the work (always be careful what you read about science in the media). Whatever you give to people that makes them relaxed and happy makes them perform better at specific tasks (refer to Chapter 20).

Getting Aggressive about Computer Games

Many people claim that children who play violent computer games or watch violent TV programmes are more likely to become violent. This myth is one of the more controversial in psychology, because of the amount of money invested into researching it and all the differing, strongly held opinions.

A great deal of research has been conducted on this topic and many studies do show a correlation between the amount of TV violence watched and aggression. A key example is that of Albert Bandura, a Canadian social psychologist. He showed some children people hitting a big doll called Bobo on a TV monitor and then let the children into the room with the Bobo doll. Many children hit it.

This finding may seem obvious, and it's where people who believe this myth stop. But if you look deeper, you find lots of problems with this work. For example, the children almost always looked at the experimenter for what to do when in the room with the Bobo doll: because there wasn't a lot else to do in the room, invariably the children hit the doll. Plus, the experiment was funded by a government lobby trying to show that media violence is bad.

Most studies that show such a correlation have problems:

✔ Most such research is funded by people trying to prove such a link exists, which isn't appropriate for scientists.

✔ The studies need thousands of participants to show an effect (suggesting that if an effect does exist, it's very small).

✔ The studies almost always ignore the parents' role, crucially excluding parental aggression. Yet parental aggression is very likely to predict aggression in children and is a stronger influence than anything else. People who experience aggression at home are more likely to seek out aggression in media, giving the impression that the violent media leads to aggression (whereas it's actually a consequence of something else).

Violent media probably changes only the *nature* of aggression in those who watch it. For some, watching aggression relieves their feelings of aggression and is therefore beneficial. For people who're aggressive anyway, media violence just shows them how.

Hunting for Free Will

Free will is possibly the most controversial idea in this chapter. Most people believe that they have *free will* – the freedom to choose how they act – and that their conscious mind decides how to act.

Yet Benjamin Libet, an American physiologist, conducted an innovative study (that has been replicated many times), in which he got participants to choose simply when to press a button that stopped a clock hand. Libet measured the activity of the person's brain when making the 'free' choice. He also asked the participant to record the time in seconds when she chose to press the button.

Libet found brain activity in the motor cortex of the brain (that started the hand movement) *before* the participant chose to press the button (and this choice occurred before the person physically pressed the button). This means that the choice of when to press the button was made unconsciously by the brain and not by the person's conscious.

The brain starts to move the hand such a long time (around 300–500 milliseconds) before the person decides to move that researchers can identify which hand the person will use! Psychologists can read people's minds, because they don't have free will.

Communicating Differently as a Man or a Woman

Many people believe that men and women communicate in a fundamentally different way, reinforced by popular books such as John Gray's *Men Are from Mars, Women Are from Venus*. The view from cognitive psychology, however, is quite different.

Male and female brains are remarkably similar in their basic wiring and function, and any differences that do emerge tend to be the result of cultural experience rather than any innate biological difference. Janet Hyde, a psychologist at the University of Wisconsin, and her colleagues examined the evidence for gender differences in verbal ability. They found that in every measure of verbal ability very little, if any, difference exists between genders.

Hypnotising You to Do Anything

Films and TV programmes often portray hypnosis, making out that someone can be hypnotised to kill: for example, in *Zoolander*. Slightly more realistic are the shows where hypnotists get members of the audience on stage to do silly things. The myth stems from a misunderstanding of what hypnosis does and how it occurs.

Whether through meditation, reading, deep thought or guidance, hypnosis puts people into a state of hypervigilance, trance-like extreme relaxation and heightened imagination, a bit like day-dreaming. In this state, you're suggestible because you're relaxed. If someone tells you something, you believe it in a similar way to how you believe something during day-dreaming.

Although you become much less inhibited, a hypnotist can't make you do things you don't want to. As in a day-dream, your body's self-preservation actions are maintained. Also, hypnosis doesn't affect your sense of morality – you're just more likely to behave in a silly manner. Plus, hypnosis can only occur to people who want it to happen, are relaxed enough to let it happen and who believe it'll work. You can't be hypnotised if you don't want to be.

Index

• W •

• X •

• Y •

• Z •

Notes

Notes

Notes

Notes

Notes

Notes

Notes

Notes

About the Authors

Dr Peter Hills completed his PhD in the development of face recognition from Cardiff University in 2007. Since then, he has been educating young eager minds in the joys of cognitive psychology at Anglia Ruskin University (where he met his co-author and spent many hours with him in the local drinking establishment) and more recently at Bournemouth University. In addition to teaching cognitive psychology, he conducts research in face recognition, colour perception and attention.

Dr Mike Pake studied psychology at the University of Stirling before moving to the Department of Artificial Intelligence and the Centre for Cognitive Science at the University of Edinburgh, where he obtained a Masters and PhD. Now at the Department of Psychology at Anglia Ruskin University in Cambridge, he teaches psychology and uses computer models to help understand human language acquisition and visual attention. He has gotten a lot more work done since his co-author left for Bournemouth.

Dedication

To all the great psychologists who have gone before and whose work we've written about here, and to all the great psychologists, including many readers of this book, to come.

Most importantly, to my wife, without whom, I couldn't complete this or any other work.

—PJH

To my parents, who brought me here. My Dad would no doubt have thought that this was all a lot of nonsense and my Mum would've found all the ungrammaticalities.

And to Middle J and Little J for being there always.

—MP

Authors' Acknowledgments

We'd like to thank the plethora of editors who have helped turn our musings into a properly formatted and accurate book: Michelle Hacker for communicating so effectively and ensuring that we kept to a timescale (mostly!); Andy Finch and Kerry Laundon for ensuring that what we wrote makes sense; and the 'seminal' Graham Hole for checking the technical aspects and gently informing us when we got it wrong!

Publisher's Acknowledgments

Executive Commissioning Editor: Annie Knight

Project Manager: Michelle Hacker

Development Editor: Andy Finch

Copy Editor: Kerry Laundon

Technical Editor: Dr Graham Hole

Production Editor: Siddique Shaik

Cover Image: © wildpixel/iStockphoto

Take Dummies with you everywhere you go!

Whether you're excited about e-books, want more from the web, must have your mobile apps, or swept up in social media, Dummies makes everything easier.

Visit Us	Like Us	Follow Us	Watch Us
Join Us	Pin Us	Circle Us	Shop Us

FOR DUMMIES®

A Wiley Brand

BUSINESS

Small Business Marketing For Dummies
978-1-118-73077-5

Pop Up Business For Dummies
978-1-118-44349-1

Starting & Running a Business All-in-One For Dummies
978-1-119-97527-4

MUSIC

Mandolin For Dummies
978-1-119-94276-4

Ukulele For Dummies
978-0-470-97799-6

Piano For Dummies
978-0-470-49644-2

DIGITAL PHOTOGRAPHY

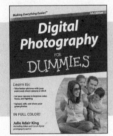

Digital Photography For Dummies
978-1-118-09203-3

Digital SLR Photography All-in-One For Dummies
978-0-470-76878-5

Nikon D3100 For Dummies
978-1-118-00472-2

FOR DUMMIES

A Wiley Brand

SELF-HELP

978-0-470-66541-1

978-1-119-99264-6

978-0-470-66086-7

LANGUAGES

978-0-470-68815-1

978-1-119-97959-3

978-0-470-69477-0

HISTORY

978-0-470-68792-5

978-0-470-74783-4

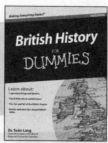

978-0-470-97819-1

Laptops For Dummies 5th Edition
978-1-118-11533-6

Management For Dummies,
2nd Edition
978-0-470-97769-9

Nutrition For Dummies, 2nd Edition
978-0-470-97276-2

Office 2013 For Dummies
978-1-118-49715-9

Organic Gardening For Dummies
978-1-119-97706-3

Origami Kit For Dummies
978-0-470-75857-1

Overcoming Depression For Dummies
978-0-470-69430-5

Physics I For Dummies
978-0-470-90324-7

Project Management For Dummies
978-0-470-71119-4

Psychology Statistics For Dummies
978-1-119-95287-9

Renting Out Your Property For Dummies,
3rd Edition
978-1-119-97640-0

Rugby Union For Dummies, 3rd Edition
978-1-119-99092-5

Stargazing For Dummies
978-1-118-41156-8

Teaching English as a Foreign Language
For Dummies
978-0-470-74576-2

Time Management For Dummies
978-0-470-77765-7

Training Your Brain For Dummies
978-0-470-97449-0

Voice and Speaking Skills For Dummies
978-1-119-94512-3

Wedding Planning For Dummies
978-1-118-69951-5

WordPress For Dummies, 5th Edition
978-1-118-38318-6

Think you can't learn it in a day? Think again!

The *In a Day* e-book series from *For Dummies* gives you quick and easy access to learn a new skill, brush up on a hobby, or enhance your personal or professional life — all in a day. Easy!

31901059698813

Available as PDF, eMobi and Kindle